365 DAYS PLAYS

I got this notion to write a play a day for a whole year. "I'm going to write a play a day for a whole year! I'll call it *365 Days/365 Plays*!" I told my husband, Paul. "Yeah, baby, that'd be cool," Paul said. And so I started writing. It was November 13, 2002. I thought about waiting until January 1 to begin, but I wanted to keep it real, so I started right where I was, working with whatever I had at the moment. So that day I began writing a series of plays called *365 Days/365 Plays*. Every day for the next year I would wake up and ask myself, "Ok, so what's the play?" and I wrote what came. The plan was that no matter what I did, how busy I was, what other commitments I had, I would write a play a day, every single day, for a year. It would be about being present and being committed to the artistic process every single day, regardless of the "weather." It became a daily meditation, a daily prayer celebrating the rich and strange process of a writing life.

—xoxoxox Suzan-Lori Parks

The 365 National Festival, co-produced by Bonnie Metzgar and Suzan-Lori Parks, will involve hundreds and hundreds and hundreds of theaters and countless folks around the country in a simultaneous and shared grassroots world premiere of these 365 plays, which will last an entire year. The Coordinator for 365U is Rebecca Rugg. The National Coordinator is David Myers. For a list of the many glorious participants, we ask you to refer to the Festival appendix.

A special thanks to Theatre Communications Group and especially Kathy Sova for working magic, moving mountains and helping it all happen.

365 PLAYS

365 DAYS/

365

SUZAN-LORI PARKS

New York 2006

Theatre Communications Group

365 Days/365 Plays is published by Theatre Communications Group, Inc., 520 Eighth Avenue, 24th Floor, New York, NY 10018–4156

This publication is made possible in part with public funds from the New York State Council on the Arts, a State Agency.

TCG books are exclusively distributed to the book trade by Consortium Book Sales and Distribution.

Library of Congress Cataloging-in-Publication Data
Parks, Suzan-Lori.
365 days/365 plays / Suzan-Lori Parks. — 1st ed.
p. cm.
ISBN-13: 978-1-55936-286-3
ISBN-10: 1-55936-286-3
I. Title. II. Title: Three hundred sixty-five days, three hundred sixty-five plays.
PS3566.A736A15 2006
812'.54—dc22
2006031006

Cover design by Mark Melnick
Cover photo by Peter Bellamy
365 Days/365 Plays logo by Jose A. Contreras
Text design and composition by Lisa Govan

First Edition, November 13, 2006
Second Printing, June 2011

For Paul Oscher

who said it'd be cool

Contents

From the Author's "Elements of Style"

I'm continuing the use of my slightly unconventional theatrical elements. Here's a road map.

■ *(Rest)*
Take a little time, a pause, a breather; make a transition.

■ A Spell
An elongated and heightened *(Rest)*. Denoted by repetition of figures' names with no dialogue. Has sort of an architectural look:

Krishna
Arjuna
Krishna
Arjuna

This is a place where the figures experience their pure true simple state. While no action or stage business is necessary, directors should fill this moment as they best see fit.

■ (Parentheses around dialogue indicate softly spoken passages (asides; sotto voce)).

■ Some plays for two characters use no character names. The performers should alternate lines. Other plays for two or more characters use no character names, but each new speech is preceded by a dash. Each dash indicates when a new speaker begins. The lines below would be read by two different speakers:

– She dont talk.
– I do so talk.

THE 3 CONSTANTS

For *365 Days/365 Plays*, I'm inviting everybody to perform these 3 Constants along with your selected plays—sprinkle them where you like.

—xoxoxox S-L P

THE 1ST CONSTANT (Remember Who You Are)

2 benches or 2 chairs. Someone on the bench (or chair).
Someone Else comes in.

Someone Else: This seat taken?
Someone: Nope.
Someone Else: You sleep?
Someone: Yep.
Someone Else: Oh. Sorry.

Someone Else goes through an elaborate before-sleep ritual. Feel free, do whatever you want. Brush yr teeth, floss maybe, pray maybe. You could stretch or gargle. Take out yr contacts, oil yr feet and hands, cold-creme yr face, roll up yr hair in curlers or wrap it in a doo-rag. Lock up yr belongings. Kiss yr beloved's image. Thank God. Do whatcha gotta do.

Someone Else
Someone Else

(Rest)

Someone Else: Yr sleeping with one eye open.
Someone: Yes.
Someone Else: How come?
Someone: To watch over you.
Someone Else: But—. But you dont even know me!!!!
Someone: I am That, you are That, all this is That, and Thats all there is.

Someone
Someone Else

(Rest)

They sleep.

THE 2ND CONSTANT (Action in Inaction)

Someone standing still. They could be dressed in mourning.
The sound of wind or whales forever.

THE 3RD CONSTANT (Inaction in Action)

Onstage are 365 things to do, that is, 365 tasks. What are the tasks? Yr choice. Lights up. Dart around trying to do all the tasks. Make it clear that you desire to complete all the tasks. Dart around as fast as possible. Do yr best. Dont be shy about going all out. There isnt anything to hold out for. This is it. Hurry hurry hurry. Lights go out long before yr done.

365 DAYS/365 PLAYS

13 START HERE

Krishna: We start here. Come on.

Arjuna: Where to?

Krishna: Does it matter?

Arjuna: Yeah. Because I have a choice in the matter and if we're going somewhere I dont like, I may choose not to go. Because I have a choice.

Krishna: You have a choice?

Arjuna: Yeah.

Krishna: Are you sure?

Arjuna: This is a free country.

Krishna: Is it?

Krishna
Arjuna

Krishna: Yr sitting down.

Arjuna: No Im not.

Krishna: Yr legs are folded underneath you and yr bottom is resting. On the ground. Where I come from we call that sitting.

Arjuna: All I know is that my legs folded and my mind stopped. And now I have a great need to cry.

Krishna: Cry? Who for?

Arjuna: Myself. My country.

Krishna: Yr *free* country.

Arjuna: Yrs too.

(Rest)

It was such a great idea. In the beginning. When they were all starting out. They had no idea that—that—. That it would end up like this.

Krishna: It hasnt ended up like this. It *is* like this. This isnt the end, its—

Arjuna: The beginning?

Krishna: Thats right. Come on.

Arjuna: Mmmm.

Krishna: Dont hold back.

Arjuna: Eeeeeee.

Krishna: Lets go.

Arjuna: Ooooooo.

Krishna: Yr having 2nd thoughts. I understand. Everything you own, everything you are, everything you know is back there, right? Yr not prepared, you think. You forgot to pack yr toothbrush. You forgot to lock the front door. You forgot to turn on the machine. You forgot to turn off the stove. You may have left the bathwater running. You dont speak the language of—wherever it is we're headed.

Arjuna: Right.

Krishna: Hear that sound?

Arjuna: Sounds like leaves moving in the wind.

Krishna: Its the sound of writing. Theyre writing yr name in the Book.

Arjuna: *My* name?

Krishna: Why not yr name?

(Rest)

Arjuna: Im afraid. A little.

Krishna: Good.
(Rest)
At the start theres always energy. Sometimes joy. Sometimes fear. By the end, youll be so deep into the habit of continuing on, youll pray that youll never stop. Happens all the time. But dont take my word for it. Lets go and youll see for yrself.
(Rest)
Get up. There you go. Breathe. Ok. Come on.

Arjuna: Where to?

Krishna: For me to know and for you to find out.

Krishna & Arjuna: Hahahahahahah.

Krishna: Come on. Not to worry. Walk with me. Keep the feet moving. And, with any luck, we'll get there.

They start out.

14 FATHER COMES HOME FROM THE WARS (Part 1)

Father: Hi honey, Im home.

Mother: Yr home.

Father: Yes.

Mother: I wasnt expecting you. Ever.

Father: Should I go back out and come back in again?

Mother: Please.

> He goes back out and comes back in again.

Mother: Once more.

Father: Yr kidding.

Mother: Please.

> He goes back out and comes back in again.

Mother: Yr home.

Father: Yes.

Mother: Let me get a good look at you.

Father: I'll just turn around.

Mother: Please.

> He turns around once. Counterclockwise.

Mother: They should of sent a letter. A letter saying you were coming home. Or at least a telephone call. That is the least they could do. Give a woman and her family and her friends and neighbors a chance to get ready. A chance to spruce things up. Put new ribbons in the hair of the dog. Get the oil changed. Have everything running. Smoothly. And bake a cake of course. Hang streamers. Tell the yard man to—tidy up his act. Oh God. Long story. Oh God. Long story. I woulda invited the neighbors over. Had everyone on the block jump out from their hiding

Father: They sent a letter saying I was coming or at least they telephoned. Maybe you didnt open the letter. I dont blame you. It could have been bad news. I see yr unopened envelopes piled up. I dont blame you. I dont blame you at all. They called several times. Maybe you were out. Maybe you were screwing the yard man. If you had known I was coming you woulda put new ribbons in the hair of the dog, got the oil changed, baked a cake and invited all the neighbors over so they could jump out of their various hiding places behind the brand-new

November

Mother (cont): places from behind the brand-new furniture with the plastic still on it and say— WHAT? Say: "Welcome Home" of course. And then after a few slices of cake and a few drinks theyd all get the nerve to say what theyre really thinking. For now itll stay unthought and unsaid. Well. You came home. All in one piece looks like. We're lucky. I guess. We're lucky, right? Hhhhh.

Father (cont): furniture purchased with the blood of some people I used to know—and some blood of some people I used to kill. Oh God. Long story. Oh God. Long story. And theyd shout at me—WHAT? "Welcome Home" of course. And then after a few slices of cake and a few drinks theyd get the nerve to tell me what they really think: "Murderer, baby killer, racist, government pawn, ultimate patsy, stooge, fall guy, camp follower, dumbass, dope fiend, loser." Hhhhh.

Mother
Father

(Rest)

Mother: I cant understand a word yr saying.
Father: I dont speak English anymore.
Mother: I dont blame you. SIT DOWN, I'LL FIX YOU SOMETHING.

He sits. She takes a heavy frying pan and holds it over his head. Almost murder. She lowers the pan.

Mother
Father

(Rest)

He sits. Again she raises the frying pan and holds it over his head. Almost murder. She lowers the pan.

Father: Where are the children?
Mother: What children?

Sound of the wind and the rain.

15 THE GOOD-FOR-NOTHING

Barker: Get yr looks. Come on, get yr looks, gather round. Step right up and see with yr own eyes up close and personal The Good-for-Nothing. It dont work, it dont reproduce, it dont even cause trouble, it dont vote, it dont complain. Its a Good-for-Nothing. Step right up and see. No admission charge, of course. Step right up.

> A Crowd gathers into a knot. From its center appears The Good-for-Nothing. They gather round and gawk.

1st Man: Holy Smokes!

1st Woman: Its a Good-for-Nothing!

Crowd: Jeeeesus! Wow!

2nd Woman: Ive seen this one somewhere before.

Good-for-Nothing: Ive been on tour. Perhaps youve seen me in another town.

2nd Woman's Husband: She never leaves this town. She always stays home. Right by my side. Every night. Isnt that right, woman?

2nd Woman: Yes, dear.

1st Man: Ah-hahahahahahahahaha!

Crowd
Good-for-Nothing

Barker: Shit.

> The Crowd disperses. The Barker and The Good-for-Nothing stand alone.

Barker: Thats the end of that, I guess. You made that man laugh.

Good-for-Nothing: I dont understand it. I come from a long line of Good-for-Nothings. My mother and father both. And their parents on both sides before them. I have my papers. Ive joined the Union—

Barker: What can I tell you? You made that man laugh.

Good-for-Nothing: Maybe it wasnt my doing—

Barker: Ive seen it happen before. Theres no use in trying to rationalize it away. News of his laughing will get around—its no use.

Good-for-Nothing: If only he had laughed *after* we passed the hat. We had a good crowd.

Barker: No use in going on about it. When I took you on I warned you this day would come.

Good-for-Nothing: We would have collected enough to eat tonight.

Barker: Dont sweat that. I know a gal in this town wholl feed us.

Good-for-Nothing: But Im not a Good-for-Nothing anymore.

Barker: Im telling you: it happens. It happened to yr parents, otherwise they wouldnt of had you, now would they of?

Good-for-Nothing: What will I do with the rest of my life?

Barker: Youve got a nice pair of legs. Maybe you could be a dancer. Yr also really good with numbers. You could be an accountant or a banker or a loan shark.

Good-for-Nothing: High finance? Me? You think?

Barker: You gotta do something with yr life.

Good-for-Nothing: But Im a Good-for-Nothing.

Barker: Not no more. Now yll make something of yrself.

Good-for-Nothing: I'll make something of myself. Yes. Why not?

> They exit happily, going to dinner at the house of the Barker's friend: a woman he used to know, his ex-wife, actually, who, after all these years is still very angry. She will slit his throat while he sleeps and spend the rest of her life in the women's prison.

16 THE WINDOW OF OPPORTUNITY

> A Window, nothing fancy, covered with a red-and-white-checkered curtain, or perhaps a gorgeous portion of purple velvet drapery.

The Window of Opportunity
The Window of Opportunity

> After a moment a person in uniform enters with great precision but no unnecessary ceremony. Kind of like the soldiers who guard the Tomb of the Unknown. This is the Window Meister. He stands at attention at the Window. Then, after checking his watch, checking his shadow against the sun, and testing the direction of the wind with his wetted finger, he takes a deep breath and, drawing the curtains, reveals the plain little Window. He then opens said Window with a great flourish and stands at attention.

Window Meister: The Window of Opportunity is now open!

He stands at ease—that is, still on the job, but a bit more relaxed. For a moment, nothing happens. Then the curtains begin to flutter in the breeze. Ever so slightly as curtains would flutter at a kitchen window in a farmhouse in Kansas, or at the window of an English manor house on a perfect summer day. The curtains continue fluttering as the Meister speaks:

Window Meister: Ellipses. Ellipses. Before. The Dawn of Time. The Creation of the Universe. Ellipses. The fish crawls out of the sea. Ellipses. Olduvai Gorge. Ellipses. Homo Erectus in God's image. Ellipses. Hunting. Gathering. War. The Wheel. More War. Ellipses. Gods, Gods and more Gods. The Rise. The Fall. Ellipses. Ellipses. Ellipses. Confucius and the Buddha. Ellipses. Jesus. Ellipses. Ellipses. United States version: Mayflower and Indians and Slavery; Washington Crossing the Delaware. Ellipses. Civil War. Ellipses. The War to End All Wars. Ellipses. Ellipses. All universal events of great significance up to and including the Present Day.

The Window of Opportunity
Window Meister

(Rest)

The Meister checks his watch. Watches the fluttering curtains. Waits. Again checks his watch. Its time. With great precision he closes the Window and draws the curtains. He stands at attention beside the curtained Window.

Window Meister: The Window of Opportunity is now closed!

The Window of Opportunity
Window Meister

(Rest)

Someone enters running at full speed. This is The One Who Got Away. He sees the closed Window and stops.

The One Who Got Away: No?
Window Meister: Sorry.
The One Who Got Away: Chuh.
Window Meister: Its not worth sucking yr teeth over.
The One Who Got Away: Easy for you to say.

Window Meister: Look at it this way: Yr "The One Who Got Away."

The One Who Got Away: Chuh.

Window Meister: Maybe next time.

The One Who Got Away: Yeah.

> The One Who Got Away leaves with a heavy heart.
> The Window Meister does not leave his post.

17 VEUVE CLICQUOT

The Condemned: Beef Bourguignonne, with the raspberry reduction, garlic mashed potatoes—and could they make them without milk?

Waiter: I'll ask.

The Condemned: Great. White poached asparagus, organic greens with a lemon vinaigrette.

Waiter: Dessert?

The Condemned: I get a dessert?

Waiter: Yep.

The Condemned: Death By Chocolate Soufflé.

Waiter: Thats funny.

The Condemned: I was a comedian. Once.

Waiter: Really.
(Rest)
What to drink?

The Condemned: Veuve Clicquot.

Waiter: Wassat?

The Condemned: Champagne.

Waiter: Why didnt you just say "champagne?"

The Condemned: Cause its called Veuve Clicquot.

Waiter: Thats yr whole entire problem, if you ask me.

The Condemned: Im not asking you.

Waiter: You think yr smarter than the rest of the general population, and *that* is yr whole entire problem.

The Condemned: Im just trying to enjoy myself is all.

Waiter: Veuve Clicquot.

The Condemned: Forget it.

Waiter: I'll see what I can do.

The Condemned: I dont want it anymore. I wanna change my order.

Waiter: I wrote everything down already.

The Condemned
Waiter

(Rest)

Waiter: I let you get away with—

The Condemned: With murder?

Waiter: Ima miss you. You make me laugh. But not in the way the others make me laugh. Yr jokes are—they always got like a twist to them.

The Condemned: Twisted jokes from a twisted mind.

Waiter: Yeah. I'll miss that.

The Condemned: Me too. I think. But I might not. Maybe missing is only something we do when we're alive. And when we're dead we are missed but dont miss.

Waiter: Yeah. Whatll it be?

The Condemned: Gimmie French fries, lotsa ketchup and hot sauce, double-decker burger with nice thick patties, root beer float and apple pie à la mode.

Waiter: Pie what?

The Condemned: "In the fashion."

Waiter: In the fashion of what?

The Condemned: For-get-it. Just bring me some apple pie with a scoop of vanilla ice cream.

Waiter: You want the ice cream on top?

The Condemned: Yeah.

Waiter: You got it.

The Condemned: And make it a cheeseburger. With bacon. And a new battery for the remote!

Waiter: Sure.

Waiter exits. A Chorus of Murdered Women comes in.

Murdered Women:
On the last day of my life
I was minding my own bizness
I wasnt doing nothing special
I wasnt eating no
à la mode.
I was washing all the dishes
I was picking up the kids
on the last day of my life
when he did what he did.

They stand there staring at The Condemned.
The Waiter comes back in with the food.

The Condemned: Microwaved?

Waiter: Yeah.

The Condemned: Like I'll be in a minute.

Waiter: Hey. Enjoy yr meal.

The Condemned: Yeah.

He eats. The Waiter exits. The Chorus of Murdered Women
stands there watching him eat. "Being a man is never
having to say yr sorry," The Condemned says. Not out loud.
Only to himself, in his head. He picks up the remote and eats
with one hand and channel-surfs with the other,
pretending theyre not staring at him but knowing that they are,
and his guilt for his crimes comes moving toward him
across the room like a shadow as the day grows longer,
moving on toward him even as the tv goes full blast.

18 HERE COMES THE MESSAGE

A Scout alone onstage,
looking off into the distance with a telescope.

Scout: Hhhhh.

He looks and looks.

Scout: Ive been looking my whole life. Thats my lot, I guess.
To look and look and never—

He looks. Becomes greatly agitated.

Scout: No. It cant be. HERE COMES THE MESSAGE! Good
God! Here it comes! HERE COMES THE MESSAGE! HERE
COMES THE MESSAGE! HERE COMES THE MESSAGE!

The stage quickly fills with Townspeople in various states.
Some are in their nightclothes, some have napkins at their necks
from breakfast or shaving, some are nursing children,
some are milking cows, women flipping pancakes,
men pitching hay—everybody is running
from something very important to come have a look.

> They stand next to the Scout and look, as the Scout looks
> into the far distance.

Man: Gimmie yr telescope.

Other Man: See anything?

Man: A man. On his way. In our general direction.

Scout: Its the Message.

Townspeople: Here comes the message! Here comes the message!
Here comes the message! Here comes the message!

> A Messenger, nicely dressed, comes toward them,
> they have formed a tight knot and he pushes through them,
> working hard to get past.

Messenger: Let me pass! Let me pass!

Scout: Hold on, man, yr the message.

Man: Weve been waiting.

Woman: Very patiently.

Other Woman: Through thick and through thin.

Other Man: For years.

Messenger: Im the *messenger*. Im not the message. If youll excuse
me. Im on official business.

> The Messenger pushes through the crowd
> and continues on his way.

Townspeople
Scout

Scout: Good scouts dont grow on trees, now.

Woman: Who says yr good? I for one says yr no good. Who seconds
me?

Townspeople: I.

Townspeople
Scout

> The Townspeople surround the Scout and stomp him to death.
> The Scout's telescope stands, like an eye,
> outside of the violent circle, looking at nothing.

19 FINE ANIMAL

> A Princess and a Prince. The Prince's arms are clasped around
> the Princess's neck in an elongated hanging-on hug.
> Every so often, the Princess pulls a day off a large calendar.

Princess: Bored?

Prince: Mmm.

Princess: Me too.

Prince: Much longer?

Princess: Not much.

> The Princess rips more days off the calendar.
> At long last, she reaches the end.

Prince: That it?

Princess: Looks that way.

Prince: Can I unclasp my hands?

Princess: What did she tell you?

Prince: She said after the time passed I could unclasp my hands.

Princess: The time's passed.

Prince: I'll unclasp then. Nervous?

Princess: A little. You?

Prince: Very. Being here, with my arms around yr neck all this time. There were several opportunities I missed out on. Several wars. And remember when my servant came by with news of that damsel in distress? And the dragons?

Princess: There will always be wars. There will always be damsels in distress. There will always be dragons.

Prince: One hopes.

Princess: Unclasp yr hands.

> The Prince unclasps himself. He looks the Princess over.

Prince: She lied.

Princess: Im sorry.

Prince: Its not yr fault. You didnt promise me anything. The witch did.

Princess: I thought you were doing this all on yr own.

Prince: I was, but, you know, at the witch's suggestion.

Princess: The witch with the funny hat?

Prince: Yeah.

Princess: Hhh.

The Princess whistles, like she's calling her dog. A Hag enters.

Hag: Yes, maam.

Prince: Thats the witch. She doesnt have her hat on, though.

Princess: You a witch?

Hag: No, maam. Im not a witch, Im a hag.

Prince: A hag? You said you were a witch.

Hag: I was just trying to find somebody for my princess.

Prince: In my country, the punishment for impersonating a witch is death by dismemberment.

Princess: But yr not in yr country. Yr in my country.

Hag: I appreciate that.

Princess: Silence.

Prince: I wanted a good-looking wife. I dont mean any disrespect.

Princess: None taken.

Hag: I was only trying to help.

Princess: Silence.

Prince: And now Ive missed out on the tournaments. And the dragons. And the damsels. And the wars.

Princess: There will be more wars and tournaments and damsels and dragons too, wont there?

Hag: Im old and Ive seen plenty.

Prince: I dont trust you, Hag.

Princess: Silence. I mean—

Prince: No worries. We're all under stress here. I had a plan and its gone to shit. My plan was to have good-looking children. They would, when they got old enough of course, be featured in all the glossy magazines. Ive got good clear eyes and a strong enough chin. I was hoping to—well—

Princess: And here youve been tricked into spending all this time around my neck. You could go and find another.

Prince: I guess so.

Hag: I could help.

Princess: Silence.

Hag: Let me speak. Please.

Princess
Prince

Princess: Speak.

Hag: Take a look at this.

Prince: Its a glossy magazine.

Hag: With a 3-page picture in it.

> The Prince opens the magazine and eyes the centerfold.

Prince: Fine animal. Oh, yeah.

Princess: Yr not leaving then.

Prince: Fine animal.

Hag: He's staying. He's yrs.

Princess: You think?

Hag: Yep. I seen it before. Congratulations.

> The Prince gives the Princess a kiss on the cheek.

Princess: Hag, go fetch the prince, my husband, some slippers, a meatloaf, lots more magazines, and a pipe howbout.

> The Hag curtsies and goes. They settle into domestic bliss.
> The Princess gazes at the Prince and
> the Prince gazes at the centerfold.

20 THE ENDS OF THE EARTH

> A Throng chases a Man. They run pell-mell. They pass a small
> nondescript sign. They stop, run back, read the sign.

Throng: This is it.

Man: What do you mean?

Throng: Arent you beat?

Man: I was just getting into it.

Throng: This is as far as we go.

Man: Have we crossed the county line or something? Dont be ridiculous! Where are you all headed? Dont turn back! You said youd hound me to the ends of the earth!

Throng: And here we are. At the ends of the earth.

Man: This isnt the ends of the earth.

Throng: Read the sign.

Man: Forget the sign. This isnt the ends of the earth.

Throng: Ever been there?

Man: No. But. Well, this is not the ends of the earth. Let-me-tell-you.

Throng: Read the sign.

The Sun
The Sun

(Rest)

The Sun: Shine! Shine! Shine! Shine!

23 THANKSGIVING? (See November 28 Again)

23 DEAD BEAUTY

> A woman, the Dead Beauty, lies on the floor covered
> with a shroud. Another Woman is brought in by 2 Men.
> She walks with difficulty.

1st Man: Stand here, maam.

> The Men pull back the shroud. The Dead Beauty and
> the Woman are the same age and look as much alike
> as possible.

Woman: My beauty.
2nd Man: We'll leave you alone with her.

> The Men exit.

Woman: My beauty. My beauty. What happened to my beauty?
Dead Beauty: You didnt feed me, so I died.

Woman
Dead Beauty

Woman: Hhhhh.
Dead Beauty: Hhhhh.

(Rest)

Woman: Traitor.
Dead Beauty: Has-Been.

> The Woman lunges at the Dead Beauty,
> the Dead Beauty leaps to her feet.

Woman
Dead Beauty

> They circle each other like 2 sumo wrestlers,
> or 2 brothers on the street with knives.
> They clutch and struggle as the lights fade.

24 THE 20th CENTURY

> A Woman stands at a velvet snake holding a ticket.
> We hear an unearthly sound—the sound of a very loud train.
> A Frozen Tableau—people and events, both famous and not,
> from the 20th Century—passes in front of her,
> like a float in a parade.
> The Tableau stops.

Conductor: The 20th Century! All Abooooooard!

> The Woman gets on the float, poses in some kind of way.

Conductor: Move to yr left.
Woman: Thats coach.
Conductor: First-class is full.
Woman: But I paid for first-class.
Conductor: All Abooooooooooard!
Woman: My ticket says "first." See?
Conductor: They oversold it. Sorry. Coach.
Woman: First!
Conductor: Coach!
Woman: First!

> Another loud train sound is heard.
> Another Tableau pulls up alongside.

Woman: What train is that?
2nd Conductor: The 21st Century! All Abooooooooooooard!

> Everything is very still.
> Then a Man leaps from one train to the other.

21st Century:
What else?
Dunno.
Here we are.
And here we go.

> The 21st Century takes off and
> the 20th Century watches it leave.

25 BEGINNING, MIDDLE, END

Traditionalist:
Beginning, Middle, End
Beginning, Middle, End.
Fresh One:
End, Beginning
Beginning, Middle
Middle, End
Middle, Fiddle
Faddle, Paddle
yr own canoe.

> They look at each other.

Traditionalist: Yrs is better than mine.

Fresh One: No its not. Its just—

Traditionalist: Fresh. And fun. Im no fun. Im stuck in a rut.
Everybody says so.

> The Traditionalist bursts into tears.

Fresh One: Forget what everybody says.

Traditionalist: I tried. I tried to be fresh. Once.

Fresh One: Howd it go?

Traditionalist: Felt lousy. Felt—fake.

Fresh One: Maybe you were trying too hard. I never try too hard.

Traditionalist: It just comes, right?

Fresh One: Kind of.
(Rest)
When I started out I looked to traditional forms. But the situations I wanted to explore, the characters I wanted to embrace didnt fit—you get the picture?—

November

Traditionalist: Sorta.

Fresh One: My stuff didnt fit traditional forms.

Traditionalist: But mine does. Most of it. Although, thinking back on it all, there have been things left out, discarded. But most things fit.

Fresh One: Then be traditional. Its not a CRIME.

Traditionalist: But being fresh is criminal.

Fresh One: In some circles.

> The Traditionalist takes out a piece of chalk.
> He considers writing the following stage direction:
> "The Traditionalist draws a circle around the Fresh One."

Fresh One: Whatcha doing?

Traditionalist: Whassit look like.

Fresh One: Yr drawing a circle around me.

Traditionalist: Mmm.

Fresh One: How come?

Traditionalist: Ha!

Fresh One: What?

Traditionalist: Nothing.

Fresh One: Wassup with the circle, pal?

Traditionalist: Im being experimental.

Fresh One: Good for you.

Traditionalist: We'll see. Heres a whistle.

Fresh One: Right.

Traditionalist: Blow it.

> The Fresh One blows the whistle. They wait.
> A Group of Riot Police come in. They eye the circle.
> They stand at the circle and beat the Fresh One.

Traditionalist:
Beginning, Middle, End.

Riot Police Captain: Says who?

Traditionalist: Says me. Says you. Says all of us. Its an accepted form.

Traditionalist
Riot Police

(Rest)

Riot Police Captain: Anybody watching?

Riot Police Lieutenant: Nope.

Riot Police Captain: Go for it.

> The Police surround the Traditionalist and beat him.
> Then they exit.

26 MRS. KECKLEY & MRS. LINCOLN

1865. Mrs. Lincoln, wife of the 16th President, and Mrs. Keckley, her Negro dressmaker and handmaid. Lots of dresses spread about. Mrs. Lincoln studies each dress in turn.

Mrs. Lincoln: I'll wear my red.

Mrs. Keckley: Yr red?

Mrs. Lincoln: Yes?

Mrs. Keckley: Yr red is very—red.

Mrs. Lincoln: You think?

Mrs. Keckley: Mmm.

Mrs. Lincoln: Theyll all be looking at me, though. The redll shut them up.

Mrs. Keckley: Theyve got things to shut them up already. Not to disagree with you, maam, but the war is preying heavy on their minds.

Mrs. Lincoln: "Preying heavy on their minds." I like that.

Mrs. Keckley: Thank you, maam.

Mrs. Lincoln: I hate when you call me that. "Maam." I want to feel young. I want to feel like I have my whole life ahead of me. I had 26 suitors. In one season. But you look down at the floor. Youve heard me tell that story already. Is that the difference between a young girl of 15 and a married woman, do you think? The young girl does not repeat herself, while the old married woman—. 26 suitors. In one season. A young girl would repeat that. Because it is worth repeating. It bears repeating. And the things I bear. And the children I have born.

(Rest)

Call me Mary.

Mrs. Keckley: What about yr blue?

Mrs. Lincoln: Are you hard-of-hearing, Mrs. Keckley? Should we call in Doctor Wilke and have you fitted for an ear trumpet?

Mrs. Keckley: Yr yellow would suit the occasion, maam.

November

Mrs. Lincoln: "Mary." I won't consider another dress or another thing, I wont move a muscle or take another breath until you call me Mary.

Mrs. Lincoln
Mrs. Keckley

(Rest)

Mrs. Keckley: Yr yellow would suit the occasion, Mary.

Mrs. Lincoln: Ah, it feels good to breathe again, Elizabeth. You are blushing. Ha. I can see the color coming up. It makes you look purple. It makes you look purple, Elizabeth.

Mrs. Keckley: You need to get dressed. Mary.

Mrs. Lincoln: We both live in this country. We both inhabit the White House. You know what its like, living here. In the joyless gloom, while the war continues. Sunshine, rain, snow, spring and still, the war continues. An admirable thing. Like a woman. War is female, wouldnt you say? Because it is so tenacious.

(Rest)

Just a little longer. Its only for fun. I'll call you Elizabeth and you call me Mary. For just a little longer. Just for fun.

Mrs. Keckley: The white, I think, Mary.

Mrs. Lincoln: Why didnt we think of that before? The white with the red roses, and cut so low that the president will look at me and his eyes will travel from my eyes down to my mouth and, then, fall into the chasm of my bosom. 26 suitors, Elizabeth, and he was the—tallest.

Mrs. Keckley
Mrs. Lincoln

(Rest)

Mrs. Keckley & Mrs. Lincoln: Hahahahahahahahahhaha!

Mrs. Lincoln: Of course I didnt know that at the time, I was only a girl.

Mrs. Keckley: You didnt know that all tall drinks of water are— (well equipped)?

Mrs. Lincoln: I'll swear an oath on my marriage bed, I'll swear that I had no idea. But on my marriage bed, Elizabeth, I tell you, Mary did discover.

Mrs. Keckley: He's a fine man, Mary.

Mrs. Lincoln: I'll give him that.

Mrs. Keckley: Lets get you dressed. We wouldnt want to keep yr president waiting.

Mrs. Lincoln: He's yr president too.

Mrs. Keckley
Mrs. Keckley

(Rest)

Mrs. Keckley: Step into yr dress. There, that's it. Pretty as a picture.

> Mrs. Lincoln steps into her white dress. Mrs. Keckley continues
> helping her get dressed, lacing up the back, etc.
> There is a sound of a gunshot.

Mrs. Lincoln: What in God's name was that?!

Mrs. Keckley: Just the sound of a car backfiring.

Mrs. Lincoln: The sound of a what-whating?

Mrs. Keckley: Just the sound of the War, maam, getting closer.

Mrs. Lincoln: I thought you said—something else.

Mrs. Keckley: Take a look in the mirror, maam. See how pretty you look.

Mrs. Lincoln: We're going to see *Our American Cousin* tonight. I wonder if its any good.

Mrs. Keckley: Its a comedy.

Mrs. Lincoln: A comedy! We are the lucky ones, Mrs. Keckley! We are the lucky ones!

> Mrs. Keckley takes a headdress of roses from a box.
> Mrs. Lincoln claps her hands in delight as
> Mrs. Keckley puts it on her head.

27 HOLE

> A Man digs a hole. He digs with great relish.
> A Woman comes up out of the hole.
> After a beat she reaches in the hole and removes her suitcase.

Woman: Whatcha doing?

Man: Digging.

Woman: You dug me up.

Man: Didnt mean to. I was just digging. You dead?

Woman: Nope.

Woman
Man

Man: I'd like to keep digging if you dont mind.

Woman: Can I watch?

Man: Whats to watch.

Woman: Yr digging.

Man: Yeah?

Woman: Yeah.

Man: Suit yrself. Its a free country.

Woman: Is it?

Man
Woman

Man: Yr one of those agitators, arentcha?

Woman: What if I am.

Man: One of those agitators, laying in wait. Hiding behind bushes, in between the wallpaper and the wall, underneath a man's own bed, underneath an honest man's own earth. Waiting for yr chance to spring up or out and—do what you agitators do.

Woman: Youve been watching too much tv.

Man: Yr one of those agitators, dont change the subject.

Woman: Dont stop digging.

Man: I dont intend to.

> He continues with his digging.

Woman: What if I were. One of those agitators?

Man: I dont got time for agitators.

Woman: What if I werent?

Man: Then youd just be some woman. Who came up crawling out the dirt. Thatd be a different story. Youd just be some woman.

Woman: Some good-looking woman.

Man: Yeah, I'll give you that.

Woman: Some good-looking woman in a low-cut blouse who likes watching you dig.

Man: Yr blouse isnt cut low.

Woman: What if it was?

Man
Woman

Man: I got work to do.

Woman: Me too.

Man

Woman

He digs with greater relish.
She watches with heightened interest.

Woman: Whats it for?

Man: The hole? Its just a job. It isnt my hole, Im digging it for a fella. A rich fella. He's got money to burn and—yeah, he's living high, lemmie tell you.

Woman: You get paid by the hour?

Man: I get paid by the hole. How about you?

Woman

Man

Woman: Im on salary.

Man: Celery?

Woman: Salary.

Man

Woman

Man: See that road right there? The wide one? Squint yr eyes up and yll see it.

Woman: I came down that road once.

Man: Everybody does. Comes down it or goes up it. Comes in on it or leaves out that way. Me, Im the exception. Ive never been further than this side of the road proper. In my whole entire life. Some would call that a rut. But some would call the road a rut and both could be right or wrong. Alls I know is that the whole world has passed me by and Ive never felt the need to join it. Ive spent my whole life right here.

Woman: Thats not what I heard.

Man

Woman

Man

Woman

(Rest)

Man: Ok, ok. I went over there. Yeah. I crossed the road and I did what I had to do, you unnerstand? You better write this down or tape-record this or document this in some fashion, take pictures or film it or—cause Im only gonna say it once. Do you shorthand? "IF-U-CN-RD-THIS-U-CN-GT-A-GD-JOB." Every woman should, you know. Every man too. Maybe if we all knew some shorthand things would be different. Thatd be a gas, right? Change the course of the world by learning secretarial skills. Thats honest work. Unless you think about who yr working for.

Woman: There aint no winning is there?

Man: Nope. Meanwhile you watch me sweat.

(Rest)

I met a guy over there who was digging a hole and it looked so—right. And I thought, sweet Jesus on the cross—are you listening?

Woman: Im listening.

Man: You dont look like yr listening. You look like yr watching more than listening. I said to myself if I ever get back, you know? I said if I ever get back thats just what Ima do. Dig a hole.

Woman: Back from what?

Man: Dont ask.

Woman: What if I did?

Man: "No comment."

Woman
Man

Woman: Youve made a career of it. Hole digging.

Man: Thats the kicker. You think one would satisfy. Wrong. Digging holes creates the need to dig holes.

Woman: Theres a word for that. A psychological term.

Man: Dont tell me the term. I just want to be.

Woman: I feel the same way exactly.

Man: Whats in the suitcase?

Woman: A bag.

The Woman opens her suitcase and takes out a big plastic bag.
Full of something. She drops it into the hole.

Man: Whats in the bag?

Woman: Mmm.

Man: Should I leave it there or should I cover it up?

Woman: Cover it up.

Man: I know the feeling.

Woman: What time you punch out?

Man: Sunset.

Woman: Wanna get a drink or a bite or a smoke or a spike or something?

Man: Thatd be nice.

> He covers the bag with dirt, pats the dirt with his spade.
> Begins digging another hole as she watches.
> After sunset they will go to a motel. She will let him
> get on top of her, and when he is inside her,
> she will look at the inexpensive nightstand and
> think of her great good fortune. When he finishes he will
> want to please her. A closeness will emerge between them.
> They will talk through the night. She will tell him of the rich man.
> And the rich man's money which was not in the plastic bag.
> It was her fondest memories that were in the bag.
> She and the rich man were lovers once. Years ago.

28 ROLL OUT THE RED CARPET

> 2 women, Dolly and Bertie, in military uniforms,
> working together, unrolling a largish red carpet.
> The carpet extends offstage so that we understand
> that theyve been unrolling it for quite some time.

Dolly: Some job, this.

Bertie: Tell me about it.

Dolly: Heavy.

Bertie: Long.

Dolly: And the heat dont help.

> They continue unrolling.

Bertie: I put on 5 pounds over the holidays.

Dolly: You dont look it.

Bertie: The waistband of this uniform is cutting into me, lemmie tell you.

Dolly: I'll hip you to something.

Bertie: Lay it on me.

Dolly: Anybody looking?

Bertie: Nope.

Dolly: Sure?

Bertie: Do they call me "Eagle Eye Bertie"?

Dolly: They do.

Bertie: Can I shoot off the head of the enemy at 10-thousand paces?

Dolly: Yr gold star proves it.

Bertie: But here we are unrolling the red carpet.

Dolly: What do you expect? Its peacetime.

Bertie: Not for long, though. Hell, gimmie a good war any day of the week.

Dolly: You dont mean it.

Bertie: I mean it.

Dolly: You dont even. You know yr crazy about yr kids. Bustling in the kitchen. I walk into yr house—no I walk by yr house—no— my dear Tom *thinks* about doing a little yardwork—finishing that moat he's digging, the one he started 3 years ago—

Bertie: Tell me about it.

Dolly: My dear Tom stands at the front door and he smells yr cooking and he gives me this *look*. And I throw up my hands, cause as hard as I try I cant outcook Eagle Eye.

Bertie: But the weight Ive gained.

Dolly: Coast clear?

Bertie: Thumbs up on the coast, thats a roger.

Dolly: Check this out.

> She lifts her jacket, showing Bertie her amended waistband.

Dolly: You get a piece of elastic, like a rubberband, right? You run the rubberband through the buttonhole then loop it around the button.

Bertie: Genius.

Dolly: Gives you breathing room.

Bertie: Geeeen-yus.

Dolly: Did Dolly crack the code used by the boat refugees?

Bertie: Yr a Geeeeen-yus!

Dolly: Come on, we got a ways to unroll yet. We dont want her arriving and walking in and us with it not all unrolled.

Bertie: Anything but that.

> Merrily they unroll along.

28 (Again) PILGRIMS' PROGRESS (For Thanksgiving)

A group of Pilgrims. Different kinds.
Pilgrims off the Mayflower of 1620, and other religious Pilgrims
of all colors and stripes: Muslims going to Mecca,
Hindus headed perhaps toward Vrindavan or Varanasi,
English folks heading to Canterbury, Christians going to Lourdes
or walking along El Camino de Santiago, or heading toward
Guadalupe. Buddhists on their way to Bodh Gaya,
Tibetan Buddhists journeying to Mount Kailash or Lhasa or
Lake Man Tso, Jews heading toward the Wailing Wall perhaps.
Pilgrims heading toward the Feast of Kumbah Mela.
Devotees walking, lying on the ground and bowing,
then walking again. Devotees whirling as they walk.
Devotees crawling on their knees as they sing.
All kinds of Pilgrims. Accommodate as many as you can.
Dont intentionally exclude anybody. The Pilgrims move very
deliberately, but also very slowly, across the stage.
Perhaps theres music to accompany the journey.
Someone and Someone Else (from "Remember Who You Are,"
the 1st of the 3 Constants) watch the procession.

Someone: All Pilgrims.
Someone Else: So different!
Someone: But all going to the same place.

Smiles all around.

29 DRAGON SONG

Narrator: This is the Song of the Dragon.

The stage fills with various players. They make a tableau.

Narrator: Once there was a virtual sailor. She had sailed the seas
without leaving her easy chair. No, thats not it. Once there was a
regular Jane who had nothing remarkable.
Jane: Nothing?
Narrator: Nothing remarkable, save one skill: she walked with her
gaze turned down to the ground because she was fond of rocks.
Jane: Im a regular Jane. Im fond of rocks.
Narrator: Her fondness of rocks led her to a cave. There she found
a chest of jewels.

Jane: Bonanza.

Narrator: She took the jewels home and put the chest under her bed. She'd look at it sometimes. The light of the jewels was very bright so she didnt look at it too often.

Jane: Bonanza. Bonanza.

Narrator: After a few years, she began having dreams. A dragon would visit her.

Dragon: Im a dragon.

Jane: Yr not only a dragon, yr an enormous dragon.

Dragon: The treasure under yr bed is mine.

Jane: Are we having an earthquake?

Dragon: No, its just my heart beating.

Narrator: Jane was forced to use her wits.

The Wits: Do yr one remarkable thing.

Jane: Im in battle with a dragon, right now.

The Wits: Do yr one remarkable thing, Jane.

Jane: You mean look down?

The Wits: Bingo.

Dragon: Give me my treasure or I'll breathe fire.

Jane: Underneath my feet is a red carpet left over from an earlier play.

The Wits: Work it.

Jane
Jane

(Rest)

Jane: Do you have any idea who I am?

Dragon: Some girl who swiped my shit.

Jane: Im—some girl *on a red carpet.*

Dragon: Yr Majesty?

The Wits: Yr Majesty!

Narrator: And all assembled, including yr devoted Narrator. We all bowed to Jane. Jane bowed back. And we made Jane queen.

Jane: And we live as happily as we can under the circumstances.

The Wits: The End.

Dragon: What about my song?

Jane: Hit it.

Dragon:
I have nothing.
Since I lost you.

The Dragon sings a torch song. Armageddon.
Civilization turns to ash. Nothing remains
of what we once knew, except that red carpet.

30 THE COMING

Except for the red carpet, the stage is bare.
An enormous stone rolls onto the stage,
self-propelled or pushed by 2 muscular men.
The rolling stone is followed by an Assistant, with a sign:
"She Has Risen." The Assistant is followed by She.
She expects to be met by a large crowd. No one is there.
She sends a Messenger into town
and they come back with news.

Messenger: The town's asleep.
Assistant: What to do?
She: Theyll wake. I'll wait.
Assistant: In the meantime, Ive got a little something.

The Assistant pulls out an entire town complete with sidewalks,
trees, picket fences, barbershops, swimming holes,
kissing lookouts, cider houses, schoolrooms,
a tomb for an unknown soldier, memories, histories,
everything a town would need, in short, the Assistant
pulls an entire town from a bag, sets it up, and immediately
it gets to the great business of living, which is to say
that the town and its folk are just like you and me.
The sun rises and sets, the moon waxes and wanes,
the seasons pass and then the years pass too. Wars, etc.
Several millennia. Through all this, She watches them
with interest, love and affection. She has forgotten about
the sleeping town, forgotten She was waiting for them to wake,
forgotten what She was waiting for and that She was waiting at all.

December
1 THE RUMOR MILL

The red carpet is still onstage, and maybe the town too,
from the last play. The Rumor Man comes onstage.
He drags behind him, on a little wheeled cart, the Rumor Mill—
a sort of bingo wheel with lots of scraps of things in it.

Townfool: Today is the "Day Without Art."

The Rumor Man: Dont be foolish! Look! The Rumor Mill has arrived!

> For a moment no one dares to move. The Rumor Man begins
> turning the wheel, thoroughly mixing the little scraps inside.
> The turning of the Mill makes a musical sound—like
> the sound of an organ grinder's organ—but much much louder.
> Folks start crowding around, almost against their will.
> They stand and watch and then, losing interest, they leave,
> watching each other as they exit. Then, all at once in a rush,
> theyre back, standing around the Mill, panting in anticipation.

Townspeople: The Rumor Mill! The Rumor Mill! The Rumor Mill!

> The Rumor Mill spits out a scrap of something. All stare at it.

The Rumor Man: You have a Reader in this town, dontcha?

Townspeople: Bring out the Reader! Bring out the Reader!

> The Reader is pushed forward, richly or poorly dressed,
> with a Servant at her elbow, or in chains and led by a master.

The Rumor Man: Yr the Reader?

The Reader: Thats right.

The Rumor Man: I hereby grant you the authority to read the Rumor.

> The Reader picks up the scrap. She clears her throat.
> She "reads":

Reader:
"The King is alive.
He's living in Vegas.
Playing the All-American slot machine
seeing if we go down for the count
or if we live up to the dream.
The King is alive. Not Elvis, but Martin.
You thought they gunned him down, right?
He's alive Im telling you.
You saw his body on the evening news
and that famous photo
of the people pointing:
'The gunshot that killed him, it came from there,'
while the King lay bleeding on the ground.
And his widow, the Queen,
in another town, but feeling it,
put her hand on her heart
and thought, 'My God.'

December

The elders among us saw this scene
with their own eyes
but it was just a version of reality
cause Im telling you, Dr. King is alive
and living in Las Vegas."

> The Reader relaxes.

The Rumor Man: The Rumor Mill has spoken!

> The Townspeople applaud enthusiastically.
> Perhaps a discussion develops in the town, long after
> this play has ended. Possible questions for discussion:
> "A physical or virtual resurrection?" and "Why in Las Vegas?"

2 ABRAHAM LINCOLN AT 89

> Abraham Lincoln, former 16th President of the United States;
> the former 1st Lady, Mary Todd Lincoln; Elizabeth Keckley,
> her dressmaker and handmaid; and other foreign
> and domestic Dignitaries, in addition to
> a respectable representation of the Local Population,
> all gathered to celebrate the Former President's birthday.

The Wealthiest Man in the World: Happy birthday, Mr. Former President! Greetings from my considerable corner of the world. You must be over a 100 by now! Happy birthday!

Lincoln: Im not over 100! Im 89!

Mary Todd Lincoln: He's funny about his age. I am too. And today's not even his birthday, either.

Mrs. Keckley: ((Dont spoil it.))

The Wealthiest Man in the World: 89! 89! Of course! Of course! Happy 89th birthday!

1st Foreign Dignitary: Thats very novel, sir, to celebrate the 89th year. In my country we would celebrate the 80th or the 90th.

Lincoln: I might not be alive that long.

Mary Todd Lincoln: Yr not alive now!

Lincoln: Mary, we have guests. My wife is not at her best. She takes the war very hard.

Mrs. Keckley: Mrs. Lincoln, I'd like you to try on the rose headdress.

Mary Todd Lincoln: I dont want to try on the rose headdress. It reminds me of a funeral wreath. It reminds me of what I was wearing. When. He. Left.

Lincoln: Mary, dont you worry about a thing. I'll handle the guests. I'll tell them the joke about how I won the presidency. Go along with Mrs. Keckley, dear, dont you worry about a thing. *(Aside)* She thinks that folks dont like my jokes. She says my jokes aren't "cultured."

3rd Foreign Dignitary: Cultured? I'll show you cultured.

> He performs a very beautiful and complicated dance
> telling the story of his national heroine and hero, how they met,
> wooed, were wed and then, owing to the evil deeds of
> the lesser of 2 evils, were torn from each other's arms.
> Her tears made the world's first oceans, his search for her
> made the world's first land masses; their separation created
> night and their ultimate and glorious reunion created day.
> It all took eons to happen and it all happened in an instant.
> An instant which ends with the birthday party of
> a Former American President: great beauty and tableau.

The Assembled Guests
The Assembled Guests

(Rest)

> Lincoln applauds. The others follow suit.
> Lincoln dabs his eyes. The others follow suit.
> He bursts into tears. The others as well.

Lincoln: Moving. Very moving. Well well well. Too bad Mary missed it.

3rd Foreign Dignitary: I'll perform it again at her request.

Lincoln: How bout we get some of these candles lit?

Candle Lighter: My pleasure, Mr. Former President.

Lincoln: And count em as you light em. I like to hear the numbers go by.

Candle Lighter: My pleasure, Mr. Former President.

> The Candle Lighter lights each candle on the cake.
> As he lights, he says the number out loud (the counting should
> continue softly underneath the remaining dialogue).
> The Assembled Guests watch the Candle Lighter for a bit
> and then, all except for Lincoln, grow bored.

2nd Foreign Dignitary: Nothing like a good war, I always say.

Lincoln: Only when we cease to fight do we truly conquer.

1st Local: Thats ridiculous, Mr. Former President.

The Wealthiest Man in the World: In my corner of the world youd be executed for yr insolence.

2nd Foreign Dignitary: Where I come from we do not invite locals to view the Former Head of State lying in state.

The Assembled Guests
The Assembled Guests

Lincoln: What did you say?

1st Local: You said, "Only when we cease to fight do we truly conquer," and I said, "Thats ridiculous."

2nd Foreign Dignitary: Im not going to repeat myself.

The Wealthiest Man in the World: Just as well.

1st Local: This is ridiculous.

Lincoln: Yep, I suppose it is. Did you ever hear how I won over my constituents? I won by a majority, because of the possum and the squirrels, and the bears and the bobcat and whatnot. It was the critters who put me in office.
(Rest)
Ha ha ha ha ha ha.

(Rest)

The Assembled Guests: Hahahahahahahahha.

> Mary Todd Lincoln reenters, in a completely different dress. Mrs. Keckley wears the dress that Mrs. Lincoln was wearing and Mrs. Lincoln wears—well, perhaps she wears Mrs. Keckley's dress.

Mary Todd Lincoln: You like it?

Lincoln: Very much. Gentlemen, my wife. Greet her in the manner of yr country, culture or social class.

> One by one each guest performs the male-female curtsy-greeting of their country, custom, culture or class. Then, all in unison, they repeat their individual curtsies, revolving around the triumphant Mary Todd Lincoln as if she were on a brilliant pedestal, or they, devotees of the maypole. As they devote themselves to her, Mary performs rhythmic breathing and various mudras. Perhaps it is all accompanied by music. This display is not at all tacky or excessive, but very devotional and a little sad.

Lincoln: This is the best birthday Ive ever had.

Mary Todd Lincoln: But you didnt live to be a 100.

The Wealthiest Man in the World: He's 89!

Mary Todd Lincoln: Its an act of self-flattery having a one-hundredth birthday party when you didnt live to be 100. He didnt live to 89, either, truth be told.

2nd Foreign Dignitary: Truth be told!!!

Lincoln: Mary, please, darling. We have guests.

Lincoln
Mary Todd

(Rest)

> The Narrator, from one of the earlier plays,
> enters from the wings.

Narrator: To be continued.

Lincoln: Really?

Narrator: You heard me.

Mary Todd Lincoln: We must be good.

Narrator: Good enough.

The Assembled Guests: All right, then!

Lincoln: We are the lucky ones!

> All are very happy. The Candle Lighter continues lighting and
> counting the candles as the lights fade.

3 IMPALA

> 2 men, Chuck and Gopher, hanging out looking
> at Chuck's vintage Chevy Impala.
> After an appropriate moment of appreciation,
> Chuck pisses on his car.

Gopher: Why you pissing on it?

Chuck: So chicks will know its mine. Dudes too. This is my Impala. Not yrs.

Gopher: It gets you pussy?

Chuck: No, man.

Gopher: No?

Chuck: It gets me *dick.* A constant hard one.

Gopher: Shit.

Chuck: Shit is right.

Gopher: Whatchu looking at?
Man: Nothing, man, nothing.
Gopher: Nothing's right, pussy.

The Man hurries on his way.

Chuck: You told him.
Gopher: Sure did.

They drink.

4 PUSSY

Gopher and Chuck hanging out at the Impala again.
Lots of time has passed, like in "Impala" it was summer
and now its winter or something.

Chuck: Whats with yr arm?
Gopher: I hurt it.
Chuck: Doing what?
Gopher: What do you think?
Chuck: Fighting?
Gopher: Shit yeah.
Chuck: Lets see.

Gopher shows Chuck his wounded arm.

Chuck: Shit, man.
Gopher: Yeah.
Chuck: Shit.
Gopher: Yeah.
Chuck: You gonna go to the hospital? I'll drive you.
Gopher: Hospital? Hells no. I aint no pussy.
Chuck: Right. Shit, man.
Gopher: Yeah.
Chuck: What was it over?
Gopher: The fight?
Chuck: Yeah.
Gopher: Nothing. Well, some girl.

Chuck: Brenda?

Gopher: Hells no.

Chuck: Wanda?

Gopher: Fuck Wanda.

Chuck: Yeah. Who, then?

Gopher: Just some chick. Some nameless chick.

Chuck: You get with her?

Gopher: Who you talking to?

Chuck: Right.

Gopher: I only lost the fight cause I wasnt going all out.

Chuck: But you got with her.

Gopher: I might be a fight-loser but I aint no pussy-loser.

Chuck: Right.

(Rest)

It hurt?

Gopher: Naw.

Chuck: It looks like it hurts. The skin's all—mangled.

Gopher: I aint no pussy.

Chuck: Right.

Gopher: Shit.

Chuck: Right.

(Rest)

Piss on my Impala.

Gopher: Shit.

Chuck: Go on.

Gopher: Its not mine. I dont even want to appear to be claiming it.

Chuck: Piss on it. Go on. Itll make you feel good.

Gopher: I dont feel bad.

Chuck: Itll make you feel better. My treat, man.

Gopher: Yeah?

Chuck: Piss on my fucking Impala, pussy.

Gopher: Cool.

Gopher urinates on Chuck's car.

Gopher: (oww)

Chuck: What.

Gopher: It hurts when—

Chuck: When you piss?

Gopher: Yeah.

Chuck: Shit, man.

Gopher: Yeah.

Chuck: From some chick?

Gopher: Yeah. From some nameless chick.

5 HOUSE OF JONES
1st Theme

> Jones rides in a cart pulled by Smith.

Jones: A General. Without a horse. Have you ever heard of such a thing, Smith?

Smith: There have been quite a few, sir.

Jones: Am I not even singular in my horseless-ness?

Smith: I dont follow you, sir.

Jones: No you dont. But if I had a horse, you would be. Following me, I mean.

Smith: I could push the cart, sir.

Jones: Give it a go.

> Smith runs to the back, pushing instead of pulling the cart. Pulling it was hard, pushing it is harder. The wheels barely turn.

Jones: What do you think?

Smith: We seem to make better progress the other way, sir.

Jones: I dont like yr tone of voice.

Smith: No offense meant by it, sir.

Jones: Go back to pulling.

> Smith goes back to pulling.

Smith: When I was a young man I thought Generals could not walk, sir. Thats what I thought because I had never seen a General walk. All the General's I'd ever seen rode. On horses, in carts or cars, or on the shoulders of their men, sir. Like in the days of the Great Triumph.

(Rest)

> Smith rests his load. Jones looks as if he's asleep.

Smith: My mother used to tell me stories. To get me to go to bed at night. Make-believe. She told me once that I was a General's son. And that Generals flew. Dont you know it, at dawn the next morning, I was jumping off the roof.

Jones: Thats what happened to yr leg.

Smith: My leg wound is from the conflict with the Northern Enemy.

> Jones draws his sword.

Jones: Yr lucky the war is over. I would have cut off yr leg for lying.

Smith: I get the storytelling from my mother, but I appreciate yr mercy, General Jones, sir.

Jones
Smith
Jones
Smith

Jones: In 10 days we'll be home.

Smith: Maybe 20.

Jones: Another war could start up in that time. The ceasefire may not hold.

Smith: We can only hope, sir.

Jones: We can only hope.
(Rest)
We'll camp here tonight.

Smith: I'll pitch the tent.

> Jones takes out his pipe and smokes it. Smith pitches the tent.

2nd Theme

Honoria: Do I look old?

Birdy: No, maam.

Honoria: But I'll look old to him.

Birdy: He'll be so glad to see you, maam. What is 20 years between 2 people who love each other. 2 people who have written each other letters. Daily. 2 people who were meant for each other. And still are. The signs were never as auspicious as they were on yr wedding day to General Jones, maam.

Honoria: He wasnt a General then.

Birdy: But the signs for his becoming a leader of men were most favorable. Remember how he used to wrestle under yr window. Most men sang, remember? But—

Honoria: "What good is singing when theres a war on," he said.

Birdy: The war made him, thats for sure.

Honoria: And will the peace un-make him? Will the peace un-make everything Ive acquired in its absence? Will his return un-make the woman Ive become?

Birdy: You are our queen.

Honoria: And when he returns I'll just be the king's wife.

Birdy: Nonsense.

Honoria: "Nonsense"? I don't like yr tone of voice.

Honoria
Birdy

> Honoria rings a bell. A Female Servant carrying a stick enters.
> The Servant holds the stick high above Birdy.

Honoria: Yr not begging for mercy?

Birdy: It wont do no good.

Honoria
Birdy

Honoria: Leave us.

> The Servant leaves.

Honoria: Damn this war.

Birdy: Yes, maam.

6 BLACKBIRD (A *Sea Gull* Variation)

> Rough and Tosha. Tosha is dressed all in black.

Rough: Ima ax you.

Tosha: Go head.

Rough: You dont want me to ax but Ima ax.

Tosha: I said go head, you deaf?

Rough: Cool.

Tosha: Ax.

Rough: So howcome you always wearing black?

Tosha: Black is beautiful, thats how come.

Tosha
Rough

(Rest)

Rough: Girl, you got to marry me.

Tosha: I dont got to marry you nothing.

Rough: We got that special something between us.

Tosha: A special something nothing.

Rough: Girl—

Tosha: I told you that this Tosha is a woman of the Movement. And you, Roughy, you are part of the stagnation. Tosha aint legally binding her womanhood into the stagnation.

Rough: Im getting on my knees till you say yes.

Tosha: Yr gonna be kneeling yr whole life.

Rough: I got a good job. Ima buy you a house in the Rolling Hills.

Tosha: Ima woman of the Movement. The Rolling Hills aint part of the Movement far as I can tell.

Rough: Power to the people!

Tosha: You dont mean it.

Rough: Power to the people!

Tosha: You just wanna get with me.

> She exits.

Rough: Power to the people!
(Rest)
Shit.

> Still on his knees, he exits following her.

7 THE CARPET CLEANER ON PEARL HARBOR DAY

> The red carpet, unrolled several plays earlier
> (see the play for November 28) is still unrolled on the stage.
> A man in a uniform, the Carpet Cleaner, comes out.
> He looks over the carpet, then exits. He returns with a vacuum
> cleaner, takes off his uniform jacket, looks around for
> an electrical plug. He whistles as he looks. At last, offstage,
> he finds a plug, plugs in, and gets to work. As he works
> he continues whistling, although we cant hear him
> over the roar of the vacuuming.

He completes a large area of the rug, say the stageright side.
Then, his offstage plugged-in power cord will not reach
any further. He tries to stretch the cord, the vacuum cleaner,
himself, the rug, then finally, he exits, unplugs the cord and,
finding an outlet offstage, say on the stageleft side,
plugs in, and gets to work, whistling all the while.
He completes another large area of the rug before
running into the same problem. After exhausting
all his options, he resigns himself to the fact that there is an
area of the carpet, exactly centerstage,
that is filthy and impossible to vacuum.
He stands there staring at the filthy spot.
He is quiet in his desperation.
He looks around.
He works the unplugged vacuum cleaner over the spot.
Whistling. The power cord flips and flops in his wake.
2 women soldiers from the earlier play, Bertie and Dolly, enter,
walking on the carpet at a brisk pace. Bertie eats.
The Carpet Cleaner, seeing them, snaps to attention.

Bertie: Some ceremony, huh?
Dolly: The food was good. Not first-class.
Bertie: But good.
Dolly: All that flag waving. Im sweating like a pig.
Bertie: Perfume?

> Dolly applies Bertie's perfume.

Dolly: Yr a godsend.
Bertie: More like a girlscout.
Dolly: We got R&R until sunset, then first watch, right?
Bertie: Thats a roger.

> They notice the Carpet Cleaner.
> A flurry of well-starched salutes.

Bertie: I like the way he works. You like the way he works?
Dolly: I like the way he works.
Bertie: We like the way you work.
Dolly: We'll recommend you for a promotion.
Carpet Cleaner: DONT!!

Dolly
Carpet Cleaner
Bertie

Dolly: Carry on.
Bertie: Yes, carry on.

> Again, they trade salutes. The women go on their way.
> He puts on his coat and leaves, heading off the other way,
> with the vacuum cleaner.

8 THE VIEW FROM HERE

She: I love a gray day. I forgot how much.
He: Me too.
She: I hope we dont move out there and miss this gray. And the view from here.
He: The view from here is great, yeah.
She: Like you said, remember? "Sometimes, nothing beats standing in the shadow of a tall building."
He: Yeah.
She: You look more like yrself against a gray sky.
He: You look good anytime.
She: Yeah?
He: In rain, in snow, in sleet, in hail.
She: My love for you will never fail, baby.
He: Who wrote that?
She: Just me, just now, with my chin on my husband's shoulder.

He
She

He:
With my head feeling like a boulder,
She:
with him taking up the rhyme,
He:
cause my wife, she dont got the time,
She:
but what I do got is the mood,
He:
whatchu saying? You wanna get screwed?

> Laughter.

9 THE PRESENTATION OF THE GRUNDIG MAJESTIC

> The Sergeant sits on a campstool. The Private comes in
> carrying something very heavy and cumbersome,
> but about the size of a breadbox. He sets it on the ground.

Private: Ive brought you something.

Sergeant: What the hell is it?

Private: A Grundig Majestic.

Sergeant: You stole it. I'll have you court-martialed for stealing.
Theyll hang you. Dont think they wont. Theyll draw-and-quarter
you. Dont think drawing-and-quartering is out of style. Theyll
put you in the stocks. Yr hands and yr feet and yr thing-thing.
Youll be the laughing stock of the entire outfit.

Private: Yes, sir.

Sergeant: You stole it.

Private: No, sir. I bought it.

Sergeant: Where.

Private: Overseas.

(Rest)

Sergeant: Overseas. Overseas. I was overseas once too. W-W-2.
Dont think you were the only one.

Private: Yes, sir.

Sergeant: You bought it.

Private: Yes, sir.

Sergeant: With what?

Private: Money.

Sergeant
Private

(Rest)

Sergeant: You been stealing from me?

Private: No, sir.

Sergeant: You bought it with money. With yr own money. Shit.
(Rest)
Bet it doesnt work.

> The Private leaps up and scurries around looking for
> an electrical source. Not a wall plug but something more
> tragic—a hand-powered army-green-colored generator that
> he plugs the radio cord into, and then cranks furiously.

365 Days/365 Plays **49**

At last the generator's green power switch lights up
and the Grundig Majestic radio starts to crackle.
The Private is as happy as he can be
and the Sergeant is as impressed as he can be,
both under the restraints of God, Country and the Service.
With great excitement the Private fiddles with the radio.
The crackling turns to static. At last he finds a station.
Sounds of bombing, air raids, death, destruction, famine
and plague are heard—the sounds and wounds of war.
As the lights dim, the 2 men listen to the radio
with rapt attention, as people in the olden days used to do.

10 THE HISTORY LESSON

Napoléon, 1769–1821, Emperor of the French,
and Wellington, 1769–1852, British, the Iron Duke.
They stand facing each other in a blizzard,
somewhere in the middle of Belgium, or Iowa even.
Their vast armies behind them,
as far as the eye can see: men, women, boys and girls,
all in uniform and bearing arms.

Napoléon
Wellington

(Rest)

Napoléon: We were born in the same year. Who would have thought.
Wellington: Dont get off the subject.
Napoléon: "The General has a battle plan, but when he is in the battle he is in the moment." Who said that?
Wellington: You did.
Napoléon: Ah, *me*. I used to love being me. I used to love my hat.
Wellington: I love my wife, my horse, my people.
Napoléon: Ah, *me*.

Napoléon
Napoléon

(Rest)

Napoléon: Are you teaching me something?
Wellington: Im not trying to.

Napoléon
Wellington

Napoléon bites his own hand, to keep from crying.

11 WHAT DO YOU SEE?

Several speakers.

– What do you see?
– Nothing.
– What else?
– What else is there?
– A blank page soon to be filled with water.
– No!
– A blank page soon to be filled with feelings.
– Tears of sadness?
– No, a murder by drowning.
– Oh.

(Rest)

– I would fill the blank page with body parts. And a list:
of the people I'd like to raise from the dead.
– Theyd stink.
– I dont smell. "Anosmia" its called.
– No smell at all?
– No.
– Never have?
– Never have.
– Never wanted to?
– Sometimes. Like roses.
– Roses.
– Yes roses. And less flowery things like piss on the subway.

(Rest)

– Whats she doing here?
– She was invited.
– Really? Does she belong?
– We're expanding our circle, dont be such a snob.

– Whats she doing over there?

– Jerking-off.

– No, she's not

– Yes she is too.

– God.

– She doesnt look like a heathen.

– Hard to say these days, everything's changed.

– Do me a favor.

– What?

– Talk to her.

– Why?

– She looks—lonesome.

(Rest)

– You should make that into the title of something. A play or something.

– You think?

– Do I think! It sounds like a money-maker.

– Not that title.

– Sure. I got a nose for money-makers.

– You dont know these days whats a money-maker and whats not. Take war for instance.

– Dont you get started talking about the war, we are sick of you talking about the war. Before we left the house you promised me you wouldnt talk about the war, in the goddamn fucking car for Christ's sake you promised me, you swore to me on everything that was sacred that you wouldnt talk about the war. Did I sell my house to get you out of the Service? Did I sell my fucking house?

– You sold yr house to yr mother.

– You wanna serve in the Service? Just say the word.

(Rest)

– Hush, both of you, people are looking.

– I want to start a family.

– Fuck you.

– I say I wanna start a family and you say fuck you.

– How else are families made, asshole.

– You dont want one. Admit it.

– All right. You wanna start a family, how about "over my dead body"?

The Assembled Speakers calmly make a circle.
Then One lunges at Another. They struggle.
Years of pent-up frustration, the mortgage on the mortgage,
the 9-to-5, the hi honey Im home, and honey wishes you werent,
the television showing you a life other than the life you or
anybody you know will ever live, the discrepancy,
the discrepancy within the discrepancy and the endless and
therefore tragic distance between a guy and his own guts.

12 JAYWALKING

1: I love the city.

2: Big C.

1: Yeah. Know why? Cause I can jaywalk here.

2: Tell me about it.

1: Cant jaywalk at home.

2: Shit.

1: Jaywalk at home and theyll fine you.

2: Fuck that.

1: Yeah. I used to fight it. I'd say I was from out of town. I'd create this elaborate identity that I had all memorized. Had it down pat. There was this town I was *really* from that nobody had ever heard of. I had a fake driver's license and a fake family tree in my wallet.

2: You radical son of a bitch.

1: I'd whip out that tree and I'd have them bamboozled.

2: *Me* thinking of what *you* did is getting *me* high.

1: Now I just come here. I fly out here and—

2: Jaywalk.

1: To my fucking heart's content.

2: Feels great, dont it.

1: You dont have to wait for the light to change. You go when YOU wanna, not when the little WHITE walking Man says WALK. I AM A MAN, GODDAMN IT, I FUCKING WALK WHEN I FUCKING WANT.

2: Once more.

1: I AM A MAN.

2: I AM A MAN TOO. Yr family know yr out here?

1: They think Im here on business.

2: Right.

December

1: I come here. Jaywalk until I get it out of my system. Then go back home and act like whoever everybody thinks I am, until I gotta come out here again.

2: Thats life.

1: I guess.

> 1 and 2 stand on the corner, lost in thought. The sign changes repeatedly from: "Walk" to "Dont Walk" with neither of them moving or noticing because theyve both been broadsided by despair—sort of like a pretty girl all dressed-up gets splashed with mud from a puddle deep-wheeled by a rich person's car.

13 LEARNING ENGLISH

English Speaker 18: Round.

Student: Woun.

English Speaker 18: Rock.

Student: Wock.

English Speaker 18: Rut.

Student: Whut?

> The English Speaker takes out a stick and the Student offers her feet for a beating.

Watcher 1: Beating like thats against the laws.

Watcher 32: Turn a blind eye.

Watcher 1: You could be locked-up.

Watcher 32: There go the Good Old Days.

> Watcher 84 struggles to his feet and sings with great feeling:

Watcher 84:
There used to be a place
where one could give a beating
and no one would see
anything wrong with that.
Those days were called the Good Old Days.

Watcher 32: Where I come from there are plenty of Good Old Days left to be had.

English Speaker 18: Next!

An Enormous Horde of Students struggles.
One is triumphant, and after taking his bows,
takes his seat in front of the English Speaker.
The play begins all over again and should continue over
and over again forever or until the English language
is less desirable to learn.

14 HIPPY

Man: Youve got yr hands on yr hips.
Woman: What of it?
Man: Yr angry.
Woman: Im not.
Man: What then?
Woman: Im thinking.
Man: About?
Woman: About William Tell.

Man
Woman
Man
Woman

Man: That guy you met at the party.
Woman: Dont be an ass.
Man: Yr thinking of swinging with him, tell the truth.
Woman: Yr such an ass.
Man: Yr standing there with yr hands on yr hips thinking of how nice it would be to swing with Big Billy Tell.
Woman: Im thinking about William Tell, stupid. How he had to shoot an apple off his kid's head cause he didnt want to salute some guy's hat. Im thinking about how he's brave. And how he lived in the 1600s or something.
Man: I'll come home one day soon and he'll be in my bed.

(Rest)

Woman: Whatever.

15 **1000 SOUTH KELLY**

> A Family: Mother, Father, 2 Daughters and a Son eat dinner.
> They all have perfect table manners.
> They all finish at the same time. They put down their cutlery.

The Family
The Family
The Family

(Rest)

Father: Seconds?

> They all look around to each other. Then the Son gets up.
> He walks toward offstage. We see that he has shackles on
> his feet and hands, and he wears a prison uniform.
> A Guard steps from the wings to receive him. They exit.

The Family
The Family

(Rest)

> They continue eating as before, but with no food on their plates,
> theyre just going through the motions.

16 **THIS IS PROBABLY NOT A PLAY**

> One speaker.

This is probably not a play.
This is probably not to be read
or said aloud or onstage even.
But there was this Vietnamese kid who
just held the door of the Uptown Number 6
for his girl and the likes of me
and the 5'11" model-looking white chick
and the brother with the diamond stud
and the happy African American buppy couple
and the Latin guy with *El Diario* under his arm.
Probably not a play.
Probably not a poem even.

But I thought,
Shit,
I dont know how to say "thank you" in Vietnamese.
So I just smiled.
We all did.

17 TREE

1: You want a tree?

2: Naw.

1: I'd get you one.

2: I dont want one.

1: A tree'd be nice.

2: I dont want a tree.

1: You bring it in the house and its nice. And it smells nice.

2: And it smells nice and then the pine needles fall off and its dead and then its a dead tree.

1: Yr right.
(Rest)
I could get a living tree or a fake tree.

2: Maybe.

(Rest)

1: Listen.

> A group sings outside. Something Christmassy.

2: Carolers. From the prison.

1: They sound nice.

> More singing.

1: You feeling the spirit?

2: Not yet.

1: But yr on yr way.

2: Im warming up to being on my way, yeah.

> They join in with the singing.

18 THE GREAT ARMY IN DISGRACE

> The Great Army walks across the stage.
> Jones and Smith from the earlier play (see December 5)
> walk along with them.

Jones: A 100,000 soldiers. All in retreat.

Smith: We're all going home, sir.

Jones: You and yr rosy glasses.

Smith: Its not what happens, sir, its how you take it.

Jones: I ought to have you shot.

> The sound of cannons. The soldiers fall on their bellies
> and crawl along. Jones stands. Then they all stand, slowly,
> not as bravely as Jones.

Jones: Is this the way home?

Smith: This is the way home.

Jones: I should be at the front of the line. I should be leading.
If I stop walking, what do you think theyll do?

Smith: They would shoot you, sir.

Smith
Jones

(Rest)

Jones: We are not headed home. There is a word for this. The
need to go home and the inability to find the way.

Smith: Lost, sir.

Jones: Lost.

> Jones unsheathes his sword. The other men watch.
> He points his sword at his own neck. The other men follow suit.
> He sees that theyre copying him. He is satisfied.
> He sheathes his sword. They follow suit.
> They all go back to walking.

Jones: The men. They love me.

19 ALL EARS

The Voices
The Voices
The Voices

(Rest)

All Ears: Ah!
Scribe: You hear them!
All Ears: No.
Scribe: Oh.

20 GOING THROUGH THE MOTIONS

A large group of people walk across the stage.
The Tour Guide holds a little flag.

Tour Guide: . . . And on our left and right, the Motions!
Tour Group *(With Tour Guide, leading)*: Oooooooooooh!
(Rest)
Aaaaaaaaaah!

Then the Tour Group whips out their cameras and clicks away.
They each go through a roll of film or the digital equivalent.
Then they all, most respectfully, move on.

21 WHERE IS THE WELL?

Head Digger: Here is the well. Dig here.

The Diggers dig. As they dig, they sing:

Diggers:
20 years
looking for a well.
Well Lord, well Lord.
20 years
looking for a well.
They say the day
I find the hole

with water, Lord,
the Motherlode.
They say the day
I find the hole
is the day I'll lay down
in my grave.
Head Digger: Well?
Diggers: Smell.

> The Head Digger smells the earth.

Head Digger: I dont smell water.
Diggers: Hell.
Head Digger: Maybe there?
Diggers: Where?

> The Head Digger points to a place very far offstage.

Head Digger: There.
(Rest)
You see the 2 mountains, not the sandy-tree-dotted ones but the rocky ones? The red-black smooth bare rocky ones? See? Not those. Those are dotted with insect colonies. The bare ones. The ones completely bare. What do you think?

(Rest)

Diggers *(Speaking)*:
When I started this line of work
I had no idea how hard it would be.
No idea that the hardest days would
look like the easiest.
Every day I wanna quit, you know?
Throw in the towel, slit my wrists.
Staple a note on my forehead: "No biggie. Just tired."
You know the feeling?
You know the feeling.
Head Digger: I know the feeling. How about we quit. But not today. We'll quit tomorrow. In the meantime we'll walk. Towards those mountains. Look! With the light on them they look like theyre kissing.

> A light—warm and not overly bright—shines on all the Diggers.

Head Digger: Come on, then.

Diggers: We'd like to sing.

Head Digger: We'll sing together.

They walk toward the mountains—all singing:

Diggers:
20 years
looking for a well.
Well Lord, well Lord.
20 years
looking for a well.
They say the day
I find the hole
with water, Lord,
the Motherlode.
They say the day
I find the hole
thats the day I'll lay down
in my grave.

22 DOES IT MATTER WHAT YOU DO?

Several different people, 5 at a time, dressed differently—
like a Doctor, Lawyer, Indian Monk, Fireman, Ballerina,
Wastrel, Mother, Wrestler, Good Clown, Boxer, Army Man,
Dramatic Actor of the National Theater of China, Failed Writer,
Bad Clown, Con Man, Child Hooker, 3rd-Rate Director,
Professional Mourner—all stand upstage. They walk, run, dance,
act, wrestle, box, doctor, lawyerize, whatever, each according
with their profession, at full speed downstage, falling into the
orchestra pit. Others appear upstage and progress downstage
at a rapid pace. Again and again with no end in sight even as
the lights fade to black, even as the curtains go down,
and even as the audience and crew
and entire world goes home.

23 THIS IS SHIT

An audience is gathered to watch a play. One person sleeps.
Another constantly refers to his program, trying to "understand"
the show. Another checks his watch. Another laughs.

December

Another weeps. Another frowns a lot, cranking her head
from side to side, trying to make heads or tails of the scenery.
Another leaps up every chance she gets
only to sit down again, embarrassed. Still another stands
and throws her program at the stage.

Program Thrower: This is shit!

Program Thrower exits. The rest give a standing ovation.

24 CHAMBER MUSIC

4 parts performed simultaneously:
1. A song sung off-the-cuff expressing the actor's feelings.
2. Radio news station (or a station chosen at random).
3. The biggest headlines of the day's *L.A.* or *New York Times* or
Times of London or *Times* of India or *Times* of Nigeria
or *Times* of Beijing or the local *Times* read over and over.
4. The caption from the same newspaper's biggest picture
acted-out as simply as possible.
Keep it clean and simple. No need to get cluttered with it.
A conductor could count time and signal the end.

25 PHOTOS WITH SANTA

A Man in a Santa suit on break with an Elf who might also be the
Santa-at-the-mall photographer.
Santa smokes or drinks from a pint bottle.

Santa: How much time we got?
Elf: Bout a minute.
Santa: Shit.
Elf: Yeah.

(Rest)

Santa: You remind me of this gal. I used to know this gal. I knew
her pretty good.

Elf: Marla?

Santa: Uh-uhnn.

Elf: Someone I know?

Santa: It was back when I lived in Artesia.

Elf: You lived in Artesia?

Santa: Yeah.

Elf: When?

Santa: When I was with this gal. It was great. She would get me anything I wanted.

Elf: Lucky you.

Santa: And it was like—she could read my mind—like she knew what I wanted before I wanted it and there itd be. Knives. Rings. Gold necklaces. Red sports cars. Silk suits. Alligator shoes. Tickets to Mexico.

Elf: Lucky you.

Santa: First-class tickets. To Mexico.

Elf: I'd get tired of that. After awhile. It aint real.

Santa
Elf

(Rest)

Santa: Yeah.

Elf: So what, you left her?

Santa: She left me. I got fat.

Elf: Yeah.

(Rest)

A Woman comes onstage backward, wagging her finger at an Unseen Child.

Woman: YOU ARE GOING TO SIT THERE AND SHUT UP AND STOP CRYING AND WAIT FOR SANTA OR I AM GONNA BREAK YR PRECIOUS FUCKING NECK. DO WE HAVE AN UNDERSTANDING?

(Rest)

Elf: Time's up.

Santa: Yeah.

26 EVEN IN A HOUSE LIKE THIS

2 People kiss passionately,
more passionately, and then suddenly stop.
They get up and run downstage and fall into the orchestra pit.
2 Others come on. They begin the kissing sequence.
Before long the first 2 People come back onstage and
sit off to the side watching the 2 new Kissers.
The Kissers get up and run downstage and fall into
the orchestra pit while the Watchers watch.
Another group of Kissers comes on.
The 2 Kissers who just exited come back on
and join the Watchers.
Repeat.
Repeat.
Repeat.

27 2 EXAMPLES FROM THE INTERCONNECTEDNESS OF ALL THINGS

2 Griot come onstage. They flip a coin to see who speaks first.

1st Griot: It was 1860 in America. South of the Mason-Dixon Line. A colored man rides into town on a handtruck, you know, one of those hand-powered carts that runs on the train tracks. His wife and child are hiding outside of town in the bushes. They are runaways. The man arrives in town. He does a little work for food. People eye him with suspicion, but he stays cool. He has come too far to break over a look someone gives him, you know what that feels like, dont you? We all know what that feels like. The man stays cool. But someone recognizes him, or thinks he does. And takes a shot and hits the man in the leg and the man runs. Theyre runaways and now theyre running. Theyre on that handtruck and the husband is bleeding to death and the child is crying and the hunters are coming and the wife works the handtruck as best she can by herself but its pretty hopeless. Until the ghosts come. Thousands of them: folks the woman recognizes and folks she's never seen. Father and mother and the grandparents and then boys wearing baseball caps on backwards and girls listening to shiny metal music boxes— future folks, they come too. They come to help the woman work the handtruck. When they reach safety, the wife tells the story of the relations coming to help out—the ghosts of the past and the future saved them, she says. The husband tells what he saw: his wife, all alone, working that handtruck all by herself, while he sang a song to the baby, right off the top of his head.

Other Griot:
Martin Luther King is alive and living in Las Vegas.
Youve heard this before? Now yr hearing it some more.
Dont laugh
I saw him there myself.
It wasnt easy to know it was him, you know to
recognize him, cause
so much time has passed
since I seen him last.
And now he's an old man
but he still had that face, those eyes that in all the drawings of
him Ive seen, no one can get right. And he was in great shape,
considering.
I know, yr thinking, that griot done gone and lost
her mind—
everybody knows the King is dead.
But Im telling you, he's alive
and living in Vegas.
Ive seen him myself.
Last night. At the Bellagio buffet.
Yr eyeing me like Im lying.
MOTHERFUCKER, WOULD I LIE TO YOU?!?!?! YOU THINK
IM LYING DONT YOU? YOU WOULDNT KNOW THE TRUTH
IF IT, IF IT, WELL, YOU WOULDNT KNOW THE TRUTH
WOULD YOU. YOU WOULDNT KNOW THE TRUTH CAUSE
YOU WOULDNT WANT TO KNOW THE TRUTH. I SEEN
HIM. I SEEN THE KING. With my own eyes, Im telling you.

Her talking turns to ranting. As she repeats:
"MOTHERFUCKER, WOULD I LIE TO YOU?!?!?!" she begins
to embarrass the 1st Griot. And the race, which up until now,
had been doing so well, takes 2 steps backward.
Still she continues to rant.
The Cops come to drag the Other Griot away.
When the 1st Griot tries to stop them, they beat the 1st Griot—
not to death, not enough to cause a riot—but just enough
to make us all doubt the interconnectedness of all things.

28 BEER POOL WINE

Man in a T-shirt: Wanna beer? No? Good. More for me. I tell you. Ima do something. Ima do something and one of these days youll hear about it. Youll be riding the bus and the driverll have the radio on: "We interrupt this broadcast for a special report," itll say. Someone has—blah buh de blah. And across the country in every city, town and village, jaws will drop. Jaws will drop across the country. And hands, sometimes alone sometimes together, will come up slow to cover said mouths. All across the country. All across the world, maybe.

(Rest)

I always wonder about that gesture. Dont you? The mouth opens wide and then—the hands cover the mouth. What the fuck is that about, huh? Goddamnit, I want answers! I demand—as a human being, I demand—

Woman: Yr talking to the tv again.

Man in a T-shirt: No Im not.

Woman: I heard you.

Man in a T-shirt: So.

Woman: So yr talking to the tv again.

(Rest)

Man in a T-shirt: Wanna beer?

The Woman looks at her watch.

(Rest)

Woman: Sure.

Man in a T-shirt: Are you gonna open it?

Woman: Not yet.

Man in a T-shirt: Its better if you open it.

Woman: Yr too much, you know that?

Man in a T-shirt: You wanna shoot pool?

Woman: Now?

Man in a T-shirt: I know a place thats open.

Woman: I cant shoot pool for shit.

Man in a T-shirt: Get yr coat.

Woman: Its 90 degrees.

Man in a T-shirt: I like to see you in it.

The Woman goes to get her coat. The Man looks around. He does the awe-jaw gesture. The Woman comes back in. She stands there watching the Man. She decides not to wear the coat, but just to hold it, or sling it over her shoulder in the style of fun-loving western people. He keeps doing the awe-jaw thing, she keeps waiting for him to quit it. They never go anywhere anymore.

29 THE KEY

An Old Well-Dressed Man or Woman: Theres a key. But to what? For years you spend yr time looking for the key and then you find the key and, guess what, youve lost the door or the box or the hatch or the window or the locket or the whatever the hell it was that you was trying to unlock in the first place. Ha. But before you found the key, things were nice. Thats what frame of mind you get into once you find the key and lose the door. You wax whatduhyacallit. Nostalgic. You wax nostalgic. And you remember. Very clearly. That every day you used to wake up and the door was there. Sometimes it was across the room and sometimes it was inches from yr face or you were in yr coffin and you were dead and the whole thing felt useless and those were the Good Old Days because you could count on things. You could count on someone to come along and say something of *relevance.* Like— like *Afghanistan.* And they would talk about *Afghanistan* and they would become quite famous—quite respected—because from their lips, from their fucking lips would issue forth *relevant* words. And before you knew it here they are—on the television— with those words coming out of their mouths and the words are like wild fire, you know—they catch on and dont stop—

A Young Man comes in. He has something he's polishing up.

Young Man: I leave you alone for one afternoon and look at you.

Old Well-Dressed: Look at me what?

Young Man: Yr ranting.

Old Well-Dressed: Im not ranting.

Young Man: Just like the fella in the last play. And the play before that too. Ranting. All of you. Whats the fucking world coming to? Jesus, I could hear you at the top of yr lungs, all the way down the hallway—

Old Well-Dressed: So.

Young Man: Out into the street.

December

Old Well-Dressed: So.

Young Man: When I got off the bus. I could hear you.

Old Well-Dressed: I am a very angry person.

Young Man: Yeah.

Old Well-Dressed: Im trying to—Im trying to get it out of my system.

Young Man: Shit.

Old Well-Dressed: They had it on the tv. An angry man. Angrier than me. Everybody—the whole crowd gathered around—everybody in the crowd said the same thing: "Get it out of yr system."

Young Man: I should get you out of the house more.

Old Well-Dressed: The man on the tv was younger than me. He said he'd been angry all his life. Since birth. I understood that. But he was younger than me. So—that makes me—

Young Man: Older.

Old Well-Dressed: Angrier.

Young Man: What can you do?

Old Well-Dressed: Eat Shit and Die.

(Rest)

Young Man: I got you something.

Old Well-Dressed: Food?

Young Man: Better. And it comes with a story.

Old Well-Dressed: Tell.

Young Man: So I go to the market.

Old Well-Dressed: To shop.

Young Man: Yeah.

Old Well-Dressed: For food.

Young Man: Yeah, but there was this guy—a little guy. Maybe foreign.

Old Well-Dressed: They all are these days.

Young Man: About 60 with his hair dyed brown. And he'd just bought—guess what.

(Rest)

Old Well-Dressed: A mint julep.

Young Man: Close. He'd just bought a miniature ceramic nigger. A figurine.

Old Well-Dressed: This is a good story.

Young Man: And he's turning it over and over in his hands. And he and his wife and someone like her sister and the sister's husband were all giggling cause this ceramic nigger was making them glad. The thing had a cap on and a gold necklace and a gold tooth and the guy whod bought him was like, "I always wanted me one of these." And then when he'd made that point he looked the thing over and said, "What he needs is some rings." And he said that over and over and over, and they was laughing like they was gonna split.

Old Well-Dressed: So what you bring me?

Young Man: A ring.

Old Well-Dressed: Classy.

Young Man: Got one for me too.

Old Well-Dressed: They look like high school graduation rings. Very classy. My day has been totally transformed.

> They sit there looking at their rings.

Old Well-Dressed: What about the figurine?

Young Man: What about it.

Old Well-Dressed: Next time get me one of those too.

Young Man: There wont be a next time.

> The Young Man stares at Old Well-Dressed until
> Old Well-Dressed can only look at his ring.
> Then the Young Man looks at his ring too.
> And together, they look at their rings as the lights fade.

30 2-FOR-1

Writer *(Writing)*: Is the rule that I have to keep writing until I think of a play?

Editor: There are no rules

Writer: What if my mind is blank?

Editor
Editor

Writer: Oh shit, its like when yr playing with yrself. Yr mind is blank and then you scroll through yr day, like a film on 2 spools and you turn a crank and watch the film and then stop—theres somebody—he'll do, or she'll do, or theyll do, him and her and that one over there or that dog or those pigeons you saw in Venice.

Editor: TMI: "Too much information."

Writer: By any means necessary, I thought.

Editor: That saying is a figure of speech.

Writer: And thats whats wrong with the world.

(Rest)

Look over there.

Editor: What?

Writer: Dust on the horizon.

Editor: Who?

Writer: Not who. What.

Editor: What?

Writer: The war.

Editor: Yeah?

Writer: Yeah. The war's coming.

Editor: Shit.

(Rest)

Why dont you write about the war coming?

Writer: Cause its coming. I dont have to write about it.

Editor: Youd rather write about pigeons in Venice.

Writer
Editor

(Rest)

Editor: I think Im going to go and buy a gun. Theres that 2-for-1 sale down the street. Want me to pick you up a couple?

Writer: Yeah. Sure. Thanks.

Editor: Keep writing.

Writer: Yeah.

> The Editor leaves. The Writer, watching the war advance, continues writing.

31 THE GREAT DEPRESSION

The One: Its hot.

The Other One: Yeah.

The One: And Dry.

The Other One: Yeah.

(Rest)

December

The One: Shit.

The Other One: Dont get antsy.

The One: Im not *antsy*—Im just—

The Other One: Antsy.

The One: "Tired of waiting," I'd call it.

The Other One: Enjoy it.

The One: Right.

> They wait.
> The One begins to hum a song and dance most splendidly.
> After a moment The Other One claps time.
> It is a beautiful thing—it reminds us of a simpler time
> when we all expected less and were—happier, maybe.
> The One stops dancing suddenly.

(Rest)

The One: Still nothing.

The Other One: Nope.

The One: Maybe there wont be one today.

The Other One: One will come—you just gotta wait for it.

The One: From which direction, you think?

The Other One: Thataway.

The One: Cool.

The Other One: You cool?

The One: Yeah.

> They wait.

January

1 HERE WE GO

> 4 People wearing 4 different historical hats.
> Maybe a Lincoln hat, a Napoléon hat,
> a President Mobuto leopard-skin pillbox-style hat,
> a Jackie Kennedy hat. A 5th Person wears a wig.

5th Person: Ready?

4 People with Hats: Ready.

One of the People with Hats: Wait!

Someone turns on music and there is a mad scramble, they exchange their hats with an intensity as yet unseen. For the most part the exchange is kindly, well-intentioned, but sometimes there is a violent outburst, nothing fatal, nothing verbal. During this exchange, The 5th Person can change or groom the wig and apply makeup or shave face. The music stops as suddenly as it started. The 5th Person puts away grooming supplies and the 4 People with Hats (or Hates) sit contentedly, wearing whatever hat they have as if theyve always worn it and will wear it forever.

(Rest)

5th Person: Ready?
4 People with Hats: Ready!
5th Person: All right. Here we go:

Everybody leans forward—the lean takes forever and is performed with great enthusiasm.

2 WE ARE FRESH OUT OF CANNED LAUGHTER, GET SOME OFF THE TELEVISION

A Kid (an adult with a doll, sucking her finger) sits on a Man's knee. They watch tv. A comedy show. Canned laughter. Every so often they laugh. When the Man laughs he slaps his knee (the one the Kid isnt sitting on). Then he jiggles his other knee (the one the Kid is sitting on). He jiggles his knee out of laughter, and then for no apparent reason. More canned laughter. The Kid laughs. The Man jiggles his knee.

Man: Horsey.

He jiggles his knee some more. The Kid laughs then—

Kid: Ouch.
Man: Whats the matter?
Kid: Im going to bed.
Man: Good idea.

The Man straightens his leg.

Man: Slide down.

Kid: No thanks.

> She hops down instead of sliding and walks offstage.
> He sits there staring at the tv with its canned laughter.
> After a moment, the Kid comes back onstage.

Kid: The door's locked.

Man

Man

Kid: The door's locked. Will you unlock—

Man

Kid

Man

Kid

> He makes a grab at her and she runs around the room,
> screaming with delight or fear—it should be hard to tell which.
> A door opens. A Woman stands there.
> The Kid hides.

Man: How was yr day?

Woman: Shitty. What are you doing?

Man: Stretching my legs.

Woman

Man

(Rest)

Woman: Im going to hang up my coat.

Man: Sounds like a plan.

> She goes offstage to hang up her coat. The Man resumes
> chasing the Kid. The Woman reappears. The Kid hides.

Woman: Wheres Clara?

Man: Clara?

Woman: Where is she?

Man: Clara's in bed.

> The Woman looks in the direction of where the Kid is hiding.

Woman: All in bed and tucked in?

Man: Yep.

Woman: And you read her a story?

Man: Am I the man of the house, or am I the man of the house?

Woman: Yr the man of the house.

Man: And I read her a story.

Woman
Man

Woman: Whats on tv?

Man: The Comedy Hour.

Woman: Im not in the mood for comedy.

Man: Watch it with me, whydontcha. A little laughter wont kill you.

> The Woman sits. After a beat, the Man sits. They watch tv.
> The Kid watches tv from her hiding place.

3 2 MARYS

> 1st Woman sits in a lawn chair. 2nd Woman comes up
> and sits in a lawn chair some distance away.

2nd Woman: How was yr vacation?

1st Woman
1st Woman

(Rest)

2nd Woman: How was—

1st Woman: Hello there.

2nd Woman: Hello. You were away. I kept an eye on yr house. The whole time. Nothing bad happened. To yr house, I mean.

1st Woman: I dont think weve met.

2nd Woman: Im yr neighbor. Ive been living over here for 3 years now. Ask anybody.
(Rest)
How was yr vacation?

1st Woman: Nice.

2nd Woman: Good for you. A nice vacation. Yr lucky. Do you know how hard it is to have a nice vacation these days, what with the world the way it is and—

Man's Voice *(From inside)*: WHAT IN THE HELL ARE YOU DOING?

2nd Woman: IM TALKING. TO THE NEIGHBOR.

Man's Voice: WHAT IN THE HELL ARE YOU DOING THAT FOR?

(Rest)

2nd Woman: IM BEING—NEIGHBORLY. *(Back to 1st Woman)* "Being neighborly." Thats one of my New Year's resolutions. Whats one of yrs?

1st Woman: Not to have any New Year's resolutions.

2nd Woman: Really?

1st Woman: Really.

2nd Woman: Thats unpatriotic. I could have you reported.

1st Woman
2nd Woman

1st Woman: What if I told you Im hoping to lose 20 pounds?

2nd Woman: A health kick, huh? Good for you. "Be more neighborly" and "Quit kicking the dog." "Quit kicking the dog" is my 2nd one. Whats yr 2nd one?

Man's Voice: WHAT IN THE FUCK ARE YOU TELLING HER?!

2nd Woman: WE'RE EXCHANGING—*PLEASANTRIES*.

Man's Voice: IM GOING TO COME OUT THERE AND GIVE YOU A PIECE OF MY MIND. AND THEN, AND THEN, AND THEN YOU KNOW WHAT I'LL DO THEN? I'LL BEAT YOU WITH A STICK.

2nd Woman
2nd Woman
2nd Woman

(Rest)

2nd Woman: Excuse me.

1st Woman: Should I call the police?

2nd Woman: Why would you wanna do that?

> 2nd Woman goes inside.

Man's Voice: DONT HURT ME! PLEASE! AAAAAAHHEEEEE!

2nd Woman: I didnt touch him. I just gave him a look.
(Rest)
They used to call me "Bloody Mary." On account of the way
I handled myself. You can fill in the blanks on yr own, right?
You know what Im talking about, dontcha? You get my drift
without me drifting too far into it, yes?

1st Woman: You worked in the—meat business.

2nd Woman: Im retired now. But back in the day, lemmie tell ya,
I could carve them up—in my sleep. "Bloody Mary" they called
me. Back in the day.

1st Woman: My name's Mary too.

2nd Woman: No shit.

1st Woman: No shit.

2nd Woman: How about that. 2 Marys. Side by side. This is what
you call an event of great singularity.

1st Woman: This is going to be a great year.

2nd Woman: You think?

1st Woman: I know. I can tell.

4 THE NEWS IS *HERE*

Woman: Look at them. Fighting in the streets. When will it end?
(Rest)
Get yr head out of that newspaper, honey. Come take a look.

Man: What are they fighting over?

Woman: Hard to tell.

The Man gets up. Looks.

Man: Looks like a child.
(Rest)
Im going out there and Im going to do something about that.

Woman: What?

Man: Watch me. And, hey take a few pictures or, you know, work
the video. This could be my moment.

The Man dashes out. The Woman watches, takes a picture or 2,
looks for the video camera and finally finds it.
The Man comes back in with something.

Woman: Dont bring it in here, huh?

Man: To the victor go the spoils.

Woman: Please.

Man: Have a heart. They woulda torn him limb from limb.

Woman: Its a he?

Man: Its got a thingy. Take a look.

Woman: Spare me. Is he white?

Man: Yup.

Woman: We're talking money.

Man: Yup yup.

Woman: We're talking a house in Lush Valley. Or at least a quonset hut in Mountain View. Away from all this action. We're talking food in the winter. We're talking—

Man: Dont even say it.

Woman: Ima say it

Man: You say it youll jinx it.

Woman: Ima say it anyway cause what the fuck.

> The Man puts the Baby down on the floor. The Man sticks his fingers in his own ears and sings. The Woman just watches him.

Man: I dont hear you I dont hear you I dont hear you I cant hear you so even if you did say it which you probably are doing right now I cant even hear you saying it so you wont jinx the good things that we might get by saying them and I cant even read yr lips saying it cause I got my eyes closed.

> The Man peeps open his eyes and then unplugs his ears.

Woman: Yr too sensitive.

Man: Did you say it?

Woman: Yeah, several times over and over, so any chance of getting anything from that baby is—

Man: Over

Woman: Sorry.

Man: Thats ok. Its not like we woulda moved anyhow. I mean, could you see me and you living in the mountains with all those—*Mountainites* or whatever the fuck theyre called?

Woman: Not in a million.

Man: The baby's probably a Mountainite.

Woman: You think?

Man: Yeah. Look at his ears. Theyre hairy like the back of my hand.

Woman: Shit. So, even if we could sell him, we'd be responsible for the carnage he'd cause.
Man: Yep. Turn on the camera.

> The Woman turns on the camera. The Man walks to the window, holds the Baby over the ledge, lets go. The Baby falls.

Man: Hit the ground and ran away. A Mountainite.
(Rest)
That was almost our chance at the brass ring.
Woman: A better chance will come.
Man: I feel a little crestfallen.
Woman: Itll fade.

> The Man goes back to reading the newspaper. The Woman goes back to sitting at the window. Everything as before.

5 THE STAR OF INDIA

Master of Ceremonies: . . . Lets have a big hand for The Cassanova Sword Swallowing Family Circus!!!!

> Amazing canned applause.

Master of Ceremonies: Theyre quite something, arent they? Do you know, I had a chance—before they went on—I had a chance to talk with Mamma Cassanova. Each Cassanova kid, on his or her first birthday is given a sword and, you know how most of us have marks on the walls where our kids grow taller and taller each year, you know, "Thats how tall Junior was on his 8th birthday!"? Well the Cassanovas *mark the sword.* Heres how much Cheeky Cassanova could swallow when he was only one, and see, the marks by his 5th birthday, already 2 inches away from the hilt! Im not kidding, they really do that. On each kid's 7th birthday, when they can swallow up to the hilt, the sword is set aflame—and then, from then on out, its not how deep but how hot, and how *many.* What a life, huh? Anyway, up next we have a male contortionist called "The Star of India." Lets give him a big hand, shall we?

> If applause from the audience is tepid, the Master of Ceremonies should turn on applause from canned applause machine by stomping on a foot pedal, to produce a great swell of artificial enthusiasm.

The Star walks on. He's Anglo American, dressed in the style of a middle management person from the middle of the Continental United States. He stands there as the Master of Ceremonies looks on expectantly.

Master of Ceremonies
Star

(Rest)

Master of Ceremonies: Do you need music?
Star: No, sir, I dont.

Master of Ceremonies
Star

(Rest)

Star: Theres a misprint in the program, sir. It should read: "Indiana." "The Star of Indiana."
Master of Ceremonies: Yr not "The Star of India"?
Star: Im the Star of *Indiana*.

(Rest)

Master of Ceremonies: Can you put yr feet behind yr head and balance on the tip of yr nose?
Star: Ive never tried, but I dont think I'd be able to, no sir. You see, Ive got this back condition. My doctor says its not serious. "Sciatica" he calls it and he says theres lots of ways to get it. I got mine from putting in long hours at my desk with my fat wallet in my hip pocket.
Master of Ceremonies: Isnt that something, folks!

Applause.

Star: I carry my wallet in the breast pocket of my suit coat now. But lets keep that *entre nous*, K?? Wouldnt want the unscrupulous types knowing where Big Daddy keeps his greenbacks. Plus the pictures of my wife and kids: Dorothy just had our latest baby—he's huge and I mean huge. And of course he looks just like—
Master of Ceremonies: Star! Of *Indiana*! How did you get that name?
Star: Ive been top salesman in my group statewide for 3 years running. I can sell almost anything.
Master of Ceremonies: Wellwellwellwell.
Star: Thats nothing to sneeze at.

Master of Ceremonies: Certainly not. Ladies and gentlemen: The Star of Indiana!

> Massive canned applause. The Star opens his wallet and an accordian flood of plastic-encased family photos spills out. The Master of Ceremonies thinks (to himself), Hasn't this Indiana guy heard of birth control? But he acts as if he's very impressed.

6 THE BIRTH OF TRAGEDY

> People gathered around a Child, Tragedy. He wears a robe, a crown on his head, and he holds a scepter. The Child sits on a Man's back. The Man is on all 4s, to make a chair.

Herald: 4 years ago today we gathered to celebrate the birth of Tragedy. And now we celebrate Tragedy's 4th birthday.

> Polite applause.

Tragedy: Where are my presents?

Herald: Theyll be presented one by one.

Tragedy: What about my cake?

Chair-Man: Made with the finest ingredients. The finest we could find.

Midwife: I remember when you were born. Yr mother was green with pain. A dark cloud passed over the sun. And its been there ever since.

> Several people begin to cry quietly.

Tragedy: What did you bring me?

Midwife: A sliver from the Root of All Evil.

Herald: Place it in the gift pile.

Tragedy: Now can I eat cake?

Herald: We have dignitaries from all over the world here to see you.

> The Dignitaries smile and bow.

Tragedy: I want my cake!

Herald: Bring the cake!

Tragedy: And—kill the dignitaries!

Herald: And kill the dignitaries!

> The cake is brought in. The Dignitaries are ushered out.

7 CALL GIRL

Sam and Dave sit in their bachelor pad. Very swank.
They eat dinner.

Sam: Howzit feel having everything you want?

Dave: I dont got everything I want.

Sam: Sure you do.

Dave: I dont got action.

Sam: The gamell be on in a minute.

Dave: Not that kind of action.

Sam: Oh. Action-action.

Dave: Yeah.

(Rest)

Sam: Pass the ketchup.

Dave: Pass yrself the ketchup.

They eat. The Phone rings.

Phone: Ring. Ring. Ring.

Dave: The phone.

Sam: Im not deaf.

Phone: Ring. Ring. Ring.

Sam: You gonna answer it?

Dave: No. Who do you think calls our home during the dinner
hour? Yr *whore*, thats who.

(Rest)

Its for you.

Sam: Hello?

(Rest)

Now?

(Rest)

NOW?

(Rest)

Yeah, I see you.

(Rest)

Gimmie—gimmie—like, 2 minutes tops.

Sam hangs up the Phone, gets his coat and leaves.
Dave eats with great concentration. He takes his plate,
goes to the window, eats and watches the scene outside.
Street lamps illuminate his face and its almost

as if he's watching tv except the street lamps cast
a yellowish light instead of a blue one.
Sound of keys in the door.
Sam comes in and goes back to the table.
He sits in Dave's spot, reaches for his own plate, eats.

Sam
Dave

(Rest)

Dave: How was she?
Sam: How do you think? You were watching.
Dave: Was that her by the street lamp?
Sam: That was her.
Dave: She looked good.
Sam: She was good.
Dave: Good.
Sam: Very.
Dave: Ketchup?
Sam: Here.
Dave: Wow.
Sam: Relax.
Dave: Shit.
Sam: Chill.
Phone: Ring. Ring. Ring. Ring.

(Rest)

Dave: Her again.
Sam: You think? She must be insatiable.
Phone: Ring. Ring. Ring. Ring.
Dave: Answer it.
Sam: Ima little tired.

Phone
Phone

(Rest)

Dave: I think Im going to buy a new lamp.
Sam: A floor lamp?
Dave: A *street* lamp. We'll put it next to the armchair. She can stand in here instead of outside.

Sam: Action.

Dave: Action-action.

> The Phone rings.

8 THERES NOTHING HERE

Dick
Jane

Jane: Theres nothing here.

Dick: No?

Dick
Jane
Dick
Jane

(Rest)

Jane: Im jumping out the window.

> She turns to go. At the last possible moment, Dick reaches out
> and grabs her hand, or arm, or the hem of her coat—
> his arm is fully extended, the muscles straining.
> Her arm, or whatever he holds onto, is straining—near the
> breaking point. Neither of them look at each other.

Jane: I saw pictures of Hiroshima. I could barely look. I thought, "No wonder they hate us." And then—that wasnt even me who did it—it wasnt me and it wasnt no one like me—my people didnt pull the trigger. We were the targets back then too. Still are. I pay first-class taxes and get second-class treatment.
(Rest)
The entire city was devastated. The whole city. There was nothing left.
(Rest)
But I cant kid myself. If we had been in power back then, we woulda been just as bad.

Dick: Come back inside.

> He pulls her to him. They hug.

Jane: Look, theres Spot. He's coming down the road. He didnt run away after all.

Dick: He probably had a night on the town.

Jane: Here, Spot! Here, boy!

Dick: Come on in, you old rascal, you!

> They clap and call for Spot as the lights fade.

9 THE PALACE AT 4 A.M.

> The Queen (a woman with a crown on her head and a purple robe over her shoulders and a big stick) sits awake.

Queen
Queen

(Rest)

> The King comes in. Stands and watches her.

King: Yr awake.
(Rest)
Come to bed.
(Rest)
(Rest)
Sitting there staring at the road wont make him come home any sooner.

Queen: He took his crown off his head. He threw it in the dirt.

King: He's young.

Queen: He took his staff and broke it in 2. Over his knee.

King: I wasnt home as much as I should have been. If I had been home more he would have—

Queen: Killed you.

King
Queen

King: You raised him. You did—a good job.

Queen: And he throws his crown in the dirt.

King: Look! The sun!

Queen: Him?

King: Another day. Sometimes you dont know if itll come or not.

Queen: Another day without him.
(Rest)
Who will rule, do you think, after we're gone?

King: The servants will rule after we're gone. Im only repeating the scuttlebutt.

(Rest)

He'll be back before we're gone, dont worry. Darling. Come to bed. I'll have the servants hang the heavy drapes and close them tightly so itll feel like night. You can sleep all day and I'll have Balthazar—

Queen: Balthazar?

King: The tall fellow. The one I pardoned just last week.

Queen: You call him by his name? A former prisoner? You call him by his name? Things are falling apart.

King
Queen

King: I'll have him stationed at yr door. No visitors: "The Queen is sleeping in today." Come on, darling.

He leads her away.

10 THINGS ARE TOUGH ALL OVER

A Woman leads a Man by the hand.
Theyve been walking for several days.

Man: Where are you taking me?

Woman: I said you shouldnt ask.

Man: Im asking.

Woman: Im taking you to see yr parents.

Man: Liar!

Woman: Im taking you to the cemetery.

Man: Im not dead. Not yet.

Woman: But you will be. And ever since they took the car and the house and the cart and the cow and the horse and the meadow— I lay awake at night for a whole month thinking, "When he goes, I'll have to carry him there, to the cemetery, on my back." This way, when we put you in the ground theyll say: "Here lies a man who came here on his own 2 feet."

Man: I can dig the hole too.

Woman: We'll do it together, howbout.

Man: Hop up. On my back.

Woman: Dont be silly.

Man: Hop up, Im telling you. I'll give you a piggy.

Woman: You wont last 10 steps.

Man: Try me.

> She hops on his back. He looks as if he'll die—
> but then the look passes.
> Then the look comes back.

Man: Oh.

> She jumps to the ground as he collapses.

Woman: Oh?

Man
Woman

(Rest)

Man: Did you miss me?

Woman: Terribly.

Man: Piggyback ride?

Woman: No thanks.

Man: Im still a man.

Woman: Sure you are. Come on.

> She takes him by the hand and they continue walking.

11 SPACE INVADERS

> A man, Shooter, with 2 pistols shoots at the sky.

Scooter: What the hell you doing?

Shooter: Target practice.

Scooter: On what?

Shooter: You got eyes? See for yrself.

Scooter: I dont see shit.

Shooter: Thats cause yr a nonbeliever.

> Shooter reloads. Scooter relooks.

Scooter: Aliens?

Shooter: You betcha.

Scooter: There aint no aliens.

Shooter: Theyre up there somewheres and when they come Im gonna be ready. And the nonbelievers, the doubting thomases like you, are gonna wish youda spent time getting ready.

Scooter: Shit.

Shooter: Where the hell you going?

Scooter: Inside. Im gonna watch tv and jerk-off.

Shooter: Suit yrself. Yll be sorry. But. Suit. Yr. Self.

Shooter keeps shooting. Scooter goes.

12 HAMLET/THE HAMLET

Somewhere in William Faulkner's Yoknapatawpha County.

Hamlet Snopes:
That barn there
I could burn it down
or I could leave it standing.
Burn it
or leave it.
But then what?
Either way Ive taken a step.
Either way Ive done something
and by that something
Ive made myself known:
Barn burner. Outlaw.
Or the kind of fella wholl take an insult
from a rich man
and not pay that rich man no mind
but let that rich man—that rich bastard—
with all the money of the world in his pockets,
use my back
and the backs of every child coming out of me,
and me and mines,
and the likes of me and me and mines
to scrape the cow and mule shit from his fancy boots.
And underneath all that,
not on top of it, but underneath all of it,
a dead father in the ground.

And up above the father,
up above the dead and rotting corpse of a man,
who is more use now than he was useful living,
still alive, an uncle walks.
My daddy's own brother,
eating supper off of my dead daddy's plate.
(Rest)
Help me God, cause life is and seems
particularly complicated just right now.

> Mother Snopes enters.

Mother Snopes: You gonna come in and eat or you gonna stand out there all night looking at that barn and talking to yrself?

Hamlet Snopes: I'll come in and eat.

Mother Snopes: Come on in then, before yr uncle eats up all the grits.

Hamlet Snopes: See that barn, Ma?

Mother Snopes: I see it but I dont see it. I see you seeing it and I dont see you seeing it neither. Folks say yr a barn burner. I call them liars.

Hamlet Snopes: Yep.

Mother Snopes: Are they liars? Are they liars, son?

Hamlet Snopes
Hamlet Snopes

(Rest)

Hamlet Snopes: Ima get me some of them grits.

> He goes inside.

Mother Snopes: God help us. Every one.

> She goes inside too.

13 MEETING BRAD PITT

2: What are you going to do today?
1: Ive got a meeting with Priscilla Presley.
2: No shit.
1: Yeah.

2: Whos Priscilla Presley?

1: This lady.

2: Cool. Then whatchu doing?

1: Then Ive got a meeting with Brad Pitt.

2: Getoutahere.

1: No shit.

2: *Getoutahere.*

1: *No shit.*

2: Is that the guy Shanta tried to clip for selling her that lame shit? He was like, "This is first-class," and it was like, *coach.*

(Rest)

1: No.

2: His name was Brad or Chad. Brad DeWit or Chad Misfit.

1: Thats a different guy.
(Rest)
How long you been out?

2: 2 days.

1: How was it?

2: Whatchu mean: "How was it?" "How was it?" Shit, it was jail. Whatchu wanna know: "Did I get raped?!" Shit.
(Rest)
Chad DeWit. Im telling you. Dont pay him top-dollar cause he dont never got nothing but coach, all right?

1: Yeah.

14 TRUST LIFE

A Woman stands onstage. She lifts her right foot
just a few inches off the floor, balancing with great difficulty.
Then she tries balancing with her right foot on the floor
and her left foot lifted.
While she's finding her balance, 2 separate Crowds of People
walk back and forth. They whisper with great energy:

2 Crowds: . . . trustlifetrustlifetrustlifetrustlifetrustlife . . .

The Crowds stop and try the balancing act,
as the Woman walks back and forth looking them over critically.
Each person, in their own moment, that is, whenever each

person feels her or his individual need, without making too much of a big deal of it, takes a breath in and a breath out. Each creates a gesture to accompany the breath. Then they all breathe and gesture together as the lights go out.

15 EMPTY

2 speakers.

Its empty.
Yeah.
Its—really—very—
Empty.
Yes.
I told you it was.
I had to see for myself.
So what do you think?
Well, its very—
Empty.
Spacious.
Right.
Airy.
Right.
Anything could happen here because—
Because nothing's happening here right now?
Yr sort of getting the hang of it. How do you feel?
Less empty. Or—empty but ok.
Yr gonna go far. I can tell.
You think?
Im betting on it.
Gee.
Yeah.
(Rest)
Tell me something. Whered everything go, you think?
Good question. Dunno.
Cool.

16 OUT TO SEA

In one corner of the stage a group of players read a section of
Fucking A, say Scene 5. Their performances are far from ready.
In another corner, a Woman stands looking out—at the sea.
A Man stands with her.

Woman: When I started this I really liked it.

Man: When did you start?

Woman: A moment ago. The page was blank and then there
were—words.

Man: And now?

Woman: And now, here we are. But everything's changed.

Man: Not the sea.

Woman: Yeah.

(Rest)

Everything's changed but the sea.

(Rest)

Not whats in it, whats in it has changed. Hundreds of thousands
of years ago there were creatures, mollusks or whatever—theyre
extinct now—and yesterday the last seal-like creature (I forget
the exact name of it, but you know what Im talking about), they
had him at the zoo and he died. The last of his kind. God.

Man: But the sea, the way you look at it—the way it makes you
feel—thats not changed.

Woman: Except that now I look at the water and think—horrible
things.

Man: Those horrible things are only in yr head. Listen to the
water. Really listen. Its only ever beautiful. Look at it and listen.
The sea!

Woman: The sea! Im going to drown myself.

Man: Thats against the law.

Woman: Im going to break the law.

Man: Dont.

Woman: Let go of me.

They struggle. She wins. She runs toward the water.
He watches her, then turns to the players, still reading.

Man: Good job with Scene 5. Gather round. I have notes.

The players gather round and
the Man gives notes as lights fade.

17 A FAST CAR GOES FAST

Honey and Sonny. 2 that hate each other, in a fast car going
fast. They dont want to be near each other, they dont want to
be in the same car. Neither is driving. There is a Driver present,
maybe he mimes the action.

Honey: A mule. A dead mule on the side of the road.
Sonny: Where?
Honey: Oh God.
Sonny: Should I have him stop?
Honey: No.
Sonny: I'll have him stop. Driver—
Honey: No.
Sonny: I need to see that up close.
Honey: Driver, keep going!

They drive along. Faster.

Honey
Sonny

(Rest)

Honey: The mule. His head and then—. And then his feet. They
were a mile apart.
Sonny: I remember that donkey in that book. A children's book.
Driver: *Brighty of the Grand Canyon!*
Honey & Sonny: Yes! Thats it.

A moment of joy peeks through the thick layer of stress
and hatred.

Sonny: And, once again, tragedy has brought us closer.
Driver: Why is that, you think?
Honey: He was talking about *us*. "Us" in the sense of him and me.
Driver: My apologies.

The car picks up speed. Faster.

18 OUTTAKES

Speaker and an Editor, listening with almost excessive attention.

Speaker:
Here it is 2003,
what does King Day really got to do with me?
I get a day off from school, so Im not making a fuss
and yeah, Im glad Im riding at the front of the bus.
King mighta worked mighty hard to make things right
but do I bow down to Edison when I turn on the light?
(Rest)
What do you think?

Editor: Its good.

Speaker: But I dont think it fits.

Editor: Me neither. But its not bad.

Speaker: I'll use it. Somewhere else. In *365* maybe.

Editor: Not bad.

Suddenly the stage is crowded with other outtakes:
The Almost Teenage Homecoming Queen from the play
"Homecoming Forever," a miscellaneous black person from
"Once Again Im the Only Black in the Audience," a lost mariachi
band member from the play "Mariachi Mania," a young man
with a gaudy golden crown from "Homecoming Forever,"
a girl holding either a live or rubber chicken from "Foul Play,"
and others, so many others, all outtakes, some characters,
some plays that werent even fully formed enough to get titles,
like little almost-birds who fall out of the nest every springtime
and litter the sidewalk.

Editor: Who are these folks?

Speaker: Outtakes from other plays.

Editor: They look sad.

Speaker: They are sad. Its hard being born and even harder when you miss the boat.

Editor: We'll call the play "Outtakes." Theyll be welcome here.

Speaker: I thank you.

19 1-2-3

1: This train is late.
2: What can you do.

1: THIS GODDAMN TRAIN IS LATE!

2: Now yr yelling.

1: GODDAMN RIGHT IM YELLING! WE'RE GONNA BE LATE FOR WHERE WE'RE GOING!

2: Yr going to attract unnecessary attention.

1: No I wont, because theyre all sleeping. Or watching tv. Or looking at the scenery.

2: Im going to look at the scenery.

1: Im going to bust a gut.

2: Oh God.

1: What?

2: A mule in 2 pieces. The body then the head. Slaughtered.

1: A kid's prank probably. They were bored or maybe the teacher told them to kill something for their homework assignment.

2: The poor thing. Whats the world coming to?

1: Whatever's coming, its coming late, I'll tell you that. Slaughtered mules and, and, and, trains that dont run on time. What next?

> The train's refusal to keep to schedule, the outburst of emotion,
> and the horrific scenery have exhausted them both.
> They sit back, too exhausted to sleep,
> the cloudy future looming up ahead.

20 WINGS

> 3 People walk along—theyre like 3 guards, or contemporary
> soldiers, walking along with automatic machine guns.
> They walk stealthlike, cause theyre on patrol.

1: Weve made our entrance into the area.

2: Thats a roger by my coordinates.

3: Check check and a double roger on this end, check.

1: Roger triple check. We are here. Secure the perimeter.

> They fan out with their guns.

2: Secure

3: Secure secure roger

1: Triple secure triple roger, over.

2: Hold on a sec.

1: Enemy?

2: Negative.

3: Looks like—shit—

1: Looks like shit?

3: Looks like a pair of wings.

2: Bird wings.

3: A big bird, not *the* Big Bird, but a big bird.

1: Wipe down for explosives. You never know.

> They wipe down for explosives.

3: Theyve got some sort of harness on them. Like theyre for wearing.

1: Stay clear. Could be dangerous.

2: Theyre wings.

3: Ima try them on. Gimmie a hand.

1: Stay clear, Im telling you. Stay clear, hear?

3: I outrank you. Help me get them on.

> 1 does not help. 2 helps while 1 keeps lookout.

3: They fit.

2: Like they was made for you.

1: What were they made for you think?

3: Wings are made for flying.

> With that, there is a sound of a great beating of wings,
> and then, 3 flies away.
> If the production of this play has a budget that does not allow
> for this stage direction, the stage direction may simply be read
> aloud by 1 and 2, and the flight of 3 can take place
> in our mind's eye. Or someone can come in
> tossing feathers like confetti.

21 CHICKEN WINGS

> A Dad and Son eating fried chicken.

Dad: You gonna eat that?

Son: I was thinking about it.

Dad: Dont get intellectual with me. You trying to tell me Im stupid?!

Son: No, sir.

Dad: "I was *thinking* about it." Well let me tell you something. I wasnt thinking about it. I was *eating* it. In my mind, my hand had already grabbed it off yr plate. My teeths had already got done chewing it. It was headed down my throat and into my guts. I'd already shit it out.

Son: Thats *thinking*, aint it?

Dad: You back-sassing me?!

Son: No, sir, I was just saying.

Dad: Keep on saying, Son. Ima eat this wing, all right?

> The Dad eats the wing.
> The Son contemplates murder, suicide,
> or just moving out of the house where he can have his own
> dinner on his own plates and eat it at his own leisure. Or maybe
> he decides, at that very moment, to join the army or become a
> movie star—that is, to make it very big and to tell his Dad:
> "I told you so," not in words, but: "I told you so," in big and
> full-blooded actions, rubbing his father's face in the reality of
> the world, until the end of both of their days.

22 BETWEEN THE 1ST REHEARSAL AND THE 2ND

> These 3 actions should be happening at the same time,
> like a triple split-screen.
> 1st: "Daphne walked me to the subway and we ran into Emily."
> So what we see is an Actress-Type
> walking along with a Writer-Type.
> 2nd: A Dishwasher washing a plate accidentally drops it when
> his friend says: "Interest rates have fallen again!'"
> 3rd: A Guy and a Gal, both drinking beer,
> talking about joining the army:

Gal: Ima join up. You?

Guy: I dunno.

Gal: I seen that Uncle Sam poster: "I want you!" I felt like he was talking to me.

Guy: You think?

Gal: I *know*.

Guy: He says: "I want you" to everybody.

Gal: It felt personal.

(Rest)

So Im joining. You?

Guy: I dunno.

Gal: I told Mom. She cried.

Guy: You tell Dad? He cry?

Gal: See this shiner? He put his tears in his fist and SOCKO.

Guy: Shit. Cant do nothing with a guy like that but love him.

> From the 1st action: the 2 women run into Emily,
> the Dramaturg-Type.
> Gleeful shouts and an embrace.
> Emily and the Actress-Type are introduced and shake hands.
> From the 2nd action: the Dishwasher sweeps up the broken dish
> as the friend holds the dustpan.
> From the 3rd action: the Guy and Gal drink up.

23 THE WAGON

> 2 people sitting.

1: You look glum.

2: You look dumb.

1: Get off it, come on, Im trying to make a connection here.

2: You dont wanna.

1: Im for real, here.

2: You wont be when you know.

1: I know all about you, so dont worry.

2: Do you know I just fell off the wagon?

1: Oh.

2: Yeah.

1: I didnt know that.

2: Yeah.

1: You dont look like—

2: What do you want—you want me lying in the gutter so all can see that I am NOT on the wagon right now?

1: No its not that—

2: So I fell off the wagon.

1: Theres worse things.

2: Like?

1: Like the Holocaust. Like the Nuclear Holocaust. Like Slavery. Like Slavery in a Nuclear Family during the Holocaust. Stuff like that.

2: Im getting personal here and yr getting universonal.
1: Personal is universonal.

1

2

1

2

2: I wont argue with you.
1: Dont sweat the wagon.
2: No?
1: You fell off the wagon, but theres another one coming around.
They pass by here every so often. No worries.
2: "No worries," he says! No worries!

> Sure enough just then the wagon comes around.
> The Wagoneer, a little old person,
> like a kindly troll or a yard gnome,
> pulls a red wagon. This should be sad and also,
> very reminiscent of childhood, like a kindly troll playing
> with yr childhood toys.

Wagoneer: All aboard.

> 2 gets on and the wagon goes along. 1 waves goodbye.
> 2 is afraid of what the future will bring, but also is
> hoping for the best.

24 BAREFOOT AND PREGNANT IN THE PARK

Guard: Just who do you think you are?
Woman: Im looking for my husband.
Guard: Likely story. Cant you read? Signs as big as Kansas, letters plain as the Plains: "No Barefoots on Grass." That means the likes of you. Guess you cant read.
Woman: I can read.
Guard: Get lost. Or I'll have to take you in. Lock you up in jail, then youll be having that baby in lockup.
Woman: My husband. He comes here. He's—he's got shoes. Harry! There he is! He left me because, well, long story and not important now is it? Ive been looking for him for 5 whole months! Im the laughingstock of our town. Harry! Harry! Its me! Harry! Harry!

Guard: You Harry?

Harry: Yeah.

Guard: You know her?

Harry: Never seen her in my life.

Harry goes on his way. The Guard blows his whistle
and 2 other Guards come in and take the Woman away.

25 CHANNEL 5 WEATHER

Man: Cold.

Woman: You betcha.

Man: Sssgonna warm up soon. In a few days.

Woman: Yeah?

Man: Channel 5 Weather says by Wednesday.

Woman: I never believe Channel 5. Remember, back in '73, when they predicted the snow?

Man: Yeah, but—that was 30 years ago. They got that doppelgänger—whatchamacallit—

Woman: Doppler.

Man: *That.* Yeah. I got faith in the doppler-thing they got.

A Street Woman, sleeping on the street,
wakes up and makes a call on her cell phone.

Street Woman: Talk to me about the weather. Yeah. I wanna know. A warming trend? In a few days? What are you, high? So you think just cause Im high I'll enjoy hearing about it. Cause of the double-going-dutch-fuck weatherman's tool? Whats it got to do with me? Oh, thats rich. Yr telling me because you care for me. Right, he's telling me because he cares for me. Right. You *what* me? You LOVE me?! Are you high? Yr not high? Really? Yeah? Shit. He loves me! He says he loves me!

The Street Woman stands and then jumps into the air,
doing several world-class ballerina moves.
The Man and Woman are shocked by the realization that
the Street Woman, in her day, was not just somebody,
but A Somebody. The Street Woman keeps leaping
and pirouetting as she gracefully and joyfully moves offstage.

Woman
Man

(Rest)

Woman: My life sucks.
Man: Yeah. Mine too.

26 ANOTHER PLAY IN THE HOUSE CALLED "HOUSE OF JONES"

Jones, a young man, married with at least 3 legitimate children,
stands above Effie, his young daughter. She sits and puts a
wooden block puzzle together or plays with a doll or plays jacks
or something. He holds a sword, high above his head, as if,
in the next second, we'll see him bring it down and
cut through the back of her neck.

Jones
Effie
Jones
Effie

Many years pass.

Jones
Effie
Jones
Effie

Many more years pass.

Effie: Father, youve got gray hair.
Jones: Yes.
Effie: And a wrinkle.
Jones: More than one.
Effie: Do I got a wrinkle?
Jones: Not yet.

Jones
Effie
Jones
Effie

Jones: Effie! My how youve grown.

Effie: Youve grown too. Old, though.

Jones: It happens.

Effie: Have I grown old?

Jones: Not yet.

Effie: At least theres that. To be happy about, I mean.

Jones: Yes, at least theres that.

(Rest)

Effie: All these years, Father, there youve stood, standing over me wielding yr sword.

Jones: The gods, you know. They said if I sacrifice you, theyd help my fleet get to the war on time. I am the General. And I am yr father. So here I stand.

Effie: The war's long over now, though. Yr troops have dispersed. One action would have opened one road. Instead, another road was opened.

Jones: The gods said—

Effie: The war's long over, Father.

Jones: That is beside the point!

Effie: Whatever.

Jones: Make a run for it, or I'll kill you.

Jones
Effie

Effie slowly crawls away. Long after she has gone,
Jones brings his sword slowly and horribly down. All in vain.

27 FATIGUE

X: Je don les fatigues parce que je suis fatigué.

Y: Nonsense. You dont put on the fatigues because you are fatigued.

X: Je don les fatigues, et maintenant, je suis fatigué.

Y: Ridiculous. And yr French sucks.

X: Im doing my best.

Y: Wheres a gun when you need one?

X: Right here.
Y: Is it loaded?
X: I think so.

> Y shoots X, killing her dead. Y stares at the body.
> X rises with difficulty.

X: That was a lame ending.
Y: What can I tell you.
X: Yr not trying.
Y: Am too.
X: Are not. Try harder.

> Y shoots X several times. Stares at the body,
> then drags the body offstage.

28 THE ARRIVAL OF THE END

> A Crowd gathered.

Man: Qu'est-ce que c'est?
Chorus of Women: C'est un bird.
Chorus of Men: Non, non, ce n'est pas un bird. C'est un avion!
All: Ooh la la!

> They all gather around in horror and wonder. They turn around
> in unison. One large horrified Crowd turning around and around
> and around and around, as if, the thing they are all fixated upon
> is circling in the sky before landing. At last the thing lands and
> approaches them from the center of the audience.
> It is a Woman, just walking.

Chorus of Men: Halt! Who goes there?!?!?
Woman *(Singing in a voice reminiscent of Leontyne Price)*:
They call me:
"The end
of the world!"

> Grand operatic fanfare as the curtain falls.

29 THE KING SLEPT HERE

Waiting Woman: Will the king come this evening, you think?

Page: Yes, its his desire to see Southcastle again before he dies.

Waiting Woman: His Majesty was in the pink last time these lowly eyes saw his right most noble visage. He was in the pink and the world was right.

Page: Youve been too long at Southcastle. Here, at Southcastle, regardless of the weather or the season, the grass is green, the roses red, the sky blue. Here, in short, everything is right with the world. But Elsewhere, things are, well, wrong.

Waiting Woman: You speak of the Pretenders.

Page: I speak of the Pretenders.

Waiting Woman: By these old work-worn hands, if I only had a pointed stick with which I would disembowel each and every Pretender.

Page: Yr voice would be a welcome guest in the king's ear.

> Unnoticed by these 2, a group of Army Men march in,
> set up camp and begin doing pushups.
> The 2 scenes proceed simultaneously.

Sergeant: 1-2-3-4. Come on, men, eat-the-dirt.

Waiting Woman: The king has naught but fops and fools for comfort. I speak not of yr kind self, of course. I remember back into the days of my own youth—

Page: Twas not so long ago—

Waiting Woman: Long enough to make me old. Those days were better. Elsewhere did not exist. Murders did not hide in the velvet curtains or creep beneath the shrubbery.

Page: The waiting woman and the page knew their place.

Waiting Woman: And never thought to climb higher.

Waiting Woman
Page

Page: Do you—

Waiting Woman: Hear voices? Yes.

(Rest)

Private Joe: Hear them voices?

Sargeant: Keep pushing up, kid.

Private Joe: Someone's talking about kings and murders.

Private Jerry: Whassit with you? Someone's always talking about weird shit.

Private John: Yr just trying to get out of the Service by hearing voices.

Sargeant: Jumping jacks, lets go!

> The Army Men do jumping jacks.
> The Page and Waiting Woman sharpen their knives.

30 3 LIVES

> 3 actors upstage.
> They perform 3 different activities simultaneously.
> To the left: a Woman sharpens a knife. Then, while holding the
> knife in one hand, she runs downstage to pet a dog or a child.

Woman: There, there, be good for Mama, huh?

> To the right: a Man moves paper from his inbox to his outbox.
> Then he runs downstage to turn on his tv.

Man: He wouldnt let me go home, so I quit! Said I could watch it at work, but—this is the first game of the series, after all! And where the hell is my beer?!

> Meanwhile, at centerstage:
> a Bathing Beauty waits; 2 Ditchdiggers are in a digging race, a
> Timekeeper blows time and the holes the Ditchdiggers have
> dug are measured. There is applause. Then the Bathing Beauty,
> in her homely swimming costume, comes forward and awards
> 1st and 2nd place.

31 IF I HAD TO MURDER ME SOMEBODY

> 1 speaker.

If I had to murder me somebody
it would be hard to choose.
On the one hand I could pick
someone nobody would miss.
Or someone lots of people would want dead.
Like the president on a bad day.
Or some other kind of motherfucker.

January

If I had to murder me somebody, it might go down like that.
If I had to murder me somebody I might, though,
pick somebody lots of people loved.
Like when that asshole shot that real nice guy. You remember?
And the whole world, was like, sad for days.
And people know his name, the killer's.
I wouldnt do it for the notoriety, though.
Im ok with my volume, I dont need to get no louder.
Not for my own self.
Whoosh.
Im like, standing here, ruminating on evil.
Thinking about murder—you go to a place in yr mind, you know?
No, you dont know. You aint been there.
Its like saying you been to Dallas and you say, yeah,
when all you seen of Dallas is, like, Fort Worth or,
at best, reruns of the tv show.
And Im in Dallas,
which is to say that I am entertaining the thought,
just for a minute,
that hurting me somebody is gonna make me feel better.
Like when you fall in love
or like when yr team wins the Superbowl or something.
Or, ok, the Stanley Cup, if thats yr thing.
Hockey aint my thing.
But it fades. The feeling.
Like this feeling I had for this woman.
Barbara.
It faded.
Then I went and murdered me somebody.
I didnt know him at the time.
I got to know him later when I seen his life story on the tv.
His story had a halo around it.
Mine had a ring of fire.
(Rest)
He was a clerk in a store
and from what they say he was a nice guy too.
Like I said, when the mood grabs you
its like the mood is doing the murdering
and you just along for the ride and happen to have a gun, but.
Its like my moms is always eating.
And she aint eating cause she's hungry, no, she's eating cause
she's mad.
What she do dont got nothing to do with food.
But it do.
Anyway. I went and murdered me somebody.
And now somebody have to murder me.

I started talking, thinking I could explain it but I didn't.
(Rest)
I got the understanding in my mouth and I cant put it into words
but that dont mean I dont got the understanding.
I just cant pull it together is all.
Well.
Peace out.

31 (Again) HORSE AND RIDER

Rider: Are we there yet?
Horse: Not yet.
Rider: Im tired. You tired?

Horse
Horse

Rider: Its hot.
Horse: Yes, its hot.

Rider
Rider

Rider: Are we there yet?—
Horse: Yes.
Rider: But, yr still walking.
Horse: Because theres walking to do, sir.

They walk on.

February
1 TURTLE SOUP

Mary, very pregnant, and Joe.

Joe: Want some?
Mary: What is it?
Joe: Turtle soup.
Mary: Sounds good.

Mary: The turtles! Theyre still alive! Jesus Christ!

Joe: I couldnt make a fire. No wood, no coal, no paper, no sticks, no stones, no matches, no knife, no nothing.

Mary: Damn, this war.

Joe: Yeah.

Mary
Joe

They sip and eat the soup.

2 SPACE

Man: You heard about the spaceship blowing up, right?

Woman: Yeah. Someone mentioned it at work.

2 Metal Bangers, drag out a big piece of metal and bang on it with hammers.

Man: Why do they go up there, you think?

Woman: Why do they go up where?

Man: Outer space.

Woman: Cause its there, I guess. Cause its there and cause they can. Sort of.

Man: Yeah.

The Metal Bangers bang louder. Sometimes rhythmically, sometimes not. Man and Woman look at each other, at the ground, at the sky, but not in unison or anything.

Man: You guys gonna bang on that all day?

1st Banger: You gonna get in my business?

Man: Could do.

2nd Banger: We're the Wright Brothers, you know.

Man: I dont give a flying fuck.

1st Banger: Would you give a flying fuck if I hit you with this hammer?

Man
The Metal Bangers

(Rest)

Woman: Look: a bird.

> They all look up. The Metal Bangers go back to their banging.
> The Man and Woman watch as the bird falls from the sky
> in a horrible ball of fire, hitting the ground and dying instantly
> on impact. The Man cant bear it, and buries his tear-stained
> face in the Woman's shoulder. She bravely stares at
> the dead bird. The bird was a bald eagle, I think.

2 (Again) GROUNDHOG (For Sova)

> Slow light fades up. The stage is bare. A Lady walks out
> onto the stage. She has on a winter coat and hat and mittens
> and scarf and galoshes, etc. She comes out not tentatively
> but not confidently either.
> She looks behind her. No shadow. She's relieved.
> As she speaks she removes her winterwear.

Lady: Good thing thats over, right? I mean, almost over.
Groundhog Day today. Groundhog, or lady in groundhog play,
walks out, and should they see their shadow it means lots more
winter is on the way. No shadow, no winter. So its over. Winter.
Most of it anyway.
(Rest)
Winter this year was hard. You know there was—

> She makes a hand to clavicle gesture expressing extreme pain
> and sadness. Pain and sadness beyond measure.

Lady: And if none of that got to you, or you know, even with bright
spots theres the—

> She makes a gesture—arm sailing away from the body
> and returning slowly.

Lady: So much of it is difficult and even more difficult to talk
about. But its over, winter is over, winter is on its way out—
almost over—and so we can finally, at last, we can finally—just
be here—without our galoshes.
(Rest)
Every day I run to the window and see if my tulips are coming
up. And soon spring green will be here. Theres nothing better
than that.

> A man walks in, shrouded in black, the Shadow.

February

Lady
Shadow
Lady
Shadow

Lady: Yr just "a" shadow, yr not "my" shadow, right?

Shadow: Sorry Im late. You were walking so fast and—I was out pretty late last night and—I was drinking. Ok. I'll admit it. Even though my wife tells me that if I keep drinking itll kill me. But—so I was out late and having a pretty good time. And I went to bed, set my alarm. But, the alarm went off, and I was dead to the world. Out cold. By the time I got myself together you were all the way down the street.

Lady: I heard hollering—

Shadow: That was me. Yeah. Hollering for you to wait up.

Lady: Yr . . . *(Gesture)* I mean, last year I saw you and you were much . . . *(Opposite gesture)* smaller.

Shadow: Ive been eating. Too much. Gaining weight. Its a little embarrassing.

Lady: I'll say.

> She turns away, then steps away. He follows her.
> When she stops he stops.

Lady
Shadow

Shadow: So you see me, right?

Lady: Yr a shadow, not my shadow.

Shadow: Come on—

Lady: Im not going back in.

Shadow: This is hard for me too.

> He takes out a pair of handcuffs, puts one around his wrist
> then one around hers. He begins to lead her away.
> She does not resist, then, dashes back to her pile of winter
> clothes, collecting them as best she can before
> he leads her offstage.

3 SANTA ANA

> A Schoolteacher with a group of Schoolchildren
> in the middle of a museum tour.

Schoolteacher: Gather round, children, gather round.

> She turns on a light. It illuminates a diorama: a girl, Ana,
> sitting by a window. She has long blackish wet hair.
> Ana turns on a fan to dry her hair. Her Mother appears.

Mother: Yr my spitting image. What do you say to that, huh?

Ana: Yr my moms, Im yr spitting image.

Mother: Ive got 20 years on you. Plus Im exhausted from raising and bearing 12 children and a crop in a dry and rocky field that would be better suited for God knows what. Ive never seen such a barren landscape. And look at you. My daughter, Ana. Who do you think you are? Drying yr hair with a fan? Whore!

Ana: Im not a whore.

Mother: But you will be.

Ana: God told me to dry my hair with the fan.

Mother: A whore and a liar too.

> The Mother beats Ana with a stick. Ana takes the blows.
> Then she begins flying around the room like a bird.
> The barren rocky fields sprout a cornucopia of delicious edibles.
> Meanwhile, the Schoolchildren are in awe.
> The Schoolteacher turns off the lights and they move on.

Schoolteacher: Right this way, children, right this way.

4 THUMP AND THUNDER

> A big callboard. A Man and Woman in a long line of people,
> all wearing numbers. Every once and awhile, someone sees
> their number come up on the callboard and they exit.
> Each exit is tearful and followed by a loud THUMP
> and THUNDEROUS applause.

Woman: How manyd you take?

Man: Not a one.

Woman: Bullshit.

Man: On my mother's grave, not a one.

Woman: You wouldnt be here if you didnt take at least one.

Man: Not a one, Im telling you. Mines a case of mistaken identity.

Woman: Too bad. I took hundreds.

Man: Guess you took one for me, then.

Woman: Guess I did.

The Woman's number is up. She exits. THUMP.
THUNDEROUS applause.

5 HAIL AND FAREWELL

4 people speak simultaneously for specific lengths of time.
Speakers should follow prompts. Use a conductor to keep time.

Hyper Woman:	Melancholy Woman:	Boastful Man	Friendly American:
For 15 seconds please describe a walk in the woods during deer season. End with: "Ha!"	Wait 5 seconds, then for 10 seconds tell how a piece of the space shuttle Challenger landed in yr yard. End with: "Oh!"	(For 15 seconds): "Huge. How huge am I? I'll tell ya! . . ." (Tell us and end with: "Yeah.")	"Hello, my name is Joe. Joe, right here on my nametag. How can I help you?" (Wait 5 seconds) "Gosh, if only you were more like us."

Repeat as necessary. End with a big smile.
Let the lights fade out.

6 WORMS

Deputy: Not again!

Walter Charles: Im just standing here.

Deputy: I told you if I ever caught you digging up worms in the colored churchyard, I'd have to lock you up. And here you are: digging up worms in the colored churchyard.

1st Dead Person rises from a grave and holds a sign:
"The theme of this play was modified
to meet industry standards."

Walter Charles: I cant help myself.

Deputy: Jesus H. Christ.

Walter Charles: Im just doing what I do. I cant help myself.

2nd Dead Person rises and rattles a sign similar to the 1st.
Walter Charles and the Deputy see it.

Deputy: I had a grand speech I was gonna give. I had it all learned and everything.

Walter Charles: Me too. I had me a grand speech too. It was about the fairness of the worm. How it eats fair and eliminates fair and—and when it crawls in the middle of the sidewalk on a rainy day, then the sun comes out and leaves them stranded, kind of like the Ancient Egyptians following the Israelites through the Red Sea, but in reverse, cause they got caught in the water but the worms get stranded in a desert of sorts, well that breaks my heart. But I—guess I wont give my speech after all.

Deputy: Me neither. Mine was pretty grand too. It was about the unfairness of the law and how it bends fair men to unfairness no matter how honest they may be. Like a temptress in a red low-cut dress on a dark and sleazy street corner.

Walter Charles: Woah.

Deputy: Yeah.

1st Dead:
Try as you might
you cant get a bite
yr fishing, my friends,
has come to bad ends.
Exeuent
or die here.

Walter Charles and the Deputy exit.

2nd Dead: Howd they get in?

1st Dead: Musta called in a favor or some shit.

2nd Dead: Aint that the way of the world.

7 THE LAKE SHORE LIMITED

A Train Conductor comes onstage and yells:

Train Conductor: The Lake Shore Limited!! All Ahbbooooooard!

The stage fills with hundreds of thousands of people. From different ethnic groups, races, social classes, dressed for different seasons, from different epochs, some in native dress of countries that have never been heard of, some from planets and solar systems and galaxies as yet undiscovered.

> Some with great bundles and packages, some empty-handed
> and bareheaded with empty pockets.
> All united in their desire to board the train.
> But there is no train.
> They wait with smiles which, after awhile, melt and turn grimy
> like old snow in upstate New York.

Man: The goddamned train is late.

Woman: Why get angry. The train is always late.

Another Man: If it was on time, I'd shoot somebody.

Another Woman: I feel like shooting somebody right now.

A 3rd Man: Patience.

(Rest)

> They wait.
> A man pushes his way to the front. He wears a suit.
> He clears his throat, then gives a Great Speech.
> The words are numerous and meaningless.
> He should have pulled his words from
> a dictionary and written them down on a series of scraps
> of paper, pulled the scraps from an old stovepipe hat,
> assembled the scraps at the last minute on a large piece
> of posterboard which his flunkie holds for him as he reads
> the words. Somewhere in the speech is the phrase:
> "The Lake Shore Limited." Each word is delivered with more
> passionate emphasis than the last.
> Someone holds up a flag. Another wipes a tear. The Man, now
> with a capital M, continues talking and, like the miracle
> of daybreak, the hopeless faces are refreshed. He continues
> talking, most likely just repeating what he's already read, as the
> mood grows quite buoyantly patriotic and the lights fade.

8 ORANGE

> A Clown, with a strapped-on red nose and
> a colorful pointed hat, comes in. He/she juggles 3 oranges.
> A Man walks by in a hurry, talking on the phone,
> not a cell phone, but an old-style rotary-dial phone with
> a long extension cord.

Man: So I told him, I said, if you think that is the way things are, youve got another thing coming, I said. I told him. Yeah, I told him. Over my dead body! I said. Oh, yeah, *I told him.* And do you know what he said to me? Not a goshdarn thing. Not one wor—

> He sees the Clown juggling. The Clown juggles in a rhythmic, hypnotic, purposeful way, as if the movement of the 3 oranges were the very thing which keeps the world revolving. Or with the intensity of a mime who thinks the job of the mime is of great purpose. He sees himself at the bottom of the pile of man, but has made his peace with that, and works steadily on, knowing the meek and quiet will inherit.
> The Man, watching the Clown, begins to weep in an embarrassed way. Trying hard not to show it. Dabbing his eyes with his perfectly pressed handkerchief, and then replacing the handkerchief to make it look as if it never left his breast pocket. This is an impossible task, and it makes him cry all the more. He blubbers and wipes his face with his sleeve as a 5-year-old child would. Then he stops.
> The Clown continues juggling.
> The Man grabs 1 of the oranges, eating it like an apple, then stuffing the leftovers in his pocket.
> The Clown continues much as before, but with just the 2 oranges.
> The Man grabs the 2nd orange. Eats it. The Clown continues with 1 orange. The Man grabs and eats the last orange, then, as the lights fade, he makes sure no one is looking as he grabs off the Clown's red nose and pointed hat and puts them on himself.
> The Clown continues juggling even though he's got nothing to work with but air.

9 THE ORIGINAL MOTHERFUCKER

> A Man comes in—he's being led by a Child. His arm is outstretched and his hand is on the Child's narrow shoulder. The Man is blind.

Child: This looks like the place.
Man: You think?
Child: From what you told me.
Man: A clearing?
Child: Yeah.
Man: And people—people out there and watching me—us?

Child: Yeah.

Man: You sure?

Child
Man
Child

Man: Its just that, last time—

Child: I aint had as much experience in the world as you. Some trees look like people, and "clearings"—how was I supposed to know what that was?

Man: You could have asked.

Child: If I had asked I wouldnt be much of a man, would I?

Man: Yr a child.

Child: Word coulda gotten out. You coulda let news of my uncertainty slip. Say you was in a bar, drinking. And say you got drunk. You coulda blabbed my business. Patrollers come looking for me, patrollers find me. Take away my chance for manhood. So I made a mistake about the "clearing" and the "audience" yesterday, so what. We're here now. Lots of space with nothing. And some folks out there.

Man: How many?

Child: You didnt ask for a guide who could count. If you wanted a guide who could count it woulda cost you more.

Man: I didnt think counting was—anything special.

Child: You aint from around here.

Man: No. No Im not.

Child: Where you from?

Man: —. Set up the campstool, please. Ive gotta do my talk then we can go back, ok?

Child: Yeah, sure.

> The Child sets up a measly campstool. The Man sits.

Child: You want the sign hung on you?

Man: Please.

> The Child hangs a sign around the Man's neck.
> The words face the Man's chest so we cant read them.

Man: Are the words facing out?

Child: Words?

Man: The black squiggles.

Child: What about the squiggles?

Man: —. Can you see them.

Child: Nope.

Man: Please turn the sign around so that you can see the squiggles.

> The Child turns the sign so that the squiggles are visible.
> The sign reads: "Oedipus, Former King."

Child: I can see the squiggles now.

Man: Good. Thank you.

Child: Now what.

Man: I wont be long.

Child: You want me to wait.

Man: I wont be long.

Child: Waiting costs.

Man: I'll pay it.

Child: Where you want me to wait.

Man: Just a stone's throw—a short stone's throw away.

Child: Ok.

> But the Child doesnt move. He stands there.

Man: I can hear you breathing.

Child: Good thing you *can* hear, right?

> The Child walks a short distance away. Fishes in his pockets,
> finds cigarettes, smokes as he waits.

Oedipus, Former King
Oedipus, Former King
Oedipus, Former King

(Rest)

Oedipus: Im Oedipus Rex. Oedipus the King. Also known as
Oedipus the *Former* King. Also know as the original mother-
fucker. Im supposed to talk about it here. Its part of the sentence
that Ive imposed on myself. A caution. But the more
I caution, the less I have to say about it all.
(Rest)
I shouldnt of married *anybody*. Or killed *anybody*. That would
have been smart. But no one told me about the oracle.
Although—Im not saying Im innocent. Just ignorant.

(Rest)

Mother knew. I mean she knew of the oracle. So she shouldnt of married anybody, especially after her husband had been killed—but think about it—he had been killed by "3 men." Thats what the reports had said. Not "1 man" but "3." So she's thinking that, after all her loss, the oracle was bullshit, not bullshit, but incorrectly read. And there she was, she'd already given her dear son away and now her husband was dead and— she was queen, but not for long, not if she didnt remarry, and this handsome stranger comes to town. And its been years since she's seen me and I dont have any memory of her at all, and so we didnt recognize each other, I mean, what mother can really imagine the man her son will become?

(Rest)

My first time with her was my first time. And it was—really something. We would sneak around before the wedding. I'd saved the whole city, I coulda had anybody I wanted, but I only wanted her. And she was the queen and she coulda had anybody or anything she wanted. And since she'd given me away, things between her and the king hadnt been the same. They hadnt had any more children, and they hadnt gotten together much. It was as if, when they gave me away, it was as if the wind stopped blowing. Although they gave me away for their own safety. Go figure. I got her pregnant and we hurried up the wedding. We were going to get married anyway, but we rushed it. She didnt want tongues wagging. And everything was great. No wars. Plenty of everything. Everybody who wanted a job had a job, everybody who didnt was taken care of too. It was all good. And then the wind started blowing again. It was the strangest thing.

(Rest)

You know and on our wedding night she was looking at my ankles. I had a woody like Texas and she's looking at my ankles and Im like, come on, little mamma, lets get busy. Funny. I called her "little mamma" even then—before I knew she was my mother. But men call their wives "mother" dont they? Whether or not they have kids. Its a term of endearment. Im just here to fill in some gaps about the play: like what the writer didnt get around to writing, or what was cut, or what the censors cut.

(Rest)

Our children were slow. I mean, they were actually mentally challenged. Because she was my mom. And—she was looking at my ankles. I shoulda let her. Instead I just took her. We were a perfect fit. And something in me knew, I knew—that fitting that good was not good. And then, the next morning. I think she knew too but. It was like she had already gotten lost. And she knew there was no way out but deeper in.

(Rest)

I knew this sailor once. He had been shipwrecked and had, for 8 whole days, been floating around in the middle of the sea with nothing to hold on to but a plank of wood. For 8 whole days. Then he was rescued. "For my whole life, I've always been a little at sea," he said. "Circumstances just took their time catching up to me." Like Mom, always a little lost—and then lost for real and in my arms that morning. No way out but deeper in.

Oedipus, Former King
Oedipus, Former King
Oedipus, Former King

(Rest)

Child: You done?
Oedipus: Yeah.

> The Child folds up the campstool and removes the sign.
> He stands in front of Oedipus.

Oedipus: Howd I do?
Child: I didnt listen. Did you want me to listen?
Oedipus: No.
Child: I could listen next time, if you want.

> Oedipus makes a vague gesture of: "Dont sweat it, kid."
> He puts his hand on the Child's shoulder and they exit.

9 (Again) SOMETIMES GOD IS A SOPRANO

> A Woman Soprano sings an Italian aria, most likely Puccini.
> She could sing it karaoke-style. She sings well. People watch.
> A radio carried by a Radio Man announces the end of the world.
> The Radio Man is followed by a group
> of Foreign-Breastbeating Mourners.
> Then a Disco King comes in with a short line of Hustlers, doing
> the Hustle to a tune that only plays in the Disco King's head.
> The Soprano keeps singing.
> People watching the Soprano either join the Breastbeating
> Mourners or the Hustlers.

10 FATHER COMES HOME FROM THE WARS (Part 2)

A Family (Mother, Father, Children) sitting. Neatly dressed.
Theyre posing for a family portrait. Painter walks in.

Painter: Lets take up where we left off yesterday, shall we?
Mother: Thatll do nicely.

Painter paints. Children fidget. Mother eyes them or slaps them
on their hands and they do their best to keep still.
Painter paints.
Soldier Man arrives, dressed in battle dress. It does not matter
from what war: the Trojan war, WWI, American Civil, Iran-Iraq,
Napoleonic, Spanish Civil, Crimean, Zulu, ANC against the
Powers that Were, whatever, the Chinese-Tibetan conflict,
the War of the Worlds, whatever, it does not matter.
Soldier Man taps the Father of the Family on the shoulder,
relieving him from duty. The Father was only a father figure, and,
very graciously bows, clicks his heels and leaves.
The Family does not flinch. The Painter continues to paint.
After posing for awhile with his Family,
Soldier Man wanders away. He puts on a record. Opera.
A Puccini aria. He starts moving around.

Soldier Man: Lets have a sing-along, shall we?

He reaches out to the Family. They cringe and shrink from his
touch. He can live with it. He dances around. Its clear
that he's missing an eye, a leg, an arm—he sings and dances,
quite beautifully, though, all the same. The Family watches him,
with mounting horror, spoiling the portrait.
The Painter turns to the audience:

Painter: Oh, this will never do!

The Family snaps back into polite alignment.
The Painter continues painting. The Soldier Man's
hearing is now gone too. He turns up the record player
and continues singing and dancing as the Family, very bravely,
you understand, holds very very still.

11 THE RIVER THROUGH ELIZABETHTOWN, NEW JERSEY

An Old Man fishes. A Young City Couple comes up to him.

Young Man: Ever caught anything?
Old Man: Nope.
Young Woman: Never?
Old Man: Nope.

(Rest)

Young Woman: Take my picture with him, honey.

The Young Man takes a couple pictures of the Old Man
and his girl, then she takes a couple snaps of her guy
and the Old Man. Theyre all very happy.

Old Man: I caught a convict once. But never no fish.

A Protester comes in wearing a sandwich board that reads:
"No Justice No Peace!"

Protester: Excuse me. There was a group I was with. They took one road, I took another.
Old Man: Yll find them down at the courthouse, I expect.
Protester: I thank you.
Young Woman: Can I take a picture with you?
Protester: I dont think so.

Protester hurries off.

Young Woman: He wasnt very friendly.
Young Man: Not everybody is friendly, hon.

The Old Man looks at the both of them and just keeps fishing.
He reels in his line, but still, nothing.

12 THE BIRTH OF ABRAHAM LINCOLN

Night. 2 men: Mr. Lincoln, Sr., and his Mystic Friend
sit in rocking chairs in a rough-hewn log cabin.

Mystic Friend: Do you think that if everyone in the world were enlightened, things would be much different?

Mr. Lincoln, Sr.: You read too many of them Hindu books, friend.

Mystic Friend: Its a simple enough question. What do you think?

Mr. Lincoln, Sr.: I think its cold for February.

Mrs. Lincoln (*Offstage*): Oh!

Mr. Lincoln, Sr.: And my wife's in there with a colored midwife cause we cant afford no better.

Mrs. Lincoln (*Offstage*): Oh God!

Abraham Lincoln, as a Newborn Baby (*Offstage*): *Waaaaaaaah!*

> Colored Midwife comes onstage carrying unseen baby
> wrapped in swaddling clothes.

Colored Midwife: Youve got a son, Mr. Lincoln.

Mr. Lincoln, Sr.: We'll name him "Abraham." "Abraham Lincoln."

Mystic Friend: Theres a glow about yr son, Lincoln.

Mr. Lincoln, Sr.: Thats just the candlelight.

Mrs. Lincoln (*Offstage*): Is he alive or is he dead? He's dead aint he? He's dead!

Mr. Lincoln, Sr.: He's alive as we are, mother.

Mrs. Lincoln (*Offstage*): I dont believe you! Let me see him!

Colored Midwife: I'll take him back to her.

> She goes.

Mystic Friend: Yr son will be a fine man someday. Maybe even a great man.

Mr. Lincoln, Sr.: Oh, you and yr Hindu claptrap.

Mystic Friend: Let us go and congratulate yr wife.

> They take the candle and head into the nursery.

13 WE WERE CIVILIZED ONCE

> A Man stands centerstage. He looks like a Farmer.
> He swings his arms.
> The stage fills with City People from New York and Los Angeles.
> They hurry back and forth. More and more come in, hurrying
> and pushing and shoving. Suddenly somebody screams and
> everybody ducks in fear and covers their heads.
> They stay ducked down and the Farmer,
> still just standing there, keeps swinging his arms.

February

A Man and Woman come in dressed for winter walking from stageright to stageleft backward.

Man: We have to walk backwards all the way to New York.

Woman: Im not complaining.

Man: Dontcha wanna know why?

Woman: Not really.

Man: The sight of it all would blind us. Or turn us to stone. Or drive us mad. I forget which.

Woman: I didnt want to know.

Farmer: Drive you mad.

Man: Thank you kindly.

Woman: I really didnt want to know.

The 2 keep walking, the others stay ducked, the Farmer keeps swinging his arms.

13 (Again) THE BUTCHER'S DAUGHTER (For Bonnie)

A Man, you know, the kindly sort, who is hardworking and who also takes pleasure in reading the kids a bedtime story or playing the slide trombone, this Man sits exhausted. He wears his Butcher's apron, and the apron, after a hard day's work, is badly stained with blood. His Daughter, the kind of kid we all were once, young and with our whole lives ahead of us, so unaware of the Danger ahead that the Danger momentarily loses faith in itself and ceases to exist— this Daughter, she wears an apron too, and hers is clean and neat. The Daughter works at sharpening a vast array of knives. The Butcher watches her with great pride. Every so often she holds out a knife blade so that he can feel its sharpness. He is most pleased.

Daughter: Hey Pop?

Butcher: Yep?

Daughter: What am I gonna be when I grow up?

Butcher: Anything you want.

Daughter: Howabout a butcher. Like you.

Butcher: "Anything you want" means anything you want, kiddo. You dont gotta follow yr old man.

Daughter: But I wanna be a butcher. I wanna wield the family knives.

Butcher: Theres nothing grand about it.

Daughter: But I—

Butcher: And have blood on yr apron all the time? Think about it. Blood on yr apron all the time.

Daughter: Blood comes off in the wash.

Butcher: Not always.

Butcher
Daughter

Butcher: Those knives were given to me by my father. His father gave them to him. And so it went on back to the beginning of our line.

Daughter: Recent historical evidence suggests that, all those years ago, they were originally found underneath a rock. In the middle of a blizzard. When there was no food but a frozen carcass. A wooly mammoth perhaps. And no way to cut it. Until the knives were found.

Butcher: Dont be silly. Not when yr telling the family story.

Daughter: I got carried away.

Butcher: Set the record straight. Go on, tell it right.

Daughter: They were hand-forged. By Great-Great-Great-Great-Great-Great-Grandpa's mother.

Butcher: And kept sharp all these years.

Daughter: And always kept together as a set. Through thick and through thin. Through all weathers.

Butcher: Thats right.

Butcher
Daughter

Butcher: You can pick one. Pick any knife you want. Take it with you. Go out into the world and cut yr own path with it.

Daughter: But I wanna—

Butcher: Go on, Im telling you! Go on! Before I change my mind.

Daughter
Butcher

> The Daughter selects a knife. Maybe the cleaver.
> Perhaps the machete. Maybe the grapefruit knife.
> Theres a chance she'll choose the breadknife,
> but theres a greater chance she'll choose the sword.

The one her Butcher-Father uses to kill the fatted calf in preparation for the Holy Days. The sword is too heavy for her to lift—now and for the first several years of her journey she will only be able to drag it.

Butcher: Let me give you my blessing.

He kisses her gently on the forehead. She gives him a hug.

Butcher: Now go.

She leaves, dragging the sword behind her. In the years to come, she'll return home, fully grown, with her sword tucked neatly in her belt and with many splendid tales from the road. He will be blind and old—very very old—but he will recognize her. And that is everything.

14 REVOLVER LOVER

He's holding a big heartshaped box of chocolates behind his back. She's holding a gun.

Man: I love you.
Woman: I love my gun.
Man: What about me.
Woman: I love my gun, I love you.

Man
Woman

Woman: I love my gun more than I love you, thats what you were gonna ask, right?

Another Man, bleeding pretty badly, drags himself across the stage. Man and Woman watch, but not too closely.

Man: He's yr backdoor man, right?
Woman: You jealous-mealous.
Man: He's yr backdoor man, Christ Almighty!
Woman: He's my target practice.
Man: Oh.
Woman: Feel better?

Man: Yeah.

The Bleeding Man stops crawling and just lies there dead.

Woman: What did you get me for Valentine's Day?

Man: Chocolate.

Woman: I got you a heart.

Man: His?

Woman: Was his, then mine, now yrs.

She hands him a bleeding heart. He is moved, but also wonders how life with this woman will turn out. This is his 7th wife. They met in rehab. She was hot for him, he was afraid of her, and initially thought his fear was desire.

15 PIG MEAT FARMING MAN

2 Society Ladies, old friends.

Society Lady 1: I have not seen you in—

Society Lady 2: Years!

Society Lady 1: Dont date us, dont date us.

Society Lady 2: Ages.

Society Lady 1: Mmm.

Society Lady 2: Married?

Society Lady 1: You betcha!

Society Lady 2: To?

Society Lady 1: You first.

Society Lady 2: I married a banker. We have several houses and several cars and a lot of money.

Society Lady 1: How is he in the sack?

Society Lady 2: Excuse me?

Society Lady 1: You know who I married? Joe.

Society Lady 2: Joe?

Society Lady 1: That pig meat farming man. No, we dont have a penny to our names but—he puts his bacon up on my plate every night, you know what Im talking about.

Society Lady 2: I think Ive mistaken you for somebody I used to know.

Society Lady 1: Ive written a song about him. Wanna hear it?

Society Lady 2: Nope. Thanks. Bye.

Society Lady 2 leaves. Society Lady 1 sings or not
(depending if performance time allows and other extenuating
circumstances like, did we have time to learn the song or,
you know, all those things like that).
The whole play could transform itself into a little blues club:
a bar with stylish barmaids, Christmas lights up,
band onstage backing up the singer.
Slow blues:

PIG MEAT FARMING MAN
All day and all night
you know a woman sure needs love.
All day and all night
you know a woman sure needs love.
Sometimes she gotta beg and plead for her sugars
sometimes she gotta fight and push and shove.
I hear women talking, they say
their men too often come up short,
a man may pay her bills all right
but he plays his love like its a sport.
But me I dont got no complaints
my man he makes my life all sweet
I got me a pig meat farming man
he gives me all I need to eat.
Theres always meat on my plate
Im saying theres always plenty of meat for me to eat.
My mother, when I was a girl,
she told me to marry a good man:
a doctor, a lawyer,
someone who understands,
a man whose hands are clean,
a man who aint never mean,
a man who dont stay out late,
a man with money in the bank,
a man who goes to church
he wont never leave me in the lurch.
But I threw all that out the window
I tossed all that good sense out the door
I got me a pig meat farming man,
and I wouldnt never want no more.

Curtain. Society Lady 1 goes back to her 9–5 life.
Everybody else stays for the 2nd set.

16 YOU WOULDNT WANT TO TAKE IT WITH YOU EVEN IF YOU COULD

People crowded together in a cave.
Every once in awhile someone gets up and walks out.
The exit causes others to scream, wail, mourn.
On another part of the stage, someone sitting in a beach chair.
One who just left the cave joins the someone.
A Waiter serves drinks.

1: I was terrified.

2: Me too.

1: I thought—I didnt know what to think.

Again, someone leaves the cave and
the huddled people scream.
The just-left one comes to join the beach-chair group.
Sits. Waiter serves a drink.

2: You bring anything with you?

1: Whats to bring?

3: A car, a lamp, yr spouse, a pair of red shoes, yr favorite book.

Waiter: Everything and nothing.

3: Cheers.

They drink to that. Then 3 goes on to recount the story of
the Hindu god who dreamed he was a pig
happily wallowing in the mud: when he awoke,
he cried for his lost pigsty until he remembered himself.
1, 2 and the Waiter join 3 in a lengthy and spirited discussion
of the nature of reality. The discussion continues forever,
through many incarnations.

17 THE PRESIDENTS DAY SALE

6 White men walk onstage. 2 of the men hold hands,
they are the 2 Bushes. There is a Lincoln,
the greater of 2 Roosevelts, Washington and Kennedy.
Each man wears a nametag sign. No need to dress up
like the guys, just wear the big nametag sign.
The 6 are escorted downstage by 2 men wearing earpieces
and dark glasses—the Secret Service.

The Presidents stand as if theyre in a lineup.
A Woman, very rich, looks them over.

Woman: Have them turn.
Secret Service: Turn!

The Presidents turn.

Woman: Once more.
Secret Service: Turn!

The Presidents turn.

Woman: Have them speak.
Secret Service: Speak yr pieces.

The Presidents all speak their spiels once through, then again,
but this time all at once and with great urgency.

2 Bushes: How many did you send to war? A lot? Wow. Ima send a whole lot too.

Lincoln: 4 score and 7 years ago our fathers brought forth our fathers.

Washington: I cannot tell a lie I cannot tell a lie.

FDR: We have nothing to fear but fear itself nothing to fear.

JFK: Ask not what yr country can do for you ask not.

(Rest)
(Rest)

Woman: How much is the Lincoln?
Secret Service: The Lincoln is not for sale.
Woman: This is a Presidents Sale.
Secret Service: The Lincoln's been bought already.
Woman: Darn. Give me the Washington, then. Wrap him up and put him in my car.

She leaves. A few other Rich People come in.

Secret Service: Speak yr pieces.

The Presidents talk again, all at once, as the lights fade.

18 THE DAY AFTER THE PRESIDENTS DAY SALE

Man: Is it my fault we took the bridge?

Woman: No its my fault. But I told you not to drive. I knew there was gonna be traffic.

Secret Service: You ready?

Man: Yeah.

> A line of white men come out wearing signs:
> Adams, Quincy Adams, Wilson, Cleveland,
> Hoover, Garfield, Madison.

Man: A bunch of nobodys! All this way and yr showing us a bunch of nobodies!

Secret Service: All the rest were sold, sir.

> Woman flips through the catalogue.

Woman: Choose the Garfield. He was killed in office, he'll be worth something one of these days.

Man: Yr a genius.

Woman: Now can we have a baby?

Man: Now? As in "right now"? Sir, we will take the Garfield. No need for giftwrap.

Secret Service: Itll save you money.

Woman: A good day after all, huh?

> Secret Service leads unsold Presidents away.
> Man and Woman circle the Garfield.

Man: He'll look great in the courtyard.

Woman: Mmm.

Secret Service: This way out, folks.

> They exit with their purchase.

19 IT WAS THE ONLY WAY, REALLY

> People run onstage with the energy of neglected youth.
> They sing:

People:
It was the only way, really
that way we met

strange
and totally by chance
it coulda been at a cocktail party
over some so-so white wine
surrounded by expensive little delicious things
but we met on a train
strange
and totally by chance
in fact, just thinking of it now
makes me feel like singing
cause it sounds like some number in a musical
dont it?
It was the only way, really
the way I met you
strange
on a train
and totally by chance
and if this were one of those numbers
it would be the moment for the dancing men to appear
theyd be wearing desert army uniforms
and the whole thing would be set in Southern California
so, theyd blend in with the scenery
and we'd just see the dust from their boots.

> Dance break:
> An American Desert Soldier, comes out and does
> a very melancholy tap dance routine. He hums the melody as
> he dances, but by the time he's finished, the people are long gone,
> each wandering offstage, bored with his best efforts and
> on to more pleasant and less dangerous things.

20 BABE CATCHER

> 2 guys stand around. 1 holds a scythe.

2nd Guy: What the hell is that?

1st Guy: What the hell does it look like?

2nd Guy: It looks like one of them—things—you know, one of them things for doing the—the whatchamacallit.

1st Guy: Its a babe catcher.

2nd Guy: Getoutahere.

1st Guy: Would I lie to you?

2nd Guy: A babe catcher? Shit.

1st Guy: Have I ever lied to you? Did I lie to you about Gloria? Did I tell you she was a—a "you know what"?

2nd Guy: She was really something else and then, poof, she left me.

1st Guy: Yll get a million Glorias with this.

2nd Guy: Sell it to me.

1st Guy: Its gonna cost.

2nd Guy: Name yr price.

1st Guy: You know that chest of gold youve got?

2nd Guy: Underneath the lone oak in the wood of Sequoia?

1st Guy: Bingo.

2nd Guy: A million Glorias, huh?

1st Guy: You have my word.

2nd Guy: Itll take a little time to dig up the gold.

1st Guy: Lots of guys are interested in this, so dont make me wait.

2nd Guy: I'll be back in 5 minutes.

> He goes.
> 1st Guy's Wife comes outside, with her hair in rollers.

The Wife: Who the hell were you talking to?

1st Guy: The troll from the southern forest. He wants to buy the lawnmower.

The Wife: Just make sure you cut the grass before you sell it, huh?

1st Guy: No sweat, babe.

> He raises the scythe and begins cutting the grass.

21 A PLAY WRITTEN ON A PIECE OF PACKING PAPER (For Victor, Riccardo, Ramon and Roberto, the 4 Guys Who Helped Us Move In)

> Ramon teaches the Woman a word or 2.

Woman: Derecho.
Ramon: Sí.
Woman: Derecho.
Ramon: Sí.
Woman: En el frente.
Ramon: Sí.

Woman: Come se dice, "Wow, yr strong"?

Ramon: Tu es fuerte.

Woman: Tu es fuerte.

Ramon: Tu hablas Español?

Woman: Un poquito.

Ramon: Está bien.

White Guy: This is exactly how I imagined it would be. Exactly how I pictured it.

Woman: Even the Spanish?

White Guy: In Spanish makes it better.

Woman: Yeah.

> They embrace. 3 people of any ethnic group,
> walk on playing guitars (3 chords, 4 bar changes).
> 3 miracles occur simultaneously: a Person of Great Compassion
> is resurrected from the dead; a Horrific Dictator,
> murderer of millions, is also resurrected;
> and a Studio Head walks on water, across his swimming pool,
> to shake the hand of a person who looks like a Writer.

22 CONEY ISLAND JOE'S

> A sign reading: "Coney Island Joe's."
> A Lonesome Man and a Pretty Waitress.

Lonesome Man: Great coffee you got here.

Pretty Waitress: Thanks.

Lonesome Man: You know how far I come to get yr coffee?

Pretty Waitress: Yr gonna tell me.

Lonesome Man: I pass by all kinds of places. Gourmet places. Yr Zabar's. Yr Gristedes. Yr Balducci's. Plus yr Upper East Side upper-echelon types of upper-upscale places. Yr West Hollywood health food hot-spots crammed with actress-chicks. I pass by the roach coaches too. I walk for blocks.

Pretty Waitress: For my coffee.

Lonesome Man: Sorta.

(Rest)

This is yr place. I come to see yr face.

Pretty Waitress: You see the sign. I look like Coney Island Joe to you?

Lonesome Man: Joe could be Josephine. You never now. You like the movies? We could, you and me, go some time.

(Rest)

Pretty Waitress: This place belongs to Coney Island Joe. And Im Joe's wife.

Lonesome Man: With all respect, maam, I dont know no Joe.

With a kindly nod of her head the Pretty Waitress acknowledges the Lonesome Man's ignorance. A Short Order Cook comes onstage playing the guitar. The Pretty Waitress begins to sing. Her song is like a Carter Family song, haunting, like the hills. Simple melody over G–D chord changes.

Pretty Waitress:

Ima tell you the story	G chord
so that yll always know	G/D
the story of my man	D
his name is Coney Island Joe.	D/G

Short Order Cook *(Echo)*:

Coney Island Joe	G

Pretty Waitress:

Joe had hisself a good wife	G
good and clean as brand-new snow.	G/D
Joe had hisself a temper	D
his fists brought many foes	D/G
to Coney Island Joe's.	G

Short Order Cook *(Echo)*:

To Coney Island Joe's.	G

Lonesome Man *(Echo)*:

To Coney Island Joe's.	G

The song ends as the lights fade.

23 PROJECT MACBETH

2 Army Guys walk along.

MacJones: How many you hit?

MacSmith: Lets talk about something else.

MacJones: You hit zero.

MacSmith: The ones I hit were for God. And country. Im a soldier.

MacJones: Im a soldier too.

(Rest)

I hit 10. You hit zero.

MacSmith: I hit 20.

MacJones: Bullshit.

MacSmith: See my gold star?

MacJones: You oughta wear it on yr chest, man! 20 towns?! You hit 20 towns?!?

MacSmith: For God. And country.

MacJones: You the man, man. Hush my mouth.

> They walk along.

MacSmith: We're the only ones who made it back in one piece. Remember when we shipped out. Thousands of guys and gals. Now only me and you are left. And the Projects. The Projects will always be here, seems like.

MacJones: Yeah.

(Rest)

Lets swear. Eternal brotherhood forever. You and me.

> They cut their hands.

MacSmith: MacSmith—

MacJones: and MacJones—

MacSmith & MacJones: Swear eternal brotherhood.

> They clasp hands, trading blood.

MacSmith: Ive changed my fate line, cutting my hand like that.

MacJones: Come on, we're almost home.

> A trio of Women appear, perhaps dressed like the Supremes.

1st Woman: Which one of you is MacSmith?

MacJones: Theyre witches. Play them off.

MacSmith: If theyre witches how come they dont know Im MacSmith?

2nd Woman: You will murder MacJones. Dont roll yr eyes at me.

3rd Woman: You will murder MacJones sure as me and my 2 weird sisters are standing here today.

1st Woman: You will murder MacJones and you will build a kingdom on his bones.

MacJones: Hold on now, ladies.

3rd Woman: Talk to the hand, man, history is in the making, and those who fall short fall silent.

MacJones: Im outa here. But I cant move.

2nd Woman: Draw yr knife, MacSmith, go on.

MacSmith: Do I have a choice?

3rd Women: We are the Fates, brother.

MacSmith: Shit.

> MacJones suddenly regains his ability to run.
> MacSmith runs after him with his knife drawn.

24 ASK THE EXPERTS!

Host: Hi, and welcome to "Ask the Experts!"

> Applause.

X & Y: We're stumped! How do we pack all this up so it will get moved from New York City to Los Angeles, California, and arrive in one piece?

Host: Would you like to Ask the Expert?

X &Y: Yes! We'd like to Ask the Expert!

Chuck: Im Chuck, the driver, and a moving expert.

> Applause.

Host: You wanna go with Chuck?

X: I'd like to know more.

Host: More will cost.

Y

X

Y: We'd like to know more.

Chuck: They call me "Lucky Chuck." Every winter I bag a buck.

> Screams from the Crowd: "Go with Chuck!"

X &Y: We're gonna go with Chuck.

Crowd: Ask the Expert!

Host: Chuck?

Chuck: Bubblewrap oughta do it.

Host: Would you like to go with the bubblewrap?

> The entire Crowd screams advice.

Crowd: BUBBLEWRAP! GO WITH THE BUBBLEWRAP!

Host: Time's up. Yr answer please.

X &Y: Well, yes, we'd like to go with the bubblewrap!

Host: Yr a winner!

> Passionate applause.

25 A MINIATURE PAINTING ON THE WALL OF THE KING PRESIDENT'S BEDROOM IN THE PLAY "DAEDALUS 800"

> The painting: 2 men, one very old and
> one very young pose in tableau.
> The Older, wielding a knife, stands above the Younger,
> ready to kill him.
> The Chorus, looking on, speaks:

Chorus:
Nothing bad
starts out badly
as in the case of
Old Jones and Younger,
Father and Son,
their lives depicted in oils by the famous painter—
his name just now escapes me—
but you art lovers
you would recognize the hand.
He is the favorite painter of the King President
and this very painting hangs
on the wall opposite the King President's bed.
Its the first thing he sees in the morning
and the last thing he sees at night.
A reminder to him
of Life.
A caution.
A line that was crossed.
A red light
that was run.

26 NEW YORK TAXI

2 Suits come in. Theyre in the middle of a knock-down-drag-out
fistfight. After a moment an Old Lady comes in and watches.

Suit: I saw it first! It stopped for me!

Other Suit: I was halfway in! Possession is 9/10ths!

Suit: Fuck yr 9/10ths! I was helping that old lady there.

Other Suit: First come, first served!

Suit: First come first served?! I'll show you first come first served!

Suit takes out a ballpoint pen and stabs Other Suit repeatedly.

Suit: Fucking piece of shit. Thought you could just take my taxi,
huh?

Old Lady: Well done, young man.

Suit: Lets share that cab downtown, shall we?

Suit gives the Old Lady his arm and they stroll off gallantly.
The World dont really give a fuck what happens to
the Other Suit. Thats what he gets for trying
to steal the guy's taxi, right?

27 PROJECT TEMPEST

Daughter: Its raining again. Gale-force winds. The streets are
flooded. The bridges are all out. The levees are all gonna break
too. Yr doing, Daddy?

Daddy: Yeah.

Daughter: I thought they burned yr book.

Daddy: Never.

Daughter: So yr spelling again.

Daddy: Get down with it, sugar. Daddy's waging war against the Man.

Thunder and lightning. Waves as tall as skyscrapers.
Not far offshore, The-Ones-Who-Stole-the-Election
are shipwrecked. They make their way to land as best
they can. Meanwhile the levees break in New Orleans and
thousands are made homeless. And once again, Daddy thinks
of burning his book, cause his storm hit the wrong town.

28 SHE BIT ME

X: Yr bleeding.
Y: Where?
X: Just there. On yr lip.
Y: Its lipstick.
X: Its running.
Y: Ha. So it is.
X: You kissed her?
Y: No.
X: Tell the truth.

X
Y

Y: I kissed her. Most passionately.
X: And she bit you?
Y: Apparently.

(Rest)

X: Its either you or her now. Yr life or her life. Choose.
Y: I choose me.
X: What are you waiting for. Go get rid of her.
Y: What with?
X: Yr call.
Y: The rope. I'll take the rope.

> Y goes. The kiss was the 1st bold thing Y ever did.
> What Y does next will be the 2nd.

29 WHAT WERE YOU WEARING FOR BLACK HISTORY MONTH? (A Play for February 29—Even Though Every Year Aint Leapyear)

1st Theme—The Man

> 2 Men.
> One wears a sandwich board that reads: "Everything."
> The other wears a sandwich board that reads:
> "Almost Everything."

They change their signs for 2 new ones. One reads:
"I Am a Man," the other reads: "I Am The Man."

2nd Theme—Because You Are Beautiful

Panther: Its Black History Month.
X: Was.
Panther: Past Is Present.
X: Right on.

(Rest)

Panther: How come you always wearing black, sister?
X: Because black is beautiful.
Panther: Right on and pass it on, right on and pass it on.

March

1 ANOTHER PLAY WITHIN THE EPIC PLAY "HOUSE OF JONES"

The Smiths.

Chorus:
God is never wrong.
But the art of divination,
that is, the craft of interpreting God,
well, thats not what you would call
an *exact* science.
There have been mistakes.
Yes, thats right, more than one
which, in great measure,
explains how weve reached this current point in time.
Smith: Take, for example, the Smiths.
Chorus: The Smiths.
Smith: My family.
Chorus: Yr family, the Smiths.
Smith: Our lives went like this:

The scene unfolds. Mrs. Smith comes in.

Mrs. Smith: 10 years of marriage, Smith, and no children.

Smith: Weve sacrificed. All the appropriate animals have been butchered in all the appropriate ways. We sleep with our heads pointing east. We wash with blessed water, burn oil in the puddles after it rains, eat pomegranates.

Mrs. Smith: I wake up and pray. I pray all day. I pray in my sleep, I think: "Dear God, bless us with a child."

Smith: What else can we do, wife? What else but wait?

Smith
Mrs. Smith

> A bell rings, like a simple triangle sounding.
> She takes his hand.

Mrs. Smith: Im with child.
Smith: Mine?
Mrs. Smith: Yrs.

> The bell rings again.

Smith: Our child will be a great peacemaker.

> The bell rings 3 times.
> A young man walks in. He is their son, Smith-the-Younger.

Younger: Mother, Father.
Mrs. Smith: How is school going?
Younger: The oracle we read in class seems wrong.
Smith: God is never wrong, son.
Younger: God is a riddler.
Smith: Watch yr mouth.

> The bell rings. Divine light cue.

Mrs. Smith: What oracle has stumped you, my son?
Younger: I copied it off the board.
Mrs. Smith: Show it to yr father.

> As Younger digs through his book satchel:

Smith: Our son will be a great peacemaker.
Mrs. Smith: Our son will make peace throughout the land.
Younger: But it will cost.
Smith: Watch yr mouth. Where are my glasses?
Mrs. Smith: Here, dear.

Smith: "Our son will be a great—warmonger. Kill him and you kill war. Forever." The oracle has spoken.

Younger: But, do I look like a warmonger?

Mrs. Smith: My baby.

Younger: Im just in school. Weve been at war for a thousand years. I didnt start it.

Smith: This is our chance to stop the war. Forever, it says.

Mrs. Smith: By killing our son?

Younger: Yr weak in the head, Dad.

Smith: I am a man of God.

Mrs. Smith: Smith! Dont!

She stands between father and son.

Smith: Get out of my way!

The bell. Divine light.
Smith kills them both. He stands there,
with his bloody sword, waiting for the war to end.

Chorus:
Peace did come
for awhile.
But the Smith Family line was over
and the wife's side, many years later,
rose up to avenge the wrongful deaths.
Was Smith wrong? Was God?
Was Smith-the-Younger a warmonger?
God is never wrong
but the art of divination
is never ever exact.

2 BURNING

A Woman in a bathrobe stands looking off into the distance.
After a long moment she's joined by a Man.

Man: Its burning.

Woman: Mmm.

Man: Why didnt you tell me?

Woman: You didnt smell it?

Man: —My cold.

Woman: I forgot.

Man: You think itll burn to the ground?

Woman: God willing.

Man: Theyre trying pretty hard to put it out.

Woman: And then we'll have the ruin of it to look at. Thatll really suck.

(Rest)

BURN!

Man: *BURN!*

> The fire, in answer to their prayers, does pick up somewhat.
> But it gets put out before the structure can completely burn,
> and the rest of their lives are lived out
> in the shadow of the ruins.

3 LUCKY DAY

> A Delivery Guy comes in with a large satchel.
> He approaches a very downtrodden guy wearing
> a nametag that reads: "Joe."

Delivery Guy: Joe?

Joe: Howdyaknow?

Delivery Guy: Yr nametag.

Joe: Oh.

Delivery Guy: Delivery.

Joe: For me?

Delivery Guy: Yeah. Here. Sign.

Joe: You sure?

Delivery Guy: See "Joe"? See this van Gogh? My orders: "Go give van Gogh to Joe."

Joe: This is a van Gogh.

Delivery Guy: Now you know.

Joe: I hate to break the rhyme-thing but—its a real van Gogh, signed and everything.

Delivery Guy: Sign here. For the delivery.

Joe: This is my lucky day. Sing a song with me or something.

Delivery Guy: Sorry, but I got other deliveries.

Joe begins to sing, and it is such a sweet scene that
the Delivery Guy cant help himself and he joins in.
It sounds like a show tune from the 40s.
Maybe his song blossoms into a full-scale musical number.

Joe:
Lucky, Im lucky
at long last Im lucky.
Just when I thought the world
had turned her back on me
now things are looking
sunshine and roses
and gift-from-God van Gogh-ses.
Lucky at long last Im lucky, hey.

4 THE PLANK

2 men walk downstage in single file. The man in the rear,
the Drummer, beats a drum. They reach the edge of the stage.

Drummer: Go head.

The Convicted: I cant swim.

Drummer: Thats not my problem. Jump.

The Convicted: No.

Drummer: Jump or I'll push you.

The Convicted: Theres sharks.

Drummer: Dont worry, they wont eat you.

The Convicted: For true?

Drummer: Read the guidebook.

The Drummer hands The Convicted a guidebook which
he reads as if it were a Bible.

The Convicted: You right. They wont eat me.

Drummer: Plus, the guidebook inflates into a life raft.

The Convicted: Thats very kind of you.

Drummer: We do what we can to make the world a better place.

The Convicted: Im a convicted murderer.

Drummer: We dont discriminate.

The Convicted grabs the Drummer, hugging him impulsively.
The Drummer may enjoy the connection, but, after awhile,
he pushes The Convicted away.

Drummer: Jump.
The Convicted: Right.

> The Convicted jumps into the sea. The guidebook does
> in fact inflate, but this is of little help as the Drummer,
> pulling out a pistol, shoots The Convicted several times.
> Then the Drummer returns to his station, drumming all the while.

5 9 BARS

> Several speakers.

– LIGHTS OUT!

> The lights go out.

– How long you been locked-up?
– You dont wanna know.
– Shit on my dick or blood on my shank.
– Please.
– Im not saying it cause I want it, Im saying it cause it sounds good.
– Pretty please, fool.
– How long you been locked-up?
– She dont talk.
– I do so talk.
– No you dont.
– I just dont talk to you but I talk. Before I came in here, Motormouth, they called me.
– SHUTUPALREADYYOUMOTORMOUTH!! LETADECENTMANGETSOMEREST!

(Rest)

– Whats yr favorite freeworld thing?
– Swimming in the creek.
– Dancing, navel to navel.
– Getting up and going to bed whenever.
– My dog, you seen his picture. If I was blind, up in here, theyd let me have him up in here.

– Dream on.

– Wearing what I want.

– The best things in life cost money. Name something. Anything. You think its free, I'll show you it aint.

– Love.

– Money.

– Honey.

– Big money.

– Head space.

– Major paper, sucker.

– Shit.

(Rest)

– I got a serious jones for some cotton candy.

– LIGHTS UP!

> The lights come up and the next play begins immediately.

6 NEITHER SNOW NOR RAIN NOR HEAT NOR GLOOM OF NIGHT STAYS THESE COURIERS FROM THE SWIFT COMPLETION OF THEIR APPOINTED ROUNDS

> A Carrier walks on. He has been walking a great distance.
> He sees the Mother and stops. He takes a meager letter
> from his thin satchel. This series of movements
> is articulated in slow-motion:
> 1. He hands the letter to the Mother.
> 2. The Mother hands the letter to her Reader.
> 3. The Reader mouths the words.
> 4. The Mother jumps for joy.
> A 2nd Carrier walks on. He has been walking a greater distance.
> He sees the Mother and stops. He takes a slim letter
> from his meager satchel. Articulated/slow-motion continues:
> 1. He hands the letter to the Mother.
> 2. The Mother hands the letter to her Reader.
> 3. The Reader pauses, looks from one Carrier to the other,
> then mouths words.
> 4. Mother faints.
> The Reader and the 2 Carriers catch her. They create a tableau
> reminiscent of the Pietà.

7 CUCKOO

3 Women and 3 Men asleep. A group of 6 people,
the Cuckoo Chorus, surrounds them. The group holds a variety
of noise-making objects. At an agreed-upon moment they
make noise in a rhythmic fashion. The Men and Women arise
and dance in a unified rhythmic belly-hula style. They sing:

Cuckoo Chorus:
Life is a dream
and
sometimes
when you wake up
it looks
like
this.

The song and music come to an end.
The Sleepers curl back to sleep again.
The Cuckoo Chorus goes back to standing in expectant attention.

8 HOLEY

Woman 1: What?

Woman 2: My "ego" I think.

Woman 1: Dropped?

Woman 2: Yep.

Woman 1: Down there?

Woman 2: Right where Im looking.

Woman 1: Thats rough.

Woman 2: Yeah.

Woman 1: Shit.

Woman 2: Yeah.

Woman 1: You call a Returner?

Woman 2: I blew my whistle.

Woman 1: It usually takes them—a day or 2 sometimes. Once
there was this guy—I wont bore you with it. Well, 2 weeks it
took. He couldnt do his thing for 2 whole weeks.

Woman 2: Shit.

Woman 1: Yeah. Whistle again.

They wait. Woman 2 whistles again. Woman 1 gets bored and
goes on her way. Woman 2 waits, whistles again,
but very much in vain.

9 FATHER COMES HOME FROM THE WARS (Part 3)

Father, surrounded by his Soldiers, stands at the door.
The Family is at dinner.

Father: Hi, honey, Im home.

The Family stares.

1st Soldier: When you hear the word "war" what comes to mind?
Father: Dont start that talk here. Im home.
2nd Soldier: You dont mind if we wait here do you?
Father: Do what you gotta do. Im home.

Father sits in his easy chair. His Soldiers wait.

Father: Come on, Junior. Lets watch some game shows.
Mother: Yr not hungry?
Sister: Mother and me made a welcome home pie for you. See the
writing: "Welcome home from the wars, Father!"
(Rest)
Yr not even looking.
Father: All I wanna do is watch some goddamn game shows.
Junior: All thats on is war movies.
Father: Fine.
Mother: Who are yr friends, honey?
Father: Turn up the volume, Junior.
Junior: Im gonna be a soldier just like yr a soldier, right, Pop?

Father
Father

Father: You betcha.

Junior turns up the volume and the Soldiers in the doorway
make loud war sounds. Father leans back and relaxes.

10 THE LEAVING

2 people sit. One gets up.

Other: Where are you going?
One: Out.
Other: Yr going out the door.
One: Yes.
Other: You cant walk out on me. Those legs youve got? Who gave them to you?! I did! When I met you—you—you—didnt have any legs.

One
One

(Rest)

One: I had legs.
Other: But you didnt use them.
One: Im going.
Other: Yll die without me.
One: Im gone.
Other: I'll die without you.
One: Its over.
Other: I'll kill you for even thinking that.

Without getting up, Other reaches for One. One runs off. Other sits there. One comes back. Peeks in. Sits back down.

Other: What?
One: Whatever.

Other leaves.

11 DRAGON KEEPER

A Woman and a Man.

Woman: What will happen today?
Man: Same old same old.
(Rest)
Oh!

Woman: What?

Man: Yr dragon keeper.

Woman: You forgot to pay him?

Man: He visits today.

Woman: To report? Oh, thats so dull. "The dragon ate a knight, miss, the dragon breathed fire and torched a village, miss, the dragon shed its skin, miss, the dragon cut yet another tooth, miss, the dragon asks after you: 'Miss? Are you my miss?' the dragon asks me. 'Im just yr keeper,' the keeper says. 'Wheres my miss, I want my miss,' the dragon screams. The dragon screams, the dragon shouts, the dragon cries hot tears." Endless.
(Rest)
How dull.

Man: He's doing more than reporting today, miss.

Woman: Im going to sit in the bath all day and read a book. When he comes, tell him—tell him Im not well or something.

Man: He's delivering today, miss.

Woman: Delivering.

Man: He's delivering its *self* today.

Woman: The dragon?

Man: Mmm.

Woman: Has it been 40 years?

Man: They sneaked up on us.

Woman: 40 years. Well. I hope its *self*—likes me.

> An old man or old woman, the Dragon Keeper, comes in leading a Dragon. The Dragon is an enormous scaly-winged fire-breathing beast on a thin and delicate leash.

Dragon Keeper: Good day, miss.

Dragon: WELL.

Man: Thats some dragon.

Woman: What he means, I think, is, that yr bigger than we expected.

Dragon: IS SHE MY MISS?

> The Dragon's breath is rather hot. The Woman does not flinch. The Man, however, steps out of range and there are fine blisters on his face from the mild burning.

Dragon
Woman

(Rest)

Dragon Keeper: Its *self* is yrs now, miss.
Dragon: MISS? *MY* MISS?
Woman: Thats right.

The Dragon Keeper takes out a guitar or a juiceharp and the Woman and the Dragon sing. The Man claps time respectfully.

Dragon & Woman:
Im having déjà vu
is it me or is it you?
Here you are, my darling darling,
but what will yr keeper do?

The song ends sweetly. Then the Dragon screams with joy.
Fires and Armageddon. Eons pass within an instant.
God blinks the Great Eye and, as the world is born anew
and creation rapidly surges forward,
evolution happens double-triple time. We're all caught up to
where we were just before this play started, but this time,
instead of burning, we'll continue to sleep,
unaware of our power.

12 TOP SPEED

A Woman sits. Someone comes in,
pulling a crown out of a paper bag.

Woman: You are—?
Troll: Im the troll.
Woman: And that is—?
Troll: This is yr crown.
Woman: Oh.

She puts the crown on her head.

Troll: We have now reached our top speed of 150 miles an hour!

The stage fills slowly with people. They walk on applauding,
and continue applauding more enthusiastically
(if thats possible) as the lights fade.

13 BOOK

Man: Am I in the Book?

Bookie: You? Nope.

Man: Aint you gonna look?

Bookie: Im looking.

Man: In the Book, not at me.

Bookie: Dont gotta.

(Rest)

Miriam!

Miriam *(Offstage)*: WHAT?!?!?

Bookie: You on yr back?

Miriam: Is the president stupid?

Bookie: Hahaha. Yr funny, Miriam.

John *(Offstage)*: I dont like her talking!

Bookie *(To John)*: Keep yr ring on, baby!

(Rest)

Hahaha, my Miriam. Best wife a guy could have.

Man
Bookie

Bookie: What?

Man: Am I in the Book?

Bookie: Yr a real hard-on, arent you?

Man: Ive come a long way. Just take a look. In the Book.

Bookie: You take the Doomsday?

Man: —Yeah.

Bookie: No wonder it took you so long. Theres quicker ways. Hey Miriam, he took the Doomsday!

Miriam *(Offstage)*: Be a sport, honey!

John *(Offstage)*: I dont like her talking!

Bookie: All the way here the slow way. I feel for you, man.

Man: If you could just look.

Bookie: Tell you what, I'll squeeze you in. Howzat sound.

Man: Now yr talking.

Bookie: We're squeezing one in, Miriam!

14 THE LINE TO LIFE

> People enter the stage one by one and mill about
> finally forming a line. A long line. They wait.
> Some more people enter and form a shorter line.
> 2 sign bearers enter. One holds a sign:
> "To Life." The Other's sign reads: "Life."

Someone in Line: The line to life is so long!
Someone Else in Line: But the life line is so short!

15 THE RUN AROUND

> The stage is dark. People enter.
> They stand—then they walk fast, faster, super fast.
> They run around darting, rushing, pushing and shoving.
> Leaping, hurrying, scurrying, etc.
> Lights up. They run offstage as fast as they can.

16 OPENING NIGHT

> Lights up.

Actress: It cant end like this!
Actor: But it must!
But it will!
But it is!
The end.

> The lights fade and the audience applauds. Shouts of bravo!
> and standing ovations are heard. An enormous Cast crowds
> onstage for an encore. Someone gives the Actress flowers.
> Shouts of: "Author!" The Dragon Keeper and the Miss come
> onstage (see the play for March 11). They take their bows and
> are gently pelted with very expensive red roses.
> The Dragon cannot believe his good fortune.

17 FEDEX TO MY EX

The Thinker is talking to himself in anticipation of a confrontation
with the clerk at the counter:

Thinker: This line's as long as hell and I gotta be standing in it.
And today of all days. Shit. Yeah, man at the front of the line,
all eyes on you cause we all envy you, yeah, you know it too.
I bet they gonna close down before I get to the front of the line.
I bet their business hoursll be over, or, like, they will go out of
business just when I get to the counter. Instead of helping me
send my package theyll all be crying over they pink slips. Just
watch and see. Im not being negative, Im being realistic. Shit
like my shit happens every day, Im telling you. No I am not
talking to myself, bitch, so quit looking at me. Looking at me
over yr bifocals when you should be helping the next customer.
No wonder this line is slow. By the time I get to the front, I bet
the world's gonna end. Thatll be just my luck. Sorry we cant
send yr FedEx cause the world is over. Yeah, right? But I'll
beg. I'll tell them that she's gotta have this today! You dont
understand—its our anniversary and I gotta get this to her.
Today. I know what yr thinking—he dont gotta pen to fill the
form out. I got a pen, I got a hundred pens, I got a pen for each
hand I got.
(Rest)
Whatcha mean you cant get this today? This is FedEx aint it?
(Rest)
"Tomorrow?! Fuck tomorrow! I want my shit today," thats what
she said. So I gotta send it today. She'll get it tomorrow, but,
cause I sent it today, she'll cut me some slack. Who is she? She's
my ex. Yes, my ex. Yeah this is a needle—a hypo yeah. Whats
she gonna shoot up with if I dont send her a hypo along with
the shit? Some people would say Im *enabling* her—but Im just
giving her what she needs so she dont call me and bitch. You
dont need to call the cops on me. Im a regular guy just like you.
A regular guy with a dope-fiend ex wife, just like a lot of guys.
And I didnt drive her to it. She was fucked-up from the day we
met. You gonna help me out, right?

A Woman walks in. Stands behind the Thinker.

Woman: Excuse me, sir, are you in line?

Thinker
Woman

(Rest)

Thinker: "Are you in line?" That is a real deep question.

Woman: Just "yes" or "no."

Thinker: I am on the line. I am not in the line, nor am I of the line.
(Rest)
She divorced me—and I loved her just the same.
(Rest)
Got any idea what thats like? You got no idea. And may you never know.

FedEx Clerk: NEXT!

18 A PLAY FOR MY BROTHER, BUDDY, ON HIS 38TH BIRTHDAY

3 women sit doing needlework. They rock back and forth.

Past: I sent him a cake.

Present: Homemade?

Future: Of course it was homemade, what do you think, she went out and got storebought?

Present: Homemade from scratch or from a box?

Past: From scratch.

Present: But you didnt mill the flour yrself.

Past: Yes. I milled the flour myself.

Present: And cut the sugarcane?

Past: No.

Present: So its not totally from scratch.

Past: I sent him a cake, K?

(Rest)

Future: How old is he?

Past: 38.

Present: Wow.

Past: I havent seen him in 20 years.

Present: Dont be so dramatic. Just last week I seen you looking at him. He was walking down the street on his way to the war, just like all the others. "Who you looking at?" I said. "My brother," you said. "I havent seen him in 20 years." You want a sympathy pageant—thats what you want.

Past: It makes a good story.

Present: Thats all it makes.

Future: You miss him?

Past: He's my only brother, of course I miss him.

> Present feels bad suddenly. She claps her hands
> and a Sympathy Pageant, albeit a modest one, comes in.
> Past is comforted.

19 NO WAR

Crowd: No war! No war! No war!

One Person: Thats not a play.

Crowd

Crowd

Crowd

(Rest)

Crowd: No war! No war! No war!

> Bombs in the distance.

20 MORE OF THE SAME

Crowd: No war! No war! No war! No war!!!

One Person: This is not a play.

Crowd: No war! No war! No war! No war!!!

One Person: And besides, its the same play you wrote yesterday.

Another Person: Arent you repeating yrself?

Crowd: No war! No war! No war! No war!!!

> Bombs in the nearer distance.

Writer: A taxi driver was the first casualty of the war.
A taxi driver told me that.
We were stuck in traffic going up 6th Avenue.
We were riding in silence at first and passing the library.
I told him that the traffic was not his fault
and he said, perhaps it was
and I laughed along with him

and then he told me about the cab driver
being the first one to die in the war
and I wondered
not out loud
but in the head space of my own head:
What would it be like
to just be riding along
working
or on yr way to work
on the way to a meeting
or on the phone
and then
—the war comes
and nothing else comes after that.

21 A PLAY FOR THE FIRST DAY OF SPRING ENTITLED "HOW DO YOU LIKE THE WAR?"

Several speakers.

How do you like the war?
Is it everything you thought it would be?
Is it as horrific as youd hoped?
Is it as beautiful as you feared?
Does it satisfy the outrage of yr imagination?
Does it satisfy
the way only a war can satisfy?
Or does yr war
fall
short
somehow
and leave
you wanting
more?

22 THE ACT OF FORGIVENESS

One Man: No War No War No War No War!

A Crowd of Kids enters, watches the Man,
who goes from chanting to ranting.

Teacher *(Crowd leader)*: Look closely and listen up, kids. This is an antiwar protester.

1st Kid: Ancient history.

2nd Kid: Old school.

3rd Kid: Heavy.

> The Crowd watches the Protester as he works himself into a lather, repeating: "No War!" in as many different ways and with as much passion, variety and commitment as he can muster, going on for as long as he can (even if he overlaps into the next several plays). When he stops to catch his breath, the Crowd of Kids walks away.

23 SNAKE

> Several come in wearing signs that read: "Snake."

1st Snake: Yr a snake.

2nd Snake: You too.

3rd Snake: Damn this president huh.

4th Snake: No War No War!

(Rest)

5th Snake: Remember the old days?

2nd Snake: What old days?

5th Snake: The days of the first skin.

1st Snake: Back in the garden.

2nd Snake: Overhyped.

5th Snake: But at least we didnt have to wear nametags.

6th Snake: The president's motorcade!

> All lie down and crawl around as an empty sedan chair festooned with flags passes and the lights fade.

24 2 MEN

> 2 men with binoculars.

Mano: You watching?

Dano: Hells yeah.

Mano: Cool huh.

Dano: Oh yeah.

Mano: Dont get more interesting than this, do it?

Dano: Sure dont.

Mano: Woo Hoo!

Dano: Woo Hoo!

Mano: Watching the war sure beats watching the game, huh?

Dano: Sure does.

Mano: Even with those babe cheerleaders.

Dano: Beats the game, sure does.

(Rest)

Mano: Yr looking at the ground.

Dano: Im not.

Mano: Yes you are.

Dano: No Im not.

Mano: Yr looking at the goddamn ground.

Dano: Now Im not.

Mano: But before—

Dano: Im watching, ok!!? USA! USA! These colors dont run! Wooo!

> They continue watching the war.

25 A PROMISE MADE IN 1863 ISNT WORTH MUCH THESE DAYS

> President Lincoln walks in with a woman dressed as a 1920s Hollywood Movie Director.

Lincoln: You gotta understand, sir, I was promised. The Mrs. and I—

Director: The Mrs. Where is she now?

Lincoln: Mother! Bring Mother in, gents.

> 2 strong Men come in carrying a birdcage with a bird in it.

Director: Im standing here waiting for Mary Todd Lincoln and Im looking at 2 strong men holding a bird in a gilded cage.

Lincoln: I can explain—

Director: You want me to call action? I cant call action. Action! There I called action but do you see anything happening?

Lincoln: There was a troll—a magical troll. He told me he could stop her yammering—but my wife, please understand, women— please understand—

> A Producer walks onstage with a phone.

Phone: Ring ring.

Producer: Its for me. Hello? Its for you. Bad news.

> Hands the phone to the Director.

Director: The draft. I gotta go.

Lincoln: Theyre calling women now too?

Director: Im sorry.

Producer: Kill one for me, huh?

> Director runs off to war.

Lincoln: I didnt think the war would last this long. None of us did.

> Bombs in the near distance.

26 POSSUM

> 2 Soldiers come in carrying a litter with 2 Bodies on it covered by a sheet.

1st Soldier: Thank God the war is over.

2nd Soldier: The war's not over.

1st Soldier: Its over in here. In my head. Tap tap tap. Any war in there? No. Thats where it matters.

2nd Soldier: Yr wacked.

1st Soldier: Helps me get through the day.

2nd Soldier: I guess.

1st Soldier: How many you kill.

2nd Soldier: At least a thousand.

1st Soldier: Me too. And didnt they say that killing a thousand would get us—wait—I got the ad here. Somewhere.

2nd Soldier: Medals. And money.

1st Soldier: I got the ad here somewhere—I wanna read you exactly what it said.

(Rest)

Shit—I was never good with paper. My wife says she's good with paper—not me.

2nd Soldier: They got the ad on the latrine wall. Lets take 5 and go check it out.

1st Soldier: And walk off the job?

2nd Soldier: Just for 5, sides—the bodies—theyll be here. Last one theres a dead enemy!

They run off.

Body 1: Coast clear?

Body 2: Hard to tell.

(Rest)

Body 1: Ima chance it.

He peeks out—looks around.

Body 2: All clear.

Body 1: Hurry.

Body 2: Whats the hurry? We're dead.

Body 1: Right.

They get up and walk toward home. They walk as the dead walk.
Conscious of the absence of time.

27 HOUSE TO HOUSE

People enter the stage. As they stand in position they say the word: "House." Before long the stage is full of People-Houses and they are all saying: "House to House." A King General enters with a 2nd King General and a Slave. The King General observes the people saying: "House to House."
He falls to his knees.

King General:
I promised them a short war.
Something easy, something quick.
Ive let them down.

2nd King General: Theyre still yr troops.

King General: They hate me.

(Rest)

Im going to fall on my sword.

2nd King General: Dont.

King General: Ive let them down.

(Rest)

Come, Slave.

Slave: Will you kill me too?

King General
Slave

(Rest)

Slave: Will he kill me too?

2nd King General: Youll hold his sword. He'll fall on it.

King General: Come, Slave.

> They exit together.
> The 2nd King General regards the People-Houses.
> The King General reenters alone.

King General:
That slave
he died for me.
It was—
whats the right word for it?

2nd King General: ((("murder")))

King General:
"Poignant."
It was "poignant."
And "patriotic"! Yes!
And "very moving."
Come on—lets rally the men.
Weve got a whole day of war ahead.
We'll fight the enemy house to house!
And tell the cook to skip breakfast.
My men fight better
when theyre hungry.

> They exit.
> The People-Houses continue to speak.

28 THE BEACH

A Man and Fallen Starlet in 1950s swimming outfits. Towels.

Man: Youll catch cold.

Fallen Starlet: I wanna watch the stars come out.

Man: Theyre out.

Fallen Starlet: Not all of them.

Man: Most of them. Come on. Youll catch yr death out here.

Fallen Starlet: Thats what I want. To catch my death. I'd be in all the papers.

Man: Yr already in all the papers.

Fallen Starlet: On the front page.

Man: Youve had too much to drink.

Fallen Starlet: Im gonna drink the ocean up. And youll pace back and forth on the bottom of the sandy floor. Watch.

Man: Someone's already done that, honey. You wont be an original.

She runs off anyway.

Man: Silly kid.

He watches her run into the water.
A few minutes later she drowns.

29 THE SEA, THE SEA

A Man and Fallen Starlet in contemporary swimming dress.
She is soaking wet.

Man: Yr cold. Take the blanket.

Fallen Starlet: No.

Man: You cant swim.

Fallen Starlet: So?

Man: And you walk to the edge of the water telling me you wanna play the part of Cassandra Spiegel in that biopic theyre making.

Fallen Starlet: I should have gotten the part.

Man: But you didnt.

Fallen Starlet: I look like her. Im not without talent.

Man: Of course not.

Fallen Starlet: I can carry a tune—

Man: —Well

Fallen Starlet: Better than that Teresa bitch.

Man: There are other parts.

Fallen Starlet: She drowned herself. How come you think?

Man: Despair. Thats what her husband—

Fallen Starlet: Cliff.

Man: —said: "I felt that we had arrived at a beginning and she felt we were at the end—not *an* end but *the* end."

(Rest)

Fallen Starlet: "Im gonna drink the ocean up. And youll pace back and forth on the bottom of the sandy floor."

Man: "Silly kid."

> He sits. She sits beside him.

Man: The stars are all out.

Fallen Starlet: But far away theyre not as bright as they are when yr up close.

Man: Did she say that?

Fallen Starlet: No, I did.

Man: Hmmmm.

Fallen Starlet: What if I dont get to be who I want to be?

Man: Youll be someone else.

> The sea is playing on the radio.
> She turns the ocean surf sounds up.
> And the Man hugs her close as she looks at the sky.

29 (Again) SOMETHING FOR MOM

> A Kid (you could even cast an actual child),
> holding a bunch of flowers, runs toward Mother.
> Mother is surprised and happy. Kid presents flowers.
> Mother admires the flowers. Then, lifting Kid,
> Mother showers love.
> This happens several times, with other Mothers and other Kids.
> And "Mothers" and "Kids" are mutating and expanding to
> include all of us, filling the stage, the theater, and the world,
> as the action continues and repeats forever.
> Even during peacetime.

30 GEORGE WASHINGTON SLEPT HERE

Tour Guide: George Washington slept here.

Surly Tourist: Bullshit.

Tour Guide: Look, the imprint of his body is still on the ground.

Easily Led Tourist: After all these years.

Surly: I see an imprint of a body—ok I'll give you that—but how do you know its Washington's?

Easily Led: Yr saying you dont believe the words of the great book?

Surly: —Im not—I was only . . .

Easily Led: You could get reported for not believing.

Surly: I believe, ok?

Tour Guide: OK! Look, next to Washington is another imprint.

Easily Led: Martha Washington!

Surly: Martha Washington never slept on the ground.

Tour Guide: Some say it was another soldier.

Easily Led: Scandal!

The Tourists take millions of photographs. Our understanding of the phrase: "George Washington Crossed the Delaware" also gets a radical reenvisioning: discussions of how the 1st American President crossed and then double-crossed the Delaware peoples—and how those lies still linger within the mantle of the presidency— oh, but thats not the scope of this play.

31 BLACK DOG

2 People look at a Dog offstage.

1: He looks like a Booger. Here, Booger!

2: He doesnt look like no "Booger." He looks like a "Lucky." Lucky! Lucky! Here, Lucky!

(Rest)

"Yogi." Thats what he looks like.

1: No way. I seen a "Yogi."

2: Yeah?

1: He was big.

2: Yeah?

1: And white.

2: Oh.

1: And—fluffy

2: Fluffy?

1: Yeah.

2: Maybe he's a "Fluffy."

1: Give it up huh?

> A Guy walks in accompanied by someone
> playing the tambourine.

Guy: Take the dog. Take the dog! The dog will change yr life.

> The Guy and the Tambourine Player exit.

1: I hate when that happens.

2: Did you hear that?

1: Yeah.

2: "Take the dog. Take the dog! . . ."

1: What, now you want the dog?

2: You heard the guy.

1: You gonna heed his cry?

2: *He was followed by a tambourine player for Christ sakes!!!*

> The Guy enters again with the Tambourine Player.

Guy: This is not a play, no fucking way.

> They exit.

1: What now?

2: Shit.

1: Go kill him.

2: Right.

> 2 goes and returns quickly.

2: Kill the guy or kill the dog or kill the tambourine man?

1: Yr choice.

2: Right.

> 2 exits. Kills one of them. Returns. Exits again. Kills the others.
> For the rest of his life he is pursued by Furies working in
> the service of the Dog, the Guy and the Tambourine Man.
> The one who egged him on lives out his life comfortably.
> So it goes.

1 GEORGE BUSH VISITS THE CHEESE & OLIVE

A Small Man with large ears wears a suit. He struggles around underneath a table at an outdoor restaurant on Venice Beach. He is surrounded by several men and women in dark suits and dark glasses. Theyre the Secret Service: the SS Chorus.

Small Man: This is not a laughing matter! This is not funny! This is no joke! I dont care if it is April Fools!

Waitress: Mr. President, my name is Joshlynn. I'll be yr server tonight. Anything you need just ask for Josh.

Small Man: I'll find him. I'll find him all right and when I do— youll see a reckoning.

Waitress: How about hearing our specials, Mr. President?

Small Man: We will not stop until we find him. We will leave no stone unturned.

SS Chorus:
Back off, Waitress
the president's busy
hunting down the weapons
of mass destruction
ferreting out the architect
of death and evil.

A Woman, the Small Man's wife, crawls to the Small Man.

Woman: Are they shooting at you?

Small Man: I got an anonymous tip that The Bad Guys are in this restaurant under one of these tables. Imagine my picture on the front page of the *New York Times* with my hands around their throats! Im gonna catch em!

Woman: April Fools, honey.

Small Man: Dadll be proud of me.

Woman: April Fools.

Small Man: Huh?

Woman: April Fools. Yr "anonymous tip" was just me and the girls funning, honey.

Small Man: Has anyone seen me under here?

Woman: No one who matters.

Small Man: I'll wait until they close and then slip out.

Woman: Youll be here for hours.

Small Man: Sit with me.

Woman: Yr the president. We'll get yr guys to spin it.

Small Man: Sit with me, hold my hand, and tell me Im not stupid.

She holds his hand.

Woman:
Yr my genius
yr my Mr. Smarts
yr my scientist of rockets
deft
in all the arts.
Yr my brainiac,
baby, I aint fooling—
take us to school cause
we all need yr schooling.

SS Chorus:
Take us to school cause
we all need yr schooling.

A big dance number. Tableau. The lights fade.
Bombs are heard in the distance.

2 GREEK TRAGEDY & JERRY SPRINGER

Host: Today we're talking with some of the "heroes" if you will of Greek Tragedy.

Applause.

Host: Introduce yrselves.

Oedipus: King Oedipus. I killed my father and married my mother.

Tantalus: King Tantalus. Dont blame yrself, Ed. I ate my own sons.

Oedipus: I blame myself.

Tantalus: I blame fate.

Cassandra: Fate. What did fate ever do that we didnt see coming?

Clytemnestra: My husband, Agamemnon, was a pig and so I cut him down like I would a rabid hog.

Host: Yr children have a different take on that.

Clytemnestra: Youve spoken with my children?!

Host: Come on in, kids. Folks meet—Clytemnestra's kids.

The Kids rush at Clytemnestra and fight with their mama.

3 FIRST BEGINNING

Drumroll and a crash of cymbals.
Fanfare of a 1000 sounds. Galactic explosion.
Performance ends.

1: Impressive.

2: I was moved.

1: Me too.

2: What do you think it means?

1: I think its supposed to be the creation.

2: Of what?

1: Of the world I guess.

The performance begins again. The performance ends.

1: Big bang and all that.

2: Wow.

1: Yeah.

(Rest)

2: What about the cosmos?

1: Who knows.

2: Big bang produced the world thats easy to understand. Some stuff blew up and made more stuff. Thats simple. But—

1: But what?

2: What made all the stuff? All the stuff that was swirling around in the first place?

They look up.

1: I dont like to think of all that stuff.

2: I do.

1: I dont.

Performance begins again.

4 LOOK

2 speakers.

– How long do I have to look at it?

– Until it looks at you.

– Huh.
– Keep looking.
– I am. Huh. How long do you think itll take?
– Depends.
– On what?

The lights go out.

– Damn.
– Keep looking.
– But I cant see.
– Keep looking.
– K.

5 STITCHES

2: Is it healed?
1: Not yet.
2: Its been weeks. Yr a slow healer—I guess.
1: Goddamn stitches.
2: Theyre holding you together.
1: Goddamn war.
2: I used to feel proud.

(Rest)

1: I laid down last night thinking its not real—wow its just a dream war. Like my shrink says, Ima big one for conflict—I'll wake up, and itll all be just a dream.
2: And you woke up and—
1: And I woke up, and I threw up.
2: Itll leave a scar but youll be healed up in a week or so.
1: But the war wont be healed up in a week or so will it?

(Rest)

2: No.
1: Timothy McVeigh and the D.C. Sniper—they were both war vets.
2: Yeah.

(Rest)

1: Im gonna watch the Home Decorating Channel. Wanna watch with me?

2: Turn it on.

> They turn on the tv. The Home Decorating Channel
> is presented live, right in front of them.
> As the Hostess mimes a segment about curtains
> or how to best display yr bric-a-brac,
> sounds of the war drown out everything she's saying.
> They drown it out so completely that it sounds like the war
> is in the living room too.

6 6´4˝

> 2 speakers.

What happened?
Dunno?
What now?
Dunno.
I used to be 6'4". It was so nice.
It was never nice.
It used to be beautiful.
Used to be!!!!

7 FATHER COMES HOME FROM THE WARS (Part 4)

> A man, the Father, comes in wearing army fatigues.

Father: Hello? Im home. Made it home in one piece! Anybody home?

> He looks for the Family, finds no one.
> Even goes looking offstage. No one. He spies a note.

Father: "Gone to the store. Back soon. Love, Family."
(Rest)
Thats nice.
(Rest)
Gives me plenty of time to change.

He opens his pack. Changes into an army-issued business suit.
Complete with army-issued shoes and socks,
a necktie, and a pipe and tobacco.

Father: Army issue. Could be worse. Made in a country I cant even pronounce. Could be worse. I got a full suit. Some guys just get the jacket or just the shoes. Some guys dont got a need for the shoes, cause they dont got feet. There was a guy I knew, he used to be 6'4". Save that story. Dont tell the kids. Dont tell the missus. Not suitable. Tell the soldiers at the VA hospital when you go in for yr shots. Right. Some lost their feet or their arms. Or their minds. Or they house. Or they wife and kids. Put that in yr army-issue pipe and smoke it. Leave yr edge at the door. Think: "Peace." Think: "Lucky You." Think: "Same Old Same Old." Sit in my favorite chair. Watch my army-issue tv. All I need is an army-issue dog. "Gone to the store. Back soon." I'll wait.
(Rest)
Im a lucky man.

8 FATHER COMES HOME FROM THE WARS (Part 5)

Cocktails before dinner. Very stylish. The den of an early 1960s
home. Sophisticated but not over-the-top. Joe and Lovey
(husband and wife) are the center of attention.

Joe: Crawling. For miles.
Host: Yr exaggerating.
Hostess: Let him tell his story.
Host: Just as long as you dont exaggerate.
Hostess: He loves tales, he hates tall tales.

Joe gives Lovey's hand a squeeze. Too hard.

Lovey: Its not a tall tale. Its the facts.
Host: Miles?
Joe: Scout's honor.

After a beat. The girls laugh in a stylish upscale manner.

Next Door Neighbor: Crawling for miles in the dirt? Go on—
Joe: In the *sand*.
Host: Tall tale.

> Joe pinches Lovey too hard.

Lovey: Not at all. He had so much sand in his boots. There was barely any room for his feet!

> More stylish laughter.

Joe: I had sand in my mouth too. And every other uniform I saw—
Next Door Neighbor: Had the enemy in it.
Lovey: Worse.
Joe: Had a dead man in it.

Joe
Joe

(Rest)

> A Kitchen Servant appears and whispers to the Host.

Host: The cook is making yr favorite dish, Joe. He wants to know how you like yr meat.
Joe: Raw.
Host: You mean rare.
Joe: I mean raw. With the skin of the animal still on it. Right, Lovey?

> He hugs Lovey too hard.

Lovey: Joe's such a kidder.

Host
Joe

Host: How about well-done, Joe?
Joe: How about well-done, Sam?
Lovey: Yr home now, Joe.
Hostess: How about well-done, Joe?
Joe: Well-done it is. Im home now. After all.
Host: 3 cheers for Joe.

> They toast Joe.

9 FATHER COMES HOME FROM THE WARS (Part 6)

The same people—minus Joe. All are many years older.

Host: 3 cheers for Joe. Come on.

They toast Joe.

Lovey: They wanted me to testify against him.
Hostess: No!
Lovey: They wanted me to say he beat me.
Next Door Neighbor: And after all he's done for this country.

Lovey
Host
Hostess
Next Door Neighbor

(Rest)

Host: Good old Joe!

(Rest)

Next Door Neighbor: Lovey, how about I sit on the picnic bench and you do for me what you do for Joe? Whaddayathink?
Lovey: I dont think so, K?
Next Door Neighbor: Dont hurt to ask, does it?

(Rest)

Hostess: Does Joe like it better at the Front?
Host: Its where he can be himself with no pretense.
Lovey: He writes to me every day. I have a whole room full of letters and theyre all love letters. And sometimes, when he writes about something—Top Secret—you know something he knows but that he's not supposed to know, something he knows that he's not supposed to say he knows, the censors crop it out. And—

Lovey
Lovey

Hostess: Well at least he doesnt come home with blood on his clothes anymore.

Host: Thats something.

Lovey: He doesnt come home at all.

> They raise their glasses and laugh politely.

10 FLAG WAVER

> Little Mikey, about 19, waves an enormous American flag with
> great ceremony—as if Wagner opera music is playing in the
> background or as if he's the head of an enormous patriotic
> parade. He may want to hum a John Philip Sousa tune.
> He plants the flag in the ground, then takes out 2 small flags—
> tabletop size. He semaphores the letters H-E-L-P.
> His Mother, wearing an apron, and his Father, holding a pipe,
> come out of the house to watch him.

Mother: Come in and eat yr supper, Mikey.

Big Mike: At first we were proud of you, but now yr disgracing us, kid.

Mother: Inside! Now! Lets go!

Big Mike: He's probably a homosexual.

Mother: What a ridiculous thing to say. Are you a homosexual, Little Mikey?

> Little Mikey continues his flag semaphore: H-E-L-P,
> over and over. Nothing more elaborate than that.
> He could say the letters aloud as he signs them.

11 BLUE UMBRELLA

> A Woman walks back and forth with a blue umbrella—
> opened sometimes, closed sometimes.
> A whole year passes.

Man: A whole year has passed. Every day you walk by with yr blue umbrella.

Woman: Yes.

Man: How come?

Woman: I dont speak—to strangers that often.

Man: Oh.

Woman: Oh!

> She winces in pain. She falls and the Man catches her.

Woman: The sky is—!

> She dies.

12 THE MR. LINCOLN ROSE

> A Knot of People doing nothing.
> A Rose Man comes in with a rosebush. A Man, standing apart
> from the Knot, takes notice.

Man: What you got there, stranger?
Rose Man: Its a Mr. Lincoln rose

> A Hard-of-Hearing Man within the Knot gets very excited.

Hard-of-Hearing Man: Mr. Lincoln rose!
Rose Man: Thats right.
Hard-of-Hearing Man: Mr. Lincoln rose! Mr. Lincoln rose from the dead!
Another from the Knot: No kidding?!?
Daughter of Hard-of-Hearing Man: My pa dont lie!
Entire Knot: Mr. Lincoln rose! Mr. Lincoln rose from the dead!

> They whip themselves up into a frenzy and rush offstage.

Rose Man: They didnt hear me right.
Man: I know. The same rumor got spread around about Jesus.
Rose Man: Smell.

> They smell the rosebush.

13 SUNSHINE

> Dark stage lights up.

Guard: Sunshine!!!

> A Horde of People rushes onstage pushing and shoving.
> They have their eyes closed against the bright light. They stand,

> sit, lie down, turning this way and that, warming themselves.
> 1 sneaks a peak at the light source.

3: Feels good.

4: Feels good—hell, feels *great*.

5: 1 snuck a peak at it.

1: Liar.

5: Snuck a peak yesterday and a peak today.

1: Bald-face liar.

3: Just enjoy it, huh?

4: Its not as warm as yesterday.

2: Its warmer.

5: I could hear you, 1—the sound of you opening yr eyes.

1: Yr ears aint that good. No ones ears is that good.

2: I brought a jar. To take some back inside.

3: That dont work.

5: Whatd you see?

1: —. Light.

5: Wow.

Guard: Sunset!

> Lights dim into darkness.

14 THE MAN UPSTAIRS

Child: Mother?

Mother: What?

Child: Where is He?

Mother: He who?

Child: The Bad One.

Mother: In hiding I guess. Father says He's hiding in a bunker. An underground shed with enough food to last Him forever, and tunnels that connect Him to every part of the world. Kind of like a gopher. When yr walking to school and you see a hole—watch out! He could pop up out of it and with His eyes command you to take up arms against yr own mother and father. As sure as yr sitting here.

Child
Mother

(Rest)

Child: Does He ever blink?

Mother: The Bad One never blinks, child.

Child: "With a blink of His eye He creates the world," thus says the Scripture.

Mother: Oh, that "One." Thats not the "Bad One" thats the "Big One." Thats "God" yr asking about.

Child: Yes.

Mother: Where is God?

Child: Yes.

Mother: God is—upstairs.

(Rest)

Drink yr milk.

Child: Upstairs.

Mother: They dont call Him "The Man Upstairs" for nothing.

> The Child looks up.

Child: Is He up there all the time?

Mother: Every minute. Even when yr sleeping.

Child: Is He up there when—

Mother: Dont mention it.

Child
Mother

Child: Is He up there when "dont mention it" happens?

(Rest)

Mother: Of course. The Man Upstairs does not leave His post.

Child: Sometimes He falls asleep though. Like when Father watches the television late at night. I wake up. The sound is loud. Advertisements for women who will come and visit you and—. Father has fallen asleep and as I walk downstairs, I see the remote-control slip from his hand and clatter to the floor.

Mother
Mother

Child: Mother, is God like that?

Mother: Its time for school.

Child: Im dressed.

Mother: Off you go, then. Kiss?

> They kiss cheeks. The Child goes.
> The Mother waves goodbye. Then she cleans the table.
> She stands holding a plate. She watches the Child
> go into the distance. The plate slips from her hand
> and crashes to the floor. Only a miracle could make things right
> again, but they say that miracles these days are in short supply.

15 MOTHER COMES HOME FROM THE WARS

> A Man looks up at the sky. A Woman enters.

Man: Yr back.

Woman: I got in last night.

Man: I heard they freed you.

Woman: Ive been doing interviews nonstop. The National Publisher wants to buy rights to my story.

Man: The National Publisher?

Woman: That means big money.

Man: Wow.

Woman: There was a picture of me on the front page of the paper.

Man: I missed it.

Woman: Ive got a copy for you.

Man: Thanks.

Woman
Man

Woman: Hon?

Man: What.

Woman: What are you looking at?

Man: God.

Woman: Youll go blind.

> The Man lowers his head—he wears black spectacles.

Woman: Yr blind already.

Man: Yep.

> The Man lifts his glasses and smiles.

Man: Just kidding.

Woman: Yr such a joker. I could have you shot. I had a lot of men shot. They were all just like you. Just like you but—

Man: Foreign.

Woman: Just like you but foreign. Yes.

Man
Woman

Man: Welcome home, hon.

> They embrace. We can see that their embrace, while warm and passionate, causes them both excruciating pain.

16 ACCIDENT

Cindy: Bill?

Bill: Yeah?

Cindy: Oh, Bill!

Bill: Yeah.

Cindy: Christ.

Bill: Whatever.

Cindy: Youd think with Easter around the corner—

Bill: As if everybody celebrates "Easter."

Cindy: Still.

Bill: Yeah

Cindy: Still, Bill.

Bill: Youve said enough.

Cindy: Ive hardly said anything. And *someone* ought to say *something*.

Bill: Yeah.

(Rest)

Cindy: You look like an accident waiting to happen.

Bill: You think?

Cindy: Yeah, I think.
(Rest)
Can I invite the band in?

Bill: You think?

Cindy: Let me invite the band in.

> Cindy pulls a string that opens a curtain.
> Behind the curtain is a Band, all set-up and warmed-up,
> tuned-up, and not too drunk yet. As if theyve played a decent
> 1st set and are in the middle of an even better 2nd one.

Band Front Woman: Requests?
Cindy: Play "Accident Waiting to Happen."
Band Front Woman: Who for?
Cindy: Play it for Bill.

> Waiter comes by, serves drinks to Cindy and Bill. 2 busboys roll
> in empty chairs and other essential club/bar decor.
> Cindy and Bill get settled as the Band plays.
> The song is torch-song blues.

ACCIDENT WAITING TO HAPPEN
I know you
a lot better
than you know yrself.
I know yr out sleeping with more than one Somebody Else.
You think that time will heal all wounds.
You think that
rain wont rain on yr parade.
I tell you
Im thinking
and things are gonna change.
You look like an accident,
Bill,
an accident waiting to happen.
You think Im kidding you, Bill,
but, Bill, baby, my lips aint just flapping.
Yeah yeah yeah yeah.
Yeah yeah yeah yeah.

> The music continues as the next play begins . . .

17 LESS AND LESS

1: I dunno.
2: You dont have to.

> End of scene.

1: What happened?
2: To what?
1: To all the—
2: People?

(Rest)

1: Yeah.
2: I dunno.

Intermission.

1: Here.
2: Thanks.
1: No sweat.
(Rest)
That all?
2: Thats all.

1
2
1
2

1: There used to be more.
2: Yeah.
1: There used to be more and more.
(Rest)
And now theres less and less and less.
2: What do you want?!?

(Rest)

1: More. I want more. Like there used to be. More and more. More overflowing.
(Rest)
(Rest)
Are you going to hit me?
2: No.
1: Youve got yr hand raised.
2: You can see it?
1: I can feel it.

(Rest)

2: I'll go get more. Hows that?

1: It doesnt have to be much more.

2: I'll go get more.

> 2 turns out his pockets. Theyre empty. He goes.

18 PROJECT ULYSSES

> A Chorus of Young Men apparently lounging around on
> a basketball court. Spy comes in. He's got news but isnt ready
> to spill it. The Young Men act like they could care less.
> Then their enthusiasm betrays their cool.

Chorus:
Spy!

Spy:
Thats my name.
From when my mother
first looked me in the face.

Chorus:
Spy!
Spill it.

Spy:
Spill what?

Chorus:
Like we all gathered here together
and sit for nothing.
Theres news.

Spy:
Says who?

Chorus:
Says, says you, thats who says.

Spy:
I aint said nothing—

Chorus:
Yet!

Spy:
If you know theres news
why dont you spill it, then?
If yr so sure and shit,
if yr so knowledgeable,

so know-it-all, so big-head,
they call you Spy?
NOT!

Chorus:
Why does he go through this every time?
I drive a cab for a living and
if I took the long way around,
Lord knows folks wouldnt like it.
Theyd take away my license.
Theyd lock me up
under the jail.
Shit.
But, Spy. He takes the long way around every time.
Making us wait to hear what we wanna know.

Spy:
Tell you what.
Ima tell you.

Chorus:
At last.
So tell.
Go on.
He back?

Spy:
Ulysses?

Chorus:
Ulysses.

Spy:
Not yet.

Chorus:
Then we still got a chance
to get with Penny, his girl.

Spy:
But Im the only one with her number.

Chorus:
We know.

Spy:
Slide me some paper
I'll call her for you.
Maybe she'll talk.

Chorus:
For true?

Spy:
Somebody's gotta get with her
maybe that somebody will be you.

Spy:
Penelope is hot.
And Ulysses is out at the war.
I got Penny's number.
And, even though she's true like Truth,
those fools keep paying me to hook them up.
Im making some cash.
Theyre playing the Lotto.
Spoils of war, folks, spoils of war.

19 KINDER LERNEN DEUTSCH

Scene 1

> A Man and a Woman sit, sharing one chair.
> The Man fishes in his pocket like he's fishing for change.
> The Woman sees this and begins rummaging around
> in her purse. At about the same moment each pulls out a sock
> and uses it as a Puppet. The Puppets, Karl and Heidi,
> are very animated while the Man and Woman
> are very bored-looking.

Karl *(Man's Puppet)***:** Why?

Heidi *(Woman's Puppet)***:** Does there have to be a why?

Karl: There has to be reason.

Heidi: Yr so—*Wie sagt man?*—linear. Youve always been so linear. When the army marched through the streets—you *cheered* them.

Karl: Because of the way they marched. They were so *orderly*. And there had been so much—disorder up until then.
(Rest)
Heidi. Heidi, look at me.

Heidi: There is no reason, Karl, It just happened.

Karl: And it will happen again.

Heidi: It could.

Karl *(With a sadness befitting a troubled nation)***:** Ah!

Lights down.

Scene 2

Lights up. The Puppets, Karl and Heidi, brandish swords. Ordinary dinner knives actually. They sword fight.

Heidi: I am a descendant of Joan.

Karl: Joan who?

Heidi: Joan of Arc.

Karl: Dont be ridiculous. Jeanne d'Arc was French. And a virgin.

Heidi: Our savior is my witness.

She stabs Karl, mortally wounding him.

Karl: Im slain! Kiss me this last time so I may take some kind of light into the hell where Im surely bound. Dont turn away from me! I bleed I die Im—

Lights dim.

Scene 3

Lights up. The Man and Woman.

Man: Wheres my other sock?

Woman: Right here.

She gives him the sock. They either match or they dont match, but he is pleased. He puts them on his feet.

Man: Every time I lose something you find it. Yr something special.

Woman: Im a witch.

Man: Yr my wife.

Woman: Yr proposing?

Man: Say yes.

Woman: Only if you take me on a honeymoon to Germany.

Man: Germany?

Woman: Ive always wanted to go.

Man: You got it.

Woman: Goody.

They kiss. Lights out.

20 (Easter) THE JESUS ROSE

> A Knot of People looking off into the far distance.
> They are desperate for news.

Masha: He up yet?

Donatolo: Not as I can see.

Max: Ask Clara to look, she's got the eyes in this town.

> Clara looks.

Masha: He up yet?

Clara: He sleeps.

Masha: Liar! I'll rip out those famous eyes of yrs.

> The entire Knot of People restrains Masha.

Masha:
He said he'd wake!
He said he'd wake!
He's not a liar!
You are!
Waah!

> They put a cloth bag over her head.
> This silences her, even though she continues to writhe.
> A Stranger walks in, she carries a rosebush.

Donatolo: That smell.

Clara: It smells like a corpse.

Max: But a sweet corpse.

Stranger: The smell is the flower from my plant.

Clara: Perhaps a sign.
(Rest)
Stranger, yr plant, whats it called?

Stranger: They call it a Jesus rose.

Masha:
Jesus rose!
Jesus rose!
Jesus rose from the dead!

> A party-frenzy atmosphere erupts as if they had just seen
> Jesus of Nazareth, crucified and dead 3 days before,
> walk from the tomb. The Stranger looks at the rosebush.

Stranger: They didnt hear me right.

Clara: I know. The same rumor went around about Lincoln. Let them have their resurrection. Why ruin it.

Stranger: Yeah. Smell.

> They smell the rose.

21 THE LITTER OF DISCONTENT

> 2 People, male and female, walk in carrying a litter.
> A Guard just happens to be passing by.

Guard: Halt! Who goes there?

Litter Man: It is he.

Litter Woman: The one we bear on this royal litter is deceased.

Guard: Anyone I know?

Litter Woman: Who do you know?

Guard: I know people. Heres a buck. Gimmie the inside scoop. Is it a famous corpse?

Litter Man: A film star.

Guard: You dont say.

Litter Woman: But foreign.

Litter Man: A foreign film star.

Guard: I dont know many foreigners.

Litter Woman: Too bad.

Guard: Well, carry on!

> They stay. The Guard goes.

Litter Woman: Set it down. My feet. These shoes.

> They set down the litter. Suddenly, a Happy Woman
> and a Happy Man run in straight out of a glamorous foreign film.
> They play with a beachball. Then they run off, leaving a radio
> behind that plays 1940s melodrama music. The music swells.

Litter Man: Yr leaving me.

Litter Woman: Because I have to, dontcha see? Yr content to walk around life dragging a corpse behind you and Im not cut from that kind of cloth.

> She walks off, leaving him to bear the corpse alone.

22 MONSTER'S MOTHER

Scene 1

> Mother and the Chorus of Woodsmen walk downstage.

Mother:
He is a great hairy beast.
As am I.
Oh!
Chorus of Woodsmen: It cant be helped.

Scene 2

> Mother with 3 Servants. The 2nd Servant holds a radio
> and the 3rd Servant holds a box of tissues.

Mother:
Turn.
Turn.
Turn.
Turn.

> The 1st Servant turns channels as instructed.

1st Servant: Yr son's rampaging
3rd Servant: All bad news.

> Mother cries. The 3rd Servant steps forward.
> She pulls tissues from the box.

Scene 3

> Mother with Pregnant Monster Mother.

Mother: When I carried him I thought only of good things.
Pregnant Monster Mother: Then he was born.
Mother: And I smiled at him.
Pregnant Monster Mother: But, still, he grew.

> Mother cries. The 3rd Servant steps forward with tissues.

Scene 4

> The 1st Servant hands Mother a tv-changer. She changes
> channels, then hands it back. She takes it back again, etc.

New Mother: He has teeth already. And his hairiness is much upon him.

Mother: I told my boy he was a prince and that the Great Wheel of Time would bring him more pleasing looks.

New Mother: He has his claws—sprang out just now.

Mother: The day came when I told my son that Time's Great Wheel had come and gone, it had rolled by and left us the life we were living. "But surely, my father—" he said, and then he knew.

New Mother:
My misfortune!
He is a great hairy beast.
As am I.
Oh!
It cant be helped.

Mother:
Turn.
Turn.
Turn.
Turn.

1st Servant: Yr sons' rampaging

3rd Servant: All bad news.

The Mothers cry.

23 MAKE ME A WILLOW CABIN AT YR GATE

Scene 1

2 men with 1 pair of binoculars.

Captain: Lemmie see—

Major: Huh?

Captain: Lemmie see—sir?

Major: Im not done yet. God bless America.

Captain: Sir?

Major: I was reminding myself why I was here.

Captain: Can I see now, sir?

Major: Be patient.

(Rest)

Do you know I had this home once. It wasnt much, but on a clear day you could see the Hollywood sign.

Captain: With yr naked eye, sir?

Major: No.

Captain: The sun's going down.

Major: Yes it is.

Scene 2

A Woman and a Crowd, and the Other Woman.

Other Woman: Yr sewing.

Woman: Me and my slaves, yes.

Other Woman: On cement? Sowing seeds?

Woman: Me and my slaves, yes.

They continue sowing/sewing with long elegant gestures.

Scene 3

Captain: Some forest, huh? Looks like theyre all weeping willows.

Major: Weeping willows. Sprang up overnight. Miraculous.

Captain: An army man dont believe in miracles, sir.

Major: I was overcome.

Captain: Neither here nor there, sir.

(Rest)

Major: Youll report me?

Captain: Its my duty, sir. But not now. Too much bloodshed now. When the war's over. Then. When people are sick of the peace— theyll be thirsty. For blood.
(Rest)
Bonocs.

The Major gives them up, then wipes the tears from his eyes.

24 TUNDRA

Scene 1

Man: Im worried.

Woman: About—

Man: About the Tundra.

Woman
Woman

Scene 5

> The Woman stands. The Man is seated, relaxed,
> maybe with the tv-clicker.

Woman: The Tundra's coming.
Man: Dont be ridiculous. At this time of day?
(Rest)
In this heat?

Scene 86

> The Woman and Man sit relaxing—with the newspaper or tv
> or both. Military Police come in and take the Man away.
> It happens with extreme violence and in extreme silence.
> The Woman makes a single gesture to help the Man,
> but it is inadequate. The MPs do not touch,
> harm or even notice her in any way.

Scene 2120

> The Woman knits. She has knit quite a lot.
> She works with great difficulty.

Woman Friend: How many days has it been?
Woman: I keep thinking—I'll send this to him and he'll hate it because its the wrong color. Silly. Right?
Woman Friend: He wont like the color and he'll send it back. No, he'll bring it back. In person. And you and me and the girls will be sitting around drinking our warm water and eating our cakes and then His Hussy will sashay in here in her high heels—
Woman: His Hussy, you really think so?
Woman Friend: It happened to me so it could happen to you.
Woman: I dunno.
Woman Friend: You dunno. Because its been all this time and you still cant admit to yrself that yr husband ran off with another woman.
Woman: Thats not what happened.
Woman Friend: What happened then?

> The Woman stares at her Woman Friend. There are words
> for what she needs to say but they are a long way in coming.

April

She opens her mouth and repeats the gesture she made
when she tried to rescue her husband. Her friend doesnt notice.
The Woman goes back to knitting. Lights fade out.

25 LIGHTS/RATS

2 city folk.

1: Its dark.
2: Very.
1: Im scared.
2: Of what?

1

2

1

A Stranger comes in with a lightbulb.

Stranger: I heard it was dark.
1: Thats right, but whats it to you?
Stranger: Ive brought a lightbulb.
2: Its beautiful.
Stranger: Its yrs to keep.

He goes. They screw it in. No light comes from it.

1: Dont work.
2: Yeah.
1: Rats.

26 GIANT STEP

Stage fills with people just milling about, going to work, school,
etc. Someone flags a taxi, 3 Kids play jumprope,
a whole mosaic of Folks—Mother tells a story to a Kid, etc.
One of the Women—as slowly as possible and
with great attention to form and breath, and at the same time
with a good enough measure of joie de vivre—
takes a great big giant step. The largest gesture/step
she can take without jumping.

As she completes the step she exhales audibly.
At the end of the exhale the mosaic of Folks applauds.

27 DIVA

Applause from April 26 continues.

She: What was that? Sounded like applause.

He: Go back to sleep.

She: It sounded like—someone or something out there was—clapping.

He: Im going back to sleep.

She: Do you know how many years its been since Ive been on the stage?
(Rest)
Do you know how much they loved me?
(Rest)
Darling?
(Rest)
Wake up.
(Rest)
They would applaud—until their hands bled. And the house manager would bring their blood-stained handkerchiefs to my dressing room as testaments.

She waits an eternity. Finally the applause comes back—
the sound crashing like waves. She goes back to sleep.

28 THE DEVELOPMENT OF TOURISM IN LOS ANGELES COUNTY

Lots of Tourists and this guy named Herbert.

Tourist: Look.

Tourist: Look.

Tourist: Look.

Tourist: Look.

Tourist: Take our picture together. Thanks.

Herbert: You all sightseeing?

Tourist: Yeah.

Herbert: Im a sight. Thats what my mother says. She says, "Herbert you are a sight!"

> Lots of pictures taken of Herbert.
> Herbert's getting tipsy from all the attention.

Herbert: I used to have a show. Know what I mean? My own show—with commercials. My. Own. Show. It was all about me. Know what Im talking about?

Mom: *Herbert!!?!??!*

Herbert: *What!!?!??!*

Mom: Dont get stuck on stupid, Herbert!!

> Herbert stands there with his mouth hanging open.
> He is embarrassed and, at the same time,
> really hungry for attention. The Tourists take lots more pictures.
> Herbert bathes in the wash of flashbulbs
> like some people bathe in sunrays.

29 PLAYING POSSUM

> 2 People and a Dog.

L: I did I did I did I did.

P: She killed a possum.

S: Oh no. A possum? Really?

L: I did I did.

P: A little baby.

L: I am. Hunter. Me. Yes.

S: A baby?

L: Me hunter. Thats me. Yes.

P: A little baby possum.

S: Lets see.

P: Come on.

L: Me too I am yes hunter.

S

L

P

(Rest)

P: See?

S: Wow.

L: See. Me. Hunter. I am. Yes.

S: LOOK!

L: Yes I am.

P: What the—?

S: Its up—its not dead its—

L: Yes yes, bow wow, bow wow wow.

P: Playing possum. The possum's playing possum.

S: Wow! How cool.

P: She didnt kill it after all.

S: How cool.

L: And on the 3rd day he rose again in fulfillment of the Scriptures. Just like a possum.

L

L

P: The dog just spoke.

S: I know.

P: Trippy.

S: Very.

30 SAINT LAZARUS POINTS OUT THE SAINTS

2 Men onstage. Offstage, horrible screams from a single Man.

Man 1: What are you in here for?

Man 2: I dont like to talk about it.

Man 1: Joe says talking can help get stuff off yr chest.

Man 2: I dont got stuff on my chest.

Man 1: Gossip with me then.

They whisper, trading secrets that we cant hear.

Man 2: No shit?

Man 1: No shit.

More gossip.

Man 2: Huh. Him?

Man 1: The screamer.

Man 2: Really?

Man 1: Theyre torturing him for it right now.

Man 2: For?

Man 1: For saint-pointing, Im telling ya.

Man 2: But he pointed at me!

Man 1: Times are rough, man, what can I tell ya.

> Man 2 spits in the direction of the horrible screams,
> like he's spitting on a conflagration—in a vain effort to keep
> the flames from reaching his house.

May

1 BONANZA

> 2 down-and-out-looking Cowboys gnawing on enormous
> bones. A Well-to-Do Cowboy with a rope approaches.

Well-to-Do Cowboy: I was on my way to the Workers' Parade. I was going to march in support of workers' rights.

Cowboy 1: Liar.

Well-to-Do Cowboy: You calling me a liar?

Cowboy 2: "Tired," we're calling you. You must be. Tired. No horse.

Well-to-Do Cowboy: He run off. My horse. He said he had to be free. I said freedom wasnt all it was cracked-up to be. You see him?

Cowboy 1: Who?

Well-to-Do Cowboy: My horse.

Cowboy 1
Well-to-Do Cowboy
Cowboy 2

> The down-and-outs go back to their gnawing.

Well-to-Do Cowboy: Well? You seen—?

Cowboy 2: Nope.

Cowboy 1: Yep, nope. We aint seen nothing.

Well-to-Do Cowboy: Is that—barbecue?

Cowboy 2: Yep.

> They keep gnawing.

Cowboy 1: Want some?

Well-to-Do Cowboy: —Nope.

They keep gnawing.

2 WORK EXPANDS TO THE TIME ALLOTTED TO IT

Work blows up a pink balloon. It gets very full.

Work: Enough?

Worker: More.

Work blows.

Work: Enough?

Worker: More.

Work blows.
This continues until Work explodes. Worker then holds
the balloon, spreading its lips and releasing the air—
letting it scream.

3 THE HISTORY OF LUCY ON HER 103RD BIRTHDAY

Lucy: Im old.

Son: Yr 103.

Lucy: Thats old.

Son: Not if yr a redwood. Redwoods have been here since the birth of Christ.

Lucy: Im not a redwood. Im old.

Son: I was just giving you some perspective.

Lucy: I dont want some perspective. I want some Maker's Mark bourbon!

Son: Howbout some church.

Lucy: I got the same birthday as James Brown! I wanna see the Godfather of Soul in concert! Ima say it loud: "Im black and Im proud!"

Son turns on the tv. Lucy mutters foul-mouthed curses at him.
Prayer sounds come from the tv.

Lucy: Im old and you dont listen to me. I got style, still. Its old but its still style.

Son: At least yr old. Yr older than I'll be when I go. Yr lucky.

Lucy: Im not "Lucky." Im "LUCY"! "Lucky" is a damn dog's name!

Son *(Leaping up)*: Hallelujah!

Lucy: I'll write you a check to send to them, but dont let them pray for the president. I want the president to rot in hell, ok?

Son: Yes, Mother.

The room is awash with divine light.

4 TITLEMANIA

A Woman sits on a grand cushion or on a simple folding chair in a grand manner: Titlematrix. Someone walks in with a flower.

Titlematrix: "The World without Me in It."

Someone: You think?

Titlematrix: I think. "The World without Me in It."

Someone: Such a grand title for such a small—

Titlematrix: Ive spoken. Crier?

Crier *(Crying the news)*: "The World without Me in It."

Titlematrix: Scribe?

Scribe *(Writing the news)*: "The World without Me in It."

Titlematrix: And so—another title. For a previously untitled—thing.

The stage quickly fills with a Crowd of Clappers all pleased and applauding. They applaud as if applauding were everything.

5 THE CLAPPER

20 years have passed between yesterday's play and this one.
The Crowd of Clappers remains.

Father: Ive put food on yr table yr whole life.

Son: Im not ungrateful.

Father: But you want to do yr—what do you call it?

Son: My "own thing."

Father: In my day, that "do yr own thing," my dad woulda called it— *(To Grandpop)* What woulda you of called it, Pop?

Grandpop: Huh?

Father: "Do yr own thing," Pop.

Grandpop: *"Masturbation."*

Son: What does Pop know?

Father: Now youve lost respect for him too, huh?

Son: I dont want to be a Clapper.

Mother: Ask Son if he's a homosexual, dear.

Father: Yr mother wants to know if yr a homosexual.

Son: I dont want to be a CLAPPER! No, that does not mean Im gay—I just—dont wanna be a CLAPPER. Spending my life in a darkened room with hundreds of others waiting on—

Titlematrix *(From yesterday's play, offstage)*: "The 12 Days of Doomsday."

> A red light goes on. The Clappers put on bright smiles and exit, clapping vigorously. They reenter walking backward, clapping a bit less vigorously.

Mother: You used to be in the front row. You were cute as a button. They said you were going to get a chance at being Crier or Scribe or—now look at you!

Father: Yr grounded.

Son: Yr crazy.

Father: One foot out that door and I'll gun you down myself.

Son: How can you do this to me?

Father: Thats how Pop helped me to see the right road. Right, Pop?

Grandpop: I had a rifle with a laser-sight thingamajiggy. I drew a chalkline 4 times, making the shape of a box, told yr father to stand in the box and dared him to step out.

Titlematrix *(Offstage)*: "One More Thing to Swallow."

> The Clappers exit, clapping as lights fade.

6 HE SLEEPS, MOSTLY

> A Man sits with Another Man on a bench.
> A 3rd man, the Running Man, runs around and around, really
> expending a lot of energy, but he doesnt get tired.

Another Man: Impressive.

Man: Not really. He sleeps mostly.

> Running Man goes nonstop. Lights go to slow fade.

7 A FLIP-OFF FLIP BOOK

Flipper comes in. Whistles a bastardized version of
the *Flipper* tv show theme. He holds one hand clearly visible
and flips the peace sign, then the finger, then peace,
then the finger, etc.
Another comes in and watches.

Another: Cool.
Flipper: You think?
Another: Yeah.
Flipper: Ima make a book. A flip-off flip book.
Another: Cool.

(Rest)

Flipper: Flip with me.

Another flips with Flipper, faster and faster, gaining momentum
and dexterity before the lights suddenly go out.

8 SINCE YOUVE BEEN GONE MEETS IRRESISTIBLE

2 Women: Younger, covered with dirt, and Elder.

Elder: How long you been gone?
Younger: —. Hard to say.
Elder: You were missed.
Younger: I was?
Elder: In a manner of speaking. Yes. You were—missed.
Younger: It was the strangest thing. One minute I was—

Younger makes a vague gesture.

Younger: And the next minute I was—. —.

Younger makes another vague gesture.

Elder: The words take awhile but theyll come.
Younger: My mouth's still got dirt in it.
Elder: It takes awhile to get the vocabulary back.
Younger: I smell less than I did.

Elder: Yr lucky.
(Rest)
You wanna take a bath?

> Church bells sound—harshly—on pots and pans.

Younger: Bells!
Elder: Sort of. You gonna bathe?
Younger: So soon?
Elder: You wanna get laid, right? You wanna get laid, you gotta wash, K?
Younger: Water. I dunno.
Elder: I'll go with you.

> Church bells sound again. More harshly.

Elder: I'll go with you. Lets go.

> Younger makes vague gesture again. Elder escorts
> the Younger roughly away.

9 THEY WERE SO SURE IN CHICAGO

> A Group runs onstage. It ejects one of its members.
> The Ejected One attempts to perform an impossible act.

Group Leader: What in God's name is she trying to do?

> Group Leader's Assistant whispers to Group Leader.

Group Leader: That's impossible!

> When unsuccessful, the Ejected One says:

Ejected One: Blow on my feet. Go on. They said to do it this way in Chicago.

> They blow on her feet, albeit reluctantly.
> The Ejected One is again unsuccessful.

Ejected One: They were so sure in Chicago. Honest.
(Rest)
Maybe blow on my hands?

The Group has become a Crowd. The Crowd becomes a Mob.

Mob Member: Maybe, rip her limb from limb?
Mob: Hmmmmmmmmm.

They advance toward the Ejected One
with outstretched scary fingers.

10 THE WRITER TURNS 40

A stage full of people. All of them sipping drinks
and chatting—a party.

Partygoers: Murmmmmmmmuruurrrrrrrrrrrrmmmmmmmmurrrrrrmm.

One Party Guest turns to Almost the Writer.

Party Guest: I saw you in that magazine and that article about
you—in the *Times*. Well, happy birthday.

All turn to Almost the Writer.

Partygoer *(Shouting)*: Happy bir—
All *(Joining in)*: —thday! Happy! Birthday!
Almost the Writer: Im not the writer—she's over there. See that
person—with the—not her—but—the other one. Just there.
There she is.

The Writer, unseen, in the far distance.
All crane their necks to get a look at her as the lights fade.

10 (Again) EVERYBODY'S GOT AN AUNT JEMIMAH

Gang Warfare: Crips against Bloods, Red States against
Blue States, North against South, Spanish against English,
Russians against themselves, Chinese against themselves,
you know, South Koreans against Northern brethren,
Germans against the world, then against the Wall,
Irish against the English, English against the French,
Chinese against Tibetans, us against them, U.S. against Iraq,
Hutu against Tutsi, Serbs against Croats,

Israeli against Palestinian, etc., you know, you know,
you know how it go, back through the beginning of time
and unfortunately out into the future.
2 Reps, one from one side, the other from the other, square off.
They are about to throw down,
and the battle's going to decide all the marbles forever.
But first, a little conversation:

A: I heard a rumor that yr my mother's sister's cousin's kid. Just a rumor. Moms made me promise to clear it up before we kill all yall, you know?

B: Yr mother's sister's cousin's kid?

A: Yep. True or false?

A

B

B: Yr mom's name Jemimah*?

A: Yeah.

B: Jemimah *Smith?*

A: Smith was her—her before-she-got-married name.

B: Her "maiden" name.

A: Thats right.

B: Jemimah Smith. Dang. "Jemimah" in our language is
_____. *(Choose word suited to you)*

A: _____, then.

B: Aunt _____.

A: Whatever.

B: Come to think of it, you do favor my daddy's great uncle's sister's 2nd cousin.

A: Yr great uncle's granddaddy on yr mother's side?

B: By his 3rd legal wife.

A: Her, I heard stories about.

B: Yeah, she was something.

A: But still family.

B: Yeah, she was family.

A: You favor *her* daddy.

B: You think?

A: His spitting image.

B: Always thought I favored Great-Great Uncle Ben*.

A: Uncle Ben, the rice man! He's worldwide?! He's kin to you?!?

B: I would lie about Uncle Ben?

A: Getoutahere!

B: Im telling the truth, so help me.

A: This is really wow!

B: Cant lie about Uncle Ben and live. Uncle to my sister's grandson's nephew. Yr uncle too?

A: He wrote my name on a piece of rice when I was born!

B: Dang! Mines too!

> The conversation continues. Roll out the relations.
> Riff, scat, freestyle, imagine, dream the bigtime,
> superstar yrself, thats right, farfetch it and go all out.
> Go all over the wall with it. And go on forever.

* If you need to, please feel free to choose yr own version of Jemimah and Ben.

11 YOU CAN SEE THE HOLLYWOOD SIGN FROM HERE

Almost the Writer: You can see the Hollywood sign from here.

Binocular Woman: OH MY GOD! Call in the Wonderville Barbershop Chorus!

Almost the Writer: But the party's over. Shouldnt we have gone home by now?

Binocular Woman: The only way out is *in*, baby.

> 4 Men dressed in striped shirts run in. They sing in harmony.

12 THE ART OF PEACE

> Do not announce the title of this play. Instead, let a Group of
> People play "Telephone" a.k.a. "Whisper Down the Lane."
> The 1st Person begins with a phrase: "The Art of Peace."
> The phrase gets telephoned along until the Last Person says
> some complicated and impossible-to-achieve version
> of what the 1st Person began with.

Last Person: _____?

> The Group of People rests, looks to the ground,
> ashamed that they have been less than successful.

1st Person:
The Art of Peace.
The Peacemaker
has a plan,
but in the Peace
she is in the moment.

13 PLAYING CHOPSTICKS (FATHER COMES HOME FROM THE WARS, Part 7)

A Soldier Dad in an army uniform, like he's just come in
from jungle combat. He's still got a camouflage suit on,
and dark paint covers his face. Maybe even jungle twigs
and branches stick out of his helmet and clothing.
He sits on a campstool, a Kid sits with him.
The Soldier Dad is teaching the Kid to use chopsticks.
They are moving a mountain of rice into another pile,
far across the other side of the stage, making another,
hopefully identical mountain.
The Soldier Dad is great with chopsticks. The Kid is hopeless.
Somewhere offstage someone plays the piano.
Theyre playing "Chopsticks" over and over.

Soldier Dad: You wanted yr dad to bring you back something from
over there. I brought you something, right?

Kid: Right.
(Rest)
Whats "gonorrhea"?

(Rest)

Soldier Dad: Thats something for adults, Kid. Lets stick to our
chopsticks.

Kid: I heard Mom telling Grandmom that you brought her some
"gonorrhea" home from the war.

Soldier Dad
Soldier Dad

Soldier Dad: I brought you something nice and yr acting like you
dont like it, Kid. Here. Watch Dad do it.

Soldier Dad effortlessly picks up a piece of rice
and walks over to the other side of the stage
where he arranges it carefully on the pile.

The Kid watches in awe and anger.

Soldier Dad: The idea is to pick up the rice with the chopsticks, carry it over here and put the rice down. And put it down in such a way as we remake the rice mountain over here.

Kid: Right.

Soldier Dad: Its good practice.

Kid: For what?

Soldier Dad
Kid

> Soldier Dad smacks Kid upside the head.
> The move comes so fast and seemingly out of nowhere.
> Like a flash flood.
> The Kid's head snaps horribly back, but then,
> just as quickly, the Soldier Dad's anger is spent.
> The Kid doesnt cry or anything.

Soldier Dad: Try it again. Go on. You gotta learn it.

> The Kid tries moving the rice with the chopsticks again.

Soldier Dad: Not much better. Ok, a little better, but, watch.

> Soldier Dad moves several pieces of rice, all one at a time,
> very quickly and with great fanfare, talking as he moves them.

Soldier Dad: Soldier Dad can move them quick. Soldier Dad can hold the chopsticks in his right hand and move rice, and he can hold them in his left hand too. Makes no difference. Soldier Dad can hold the sticks behind his back, he doesnt have to look, its just that easy. And every piece of rice gets put in its place!

> The Kid watches with mounting awe and mounting anger.
> Offstage the piano playing gets louder.

Soldier Dad (*Yelling to the offstage piano*)**:** CUT THAT OUT, HUH? HOW AM I SUPPOSED TO FUCKING THINK WITH YOU FUCKING, FUCKING THAT MUSIC UP??!!

> The music stops.

Kid
Soldier Dad

Kid: You want me to try it again?

Soldier Dad: Yr mother used to be a concert pianist.

Kid: You want me to try it again?

Soldier Dad: Yeah. Go ahead.

The Kid tries moving the rice again. He's much better this time—
like a miracle happened—and now he's actually pretty good.

Soldier Dad: Wow! Great job, Kid.

Kid: Thanks.

Soldier Dad: Chip off the old block after all. I was worried. I'd been away for so long and you—you couldnt do the rice thing.
(Rest)
It was the only thing I brought you back and you couldnt do it and I was worried. But you can do it. My Kid's my Kid! Good. So lets get to work, huh?

The music starts up again and the Kid and Soldier Dad
get back to work. Each is amazing at moving the rice.
And they are enjoying themselves. It is horrible to see them
enjoying themselves doing such a pointless task.
But they are building a monument together—
and this monument will be a fortress against the future pain.
And the music, playing all the while, seeps into the walls
of the fortress, seeps in and holds it like stone.

13 (Again) LANDSLIDE

She runs in, grabs a brick, repeatedly hits her head against it.
2 others amble in. They regard her.

1: This isnt a play. Whatchathink?

2: You gonna tell her that?

1: This isnt a play, you!

She stops, regards the 2,
then returns to the head-brick pounding.

14 TOMATOES

A Strongman sits. People come in and throw tomatoes.
He takes it on the chin. They go. He bursts into tears.

15 ALL THE ANSWERS

The Strongman still sitting there although he's no longer crying.
A Speaker comes onstage.
A Crowd listens.

Speaker: Ive got all the answers. Heres a selection:
Learn to say no.
Learn to say yes.
Roll with the punches.
Show up but also
know when to go.
Exercise.
Vote!
Celebrate yr birthdays.
(Rest)
Show up.
Work with whatcha got.

As the lights dim, the Crowd, ceremoniously,
tears the Speaker limb from limb.
The Strongman starts crying again.

16 THE TURKEY VULTURE

3 Birdwatchers with binoculars.

Birdwatcher 1: See the turkey vulture! Whats left over by her is devoured and transformed!

Birdwatcher 2: See how she mutates and digests!

Birdwatcher 3: See how see she takes the poison and turns it into a veritable nectar.

All *(In awe)*: Awe! The turkey vulture! Let her ways be a lesson to us!

An Angry Woman shoots the bird dead.

Angry Woman: Im going to stuff this bird, charge 10 cents a head viewing price, and make me a mint. Any questions?

17 GOODBYE, CHILDREN

Sound of children playing. A Woman waves goodbye.
She waves until she is exhausted. She uses one hand,
then the other, then her arms, then her legs.
Finally she stops waving.
The sound of the children fades into the distance.

Man: Theyve gone.

Woman: Thank God.

Man: Theyll be back. Or others will come, to take their places.

Woman: Less of me will be here to greet them, Im afraid.

Sound of the playing children builds again, getting louder
as the children come nearer. The Woman and Man, horrified,
cover their ears as they resist the urge to flee.

18 FOWL PLAY

A Black Woman Desk Attendant, with an attitude,
working the desk of the Ritz.

Black Woman: I have a reservation.

Black Woman Desk Attendant: No you dont.

Black Woman: My name is—

Black Woman Desk Attendant: We dont have you down.

Black Woman: Im gonna give a speech?

Black Woman Desk Attendant: Would you like to speak with the manager?

Black Woman: Not really—I just want my room.

Black Woman Desk Attendant: Chuh.

Black Woman: Dont suck yr teeth at me.

The Black Woman Desk Attendant looks the Black Woman
up and down several times, then several times more.
Her look has its own special rhythm, like hen-pecking,
only better, or worse—it started sometime just after the fall of
Atlanta during the 1st Civil War when the freed slaves
created a new system to replace the oppressive white one
which at that time was going up in smoke.
You could fill the stage with black women and have them
do this lookover-work-the-neck move.

You could do it to music. Or you could just keep it sad
and fucked-up and simple like it is here.

19 A SCENE FROM THE GREAT OPERA

An endless Line of People.
Each person has some sort of suitcase—a rolling suitcase,
a laptop case, some carry-on stuff. And they walk along—
or stand still, barely moving—like cars going to work on
the 405 in L.A. at 6 a.m., or cars headed on the same highway
but in the opposite direction 8 hours later.
Anyway, the people move along by barely moving.
Opera music comes up: something gorgeous like
Kiri Te Kanawa singing Puccini's "Vissi d'Arte" from *Tosca*.
It gets good and really loud, really full
and swelling and gorgeous, then slowly quiet.
2 Strangers—nothing at all alike—
slowly turn to each other during the Puccini swell.

Stranger 2: Its very beautiful somehow.
Stranger 1: At least its moving.
Stranger 2: Right.

The music grows louder again and the People inch along.

20 BETTER THAN CHITLINS

A Man comes in wet from head to toe.

Wet Man: Do you know that in Mississippi everybody eats chitlins?
Woman: Not everybody.
Wet Man: Yes. Everybody.

The Woman claps time. The Wet Man begins to dance.

Woman: This is awful.
Wet Man: Cant be helped.

The Wet Man realizes that this dance is the endpoint
of his entire life. He goes all out.
It is beautiful and awful, desperate, but all right too, somehow.

21 NOWHERE

A Juggler comes on with a painted smile or lots of lipstick,
a red clown nose, a funny hat, juggling balls or scarves.
But before that or during that, Someone comes on
with a sign that says: "Nowhere." Then a clutch of people
come on. They whip out cricket lighters and light them
like they would at an 80s rock concert.
Maybe an 80s love ballad plays on the radio
or karaoke style far upstage.

22 THE GOOD COOK OF SZECHUAN

Loudmouth: "THE GOOD COOK OF SZECHUAN."

Good Cook of Szechuan: Dont yell it so loud.

Loudmouth: You want people to know, dontcha?

Good Cook of Szechuan: Im in bed.

Loudmouth: Its Friday night and I get paid on how many people
come through that door. Shit I shoulda known there was a catch.
"Just stand here and yell it," the Rich Lady said. And those
rings she had on. Theyre real diamonds. And that dress she was
wearing—pure silk. And that fur, slung so devil-may-care across
her shoulder. Shit. I come from the north. Do you know how cold
it is up there. Everybody's dick gets frostbit. Thats how cold.
And a fur like she was wearing. We would kill for that. And
I thought of killing the Rich Lady, taking her fur, and, ok, her
diamonds too, and her silk dress for my mother—wouldnt my
mother be amazed when she sees me coming home with that
dress. And then the shame that would follow, cause Mama would
know I'd stolen it—we are an honest people, us northerners.
Cold, but honest.
(Rest)
Its Friday night. Yr the Good Cook of Szechuan. You gotta get up
and cook, huh?

Good Cook of Szechuan: Leave me be, you loud poor person! Im in
bed with my whore!

Loudmouth: "A penny a head," the Rich Lady says she'll pay me.
And Im thinking, "Easy money." I shoulda known.

Good Cook of Szechuan: Even when you talk regular you sound loud.
You got a problem, you know that? And with all that loudmouthing
yr doing, guess what? All yr loudmouthing's making it impossible
to have my fun in here, get it?

Loudmouth: Yr the Good Cook of Szechuan. There are people depending on you tonight. People are coming from all over to eat here. If yr not up and cooking, there will be—long faces.

Good Cook of Szechuan: Im going to long yr face!

> The Good Cook of Szechuan leaps from his bedchamber and, as his whore watches, he runs around the room chasing the Loudmouth with a cooking instrument that can also double as a weapon. Like a big knife, or a cast-iron skillet. He runs around and around and finally he catches the Loudmouth. The Good Cook of Szechuan holds the weapon aloft, and the Loudmouth shivers in fear.

Good Cook of Szechuan: Cutie Pie?

Cutie Pie: What now?

Good Cook of Szechuan: Hold this for me.

> Cutie Pie, his paid-for lover, comes out of the bedchamber and holds the cooking tool-weapon while the Good Cook of Szechuan rapes the Loudmouth. He finishes up, then he and Cutie sit on the bed and smoke. Loudmouth pulls himself together.

Loudmouth:
The Good Cook is not a good person.
So, just because a man is kind,
does not mean he can cook.
And, just because a man can cook,
does not mean he is kind.
Goodness in one area
does not translate into goodness in another.
Although, especially these days,
we wish it would.
Yes, especially these days,
we wish for more good.

23 FRIES WITH THAT

> 2 women sit eating French fries.

1st Woman: How long's it been?

2nd Woman: Long.

1st Woman: Should we be talking?

2nd Woman: I dunno.

1st Woman: What were you thinking?

> 2nd Woman shrugs and eats fries by 2s and 3s.

1st Woman: I mean, really—what were you thinking?

> 1st Woman joins in the fry eating.

2nd Woman: I was lonesome.

1st Woman: And he was married.

2nd Woman: And he was married.

1st Woman: And he was married to me.

2nd Woman: Yeah.

> A Man walks onstage. He is either on fire or
> theres a lot of smoke coming off him.
> He holds a long extension cord.

Man: Can we go home now?

1st Woman: No.

> The Women keep eating. The Man keeps smoking.
> 1st Woman gives 2nd Woman a look, like: "Yr next."
> 2nd Woman takes up extension cord. Fade to black.

24 SUPERSIZE

> A Signer stands holding an enormous sign advertising
> something ridiculous, like: "Migrants for Sale,"
> "Own Yr Own Slave" or "Right Here, Right Now,
> Get Yr Chance to Win a New—" (the sign cuts off).

Man: You been working long?

Signer: Forever.

Man: Today? How long today?

Signer: Just a few hours, man, but it feels like forever.

Man: I know the feeling, I know the feeling.

> People and cars pass by
> and the Signer angles the sign for all to see.

Man: Yr 9 to 5?

Signer: 7 to 6.

Man: Shit.

Signer: It pays good. And it helps me, you know, bulk up my arms. And the wife cant say Im not working right?

Man: Tell you what Im gonna do. Im gonna go over to the place and buy whatever theyre selling and say if it hadnt been for you, the Sign Guy on the corner of 3rd and Figueroa, I wouldnt be buying.

Signer: Yr all right.

Man: Ima buy a lot.

Signer: Yr the best.

Man: Its the least I can do, man, cause you deserve it, right?

Signer: —I guess.

Man: Ok!

> The Man goes. The Signer stays on the job. People pass, most dont even glance at his sign.

25 I COULDA DONE THAT

> A huge amount of noise. City sounds and somebody playing the gamelan and somebody singing an opera aria and a jet plane taking off and a mom yelling at her 10 kids and CNN going full blast and army guys sounding off. The Author, promoting her book at a little measly table. She looks very calm. People walk past. No one notices her. Suddenly an Old Friend stops by. The Author pushes a button and the noise stops.

Old Friend: Sign my book?

Author: Sure.

(Rest)

Old Friend: Thats yr signature?

Author: Yeah.

Old Friend: I coulda done that.

Author: Then why didnt you?

Author
Old Friend

Old Friend: Dont you recognize me?

Author: From—Cleveland?

Old Friend: "From Cleveland?" Jeez. Cleveland? You know me from back in the day. From school.

Author: Right. From school. I remember now. Hows it going?

Old Friend: Great. But not as great as you. Tell me. How did you get to be so wise? I mean, back in the day, you were just—average.

Author: What can I tell you.

Old Friend: Tell me how you did it.

Author: Did what?

Old Friend: Come on, you got the world at yr feet. I mean—Im exaggerating, but, you gotta admit, you got it together, you got it going on, you got to admit, you got it, right?

Author: I guess.

Old Friend: So how did you get it? Come on. I knew you back in the day. We're old pals—I mean—we knew each other way back when, right? Someone coming upon us right now and hearing how we took some of the same classes—theyd believe we were old friends, right? So give yr old friend the inside scoop, huh?

Author: I'd tell you but then I'd have to kill you.

Old Friend: You were always such a kidder.

Author: Not anymore Im not.

Old Friend: So tell me. Im desperate.

Author: Ok. Its simple. I just listen.

Old Friend: "You just listen"! Brilliant. Im gonna use that, ok?

Author: Ok.

> The Old Friend exits joyously. But as she does,
> the Author snaps her fingers, alerting an Executioner Guy
> (traditional black hood and big axe). At a pretty fast clip,
> the Executioner Guy hurries after the Old Friend.
> The Author presses the button, restarting the enormous noise.

26 MY FATHER WAS A FAMOUS MOTHER

> Rachel walks in with a paper bag.

Hank: Where the hell you been?

Rachel: Out spending yr hard-earned money, where the hell do you think Ive been?

> Hank watches Rachel walk around with her bag. She's pregnant.
> Its love or something like it.

Hank: How much you spend?

Rachel: Yr gonna cry when the bill comes in the mail.

Hank: Did you get my beer?

Rachel: Nope.

(Rest)

Hank: I was thinking about Pop.

(Rest)

Rachel: Pop? What Pop? Yr pop? Yr father?

Hank: Thats right. My father. My father was a famous mother. And the more I thought of Pop, the more I started thinking. You wanna know what I started thinking? I started thinking, I started thinking about taking up a life of crime. Give Junior an old man his friendsll be scared of. Give Junior a mother like my father gave me.

Rachel: You promised me you wouldnt.

Hank: Im breaking my promise.

Rachel: Yr a jerk, Hank.

Hank: Im a 2-bit CPA!

Rachel: But yr honest and good and clean and you dont have to watch yr back, and when yr head hits the pillow at night, Hank, its a white pillow, not a black one.

Hank: But you treat me cruel.

Rachel: Its just my nature. I was a tramp when you met me. Getting the tramp out of my blood is gonna take some time. Hey, you know I love you, Hank.

Hank: Do you think Junior will look up to me?

Rachel: Oh, Hank. Yr an honest Joe, Hank. And Junior will love you. Of course he will.

> They embrace. He puts his hand on her belly even though
> they both know that the unborn child isnt his.
> Music swells underneath. Its well-fed, nourishing,
> 1950s tv music full of solid Nuclear American Family Values.

27 BOOTS

> 2 Men sit in an airport. One wears boots. People pass by
> in a hurry. Each stops briefly glancing at the Man's boots,
> then continues on.

Various People in a Hurry:
Nice boots.
Nice boots.
Nice boots.
Nice boots.

(Rest)

Boot Man: You like my boots?
2nd Man: Yr what? Yr *boobs?*
Boot Man: My boots.
2nd Man: Theyre—"nice."
Boot Man: You gotta get yrself some—
2nd Man: Im not the type.
Boot Man: And a hat and a rope and a horse to go with it.
2nd Man: You think?
Boot Man: Itll give you confidence. With the ladies. You know what Im talking about?

2nd Man
2nd Man
2nd Man

(Rest)

2nd Man: Yeah. *(Sigh)*

28 EL FÉNIX

Great fanfare—symphony and kettledrums, etc.

El Fénix: I am El Fénix!

The curtain comes down.

(Rest)

Writer: Not enough, I guess.

Writer scribbles, passes paper to the waiting hand of El Fénix.
Curtain rises, fanfare again.

El Fénix:
I am El Fénix, see my wings!
HARK!
The Herald Angel sings!

The curtain comes down. Wild applause. A Small Child from the Village presents El Fénix with a bouquet of indigenous wildflowers.

29 ARE WE IN BUSINESS OR WHAT?

2 people sit on a park bench.

Man 1: Nice day.
Man 2: You betcha.

They sit and enjoy the day. Suddenly Man 2 puts on a knit cap, tucking in his hair. He puts socks on his hands and double-ties his shoes. He smears his face with vaseline. Looks around.

Man 1: Are we in business or what?
Man 2: Damn straight, man.
Man 1: You never know, huh?
Man 2: Damn straight. You. Never. Know.

30 THE WAR TO END ALL WARS IS ALMOST OVER

A Man and Woman each perform this simultaneously, but are unaware of each other—each vigorously fights with himself/herself, then when the energy is spent:

Man & Woman: Whew.

Each works to catch his/her breath, then, each starts fighting with himself/herself again. Forever. Well, almost forever.

31 WAVE

A Student and a Teacher staring out. Sounds of the sea.

Teacher: What do you see?
Student: Water.
Teacher: Good. What else?
Student: Waves.

Teacher: Whats making the waves?

Student: —. My dad.

Teacher: Yr dad?

Student: He's ill and—today's his birthday. Happy birthday, Dad! God bless you!

Teacher: And he's making waves?

Student: No. God bless him. The water's making the waves. I think.

Teacher: Almost.

Student: The water, but more than the water.

Teacher: Good. The *Everything* makes the waves. We cannot see the Everything, but we can see the water. The water is the part of the Everything that we can see.

(Rest)

You can fight the waves—sure. But you will not win. So its best not to waste yr time and energy fighting it.

Student: So just go with it.

Teacher: Yes.

> The sea sounds grow louder.
> As the Teacher continues to talk she moves
> her hands elegantly. Its clear she's speaking with great wisdom,
> but, alas, we cant hear a word she's saying.

June

1 THE RED BLANKET

> 2 chairs, one has a tiny folded red blanket on it.
> 2 people come to sit. One takes the blanket off the chair.

Other: That was my blanket.

One: No—

Other: It was on my chair.

One: First come first—

Other: BULLSHIT.

> Other grabs One by the throat
> and raises his free hand in the air, making a fist.
> One's hands go to his neck in the universal sign of choking.
> Tableau.

Then, the Peace Dove passes overhead,
and onstage falls another red blanket—
gently and completely from God's grace—as if the red blanket
was one of the Dove's feathers,
which the Dove gracefully discarded as it passed by.
One and the Other watch the blanket descend toward them,
then slowly move from their war tableau
into a double-blanketed tableau, a tenuous peace—
looking like 2 bears listening to
the sounds of winter from a cave.

One: Goodnight.
Other: You too.

2 THE PRESIDENTIAL RACE, CIRCA 1972

3 Men upstage center. They run the 50 yard dash in slow
motion straight downstage. The Black Man wins.
(Did I say there was a Black Man? There is a Black Man,
by the way.) Its like the Olympics. A garland for his head.
Then he takes the Presidential Oath of Office with his Wife
at his side. Someone walks across the stage
with the race tape (the one they broke when they won).
They run the tape through their fingers,
reading it like its a ticker tape fresh from Wall Street.

Writer as a Small Child: When I was a kid I thought the presidential
race was like a race in the Olympics so I couldnt understand
why there werent any black presidents.

3 THE SCRIPT

2 strangers on a bench.

1: Woe is me.
2: Yeah.
1: Shit was out of the blue—
2: Yeah?
1: Yeah.
2: You dont read yr script?

1: My script?

2: Open yr hand. I'll read yr lines.

(Rest)

You grew up in the rough hood. Didnt learn to read. The script.

1: How do you know that about me?

2: Its yr script.

1: You been spying—

2: I see infidelity brewing.

1: Thats my wife yr talking about.

2: Change the script. Its easy.

Palm Reader/Rod Serling: The Reader slices the Nonreader's palm with an enormous knife. Blood spurts everywhere and I mean *everywhere*. Nonreader freaks out. You see, our lifelines are constantly changing. If we could see the change in action it would be as dramatic as this. But then we'd be freaking out and squirting blood everywhere, so the changes present themselves to us in a somewhat lower key. One we can hear. One we can bear hearing. Anyway. Back to scene:

1: *Thanks.*

2: My pleasure.

Palm Reader/Rod Serling: They shake hands. They dont wipe the blood off. They go offstage where they become the best of friends, although, as fate would have it, Reader does in fact end up sleeping with Nonreader's wife.

4 THE COURT OF THE EMPEROR

A Painter paints a tree. The sun rises and sets.
He works without stopping but he does not rush.
At last he is finished. He rings a bell.
The Critic enters and looks at the painting.

Critic: Hmmm.

The Critic looks at the Painter.

Critic: Hmmm.

Painter: Hmmm?

Critic: Hmmm.

The Critic rings another bell and several Critics come onstage.

Chorus of Critics:
We heard a bell most distinctly.
We wanna know
does it ring true?

> They regard the painting for many years.

Painter *(To the audience)*: Some say yes, some say no.

5 THE TRAGEDY OF THE LEAST FAVORITE

Emperor's Wife: I wasnt really his wife. We werent legally married.
Guard: Sorry.
Executioner: I aint got all day, lady.
Emperor's Wife: I was his least favorite. I lived at the foot of his bed.
Guard: Im so sorry.
Emperor's Wife: Like a *dog*!
Executioner: Head on the block, baby, lets go!
Emperor's Wife: You cant.
Guard: If it were up to me, maam—
Executioner: But it aint, is it, pal? Lets hit it and quit it, mamma!
Emperor's Wife: They do not know what theyre doing! Alas!
Guard: Alas!

> She approaches the block with majesty far above
> her lowly birth. Even the Executioner is moved,
> although he tries his best to play it off. She sadly puts her head
> on the block. The Executioner cuts off her head.
> A blue hydrangea sprouts from the trunk of her neck.
> The birds sing.

Guard: We were wrong to blame her! The rebellion against the
emperor was not her fault.
(Rest)
And she left a son!

> The music swells.

Executioner: Next!

6 APPLES AND TREES

Daughter: Mother?

Mother: Yes dear?

Daughter: Theres something out there on the stoop.

Mother: A puppy?

Daughter: A baby looks like.

Mother: Oh dear. Wheres my knitting?

Daughter: Whatcha making this time?

Mother: Another washcloth.

Daughter: For the boys and girls at the front?

Mother: Who else? Whats this world coming to is all I want to know.
(Rest)
Youve lost interest in yr needlepoint.

Daughter: Tv's more fun.

Mother: Whats the world coming to is all I wanna know. Next thing youll wanna do is go outside and get that baby.

Daughter: Can I?

Mother: Could be a bomb.

Daughter: Yr right.

Daughter turns on tv. Mother knits.

7 SOFA SCENES

3 chairs together like a sofa. Someone walks in with a sign that reads: "Imagine a Sofa." A 2nd someone enters with another sign reading: "Imagine the Sofa Converts into a Bed." A 3rd someone walks in with a sign that says: "Imagine the Sofa Bed Stained in Blood." Downstage lights come up quickly. Ma and Pa testify:

Ma: He didnt even know her.

Pa: I could almost understand the crime if he knew her. But he didnt—

Ma: He didnt even know her. As God is my witness.

The Son comes onstage with a noose around his neck. A Signholder's new sign: "Imagine the Son Killing Himself After Murdering a Girl that He Didnt Even Know." Ma and Pa look and then look away.

Lights out.

8 THE BOSS OF EVERYTHING

4 Servants come in.

Most Senior: He hasnt been himself.
2nd Senior: Really?
Most Senior: Its hard to say.
3rd Senior: Its not hard to say, but it is hard to watch.
4th Senior: Here he comes.

They blow great fanfare on kazoos.

Most Senior: Behold! The Boss of Everything!
Boss: Gimmie da map.
Most Senior: Sir?
Boss: What, you dont got ears no more? Da map, da map, da map.
Most Senior: You are remarkably Italian today, sir.
2nd Senior: Heres the map of the world, sir!
3rd & 4th Senior: Allow us to unroll it.
Boss: Im the Boss of Everything.

Astronomer rushes in.

Astronomer: Ive just discovered a new—WOW—look!

They all look. Theyre filled to the brim with awe and wonder.

Boss: Im the Boss of that too!

A Group of Folks enters. One of them is a Bear.

Boss: What?
Group of Folks: We're the next play.
Boss: Well, Im not through yet.

His Servants leave.

Boss: Ive got a whole epic ahead of me—

Boss
Group of Folks

Boss: Shit.

He stands there. The next play begins.

9 STAR SEARCH

The Group of Folks from yesterday's play
still lounges around with the Boss.

Headman: Come on, lets get going. That means you leave.

Boss: I aint moving.

Headman: Fine. *We'll* split then.

They go. An Older Woman from the Group remains.
She lights up a cigarette, looks bored. The Bear remains.
Boss remains too, looking up at the bright lights.

Boss: When I was a kid all I wanted to be was famous. Good-looking,
tall, talented—forget it. Just famous is all I really wanted.
I would go outside at night on our street, there was this one
street lamp and I would stand there underneath it grinning.
Pretending I was a star. My mother would yell—

Mother *(Yelling)*: Get the hell offstage, you loser.

Boss exits, pursued by the Bear.

10 SAFEGUARDING THE PRIME MINISTER OF GRENADA

2 Secret Service Agents.

1st Agent: All clear.

2nd Agent: Thats a roger.

1st Agent: We're ready for the prime minister.

They stand in readiness.
After a moment, a Secret Service Agent
with an open umbrella comes in.
After him enters a Woman with a Baby in her arms. They wait.
Someone enters playing music.

Woman: Where is the double?

1st Agent: On its way.

A Double Woman comes in with an identical Baby
and Umbrella Agent.

1st Agent: Lets move out.

Woman: Its not easy running a country. You do yr best to get elected. Do you know how many hands Ive glad-handed. And I spend my term in disguise because—well there are lots of reasons. Most of them I dont understand. And, well—

Double Woman: The People.

Woman: The People.

Agents: The People.

Woman: The People want to blow my head off.

> They walk. Sniper shots ring out. They all hit the deck
> and crawl offstage. The 1st Umbrella Agent crawls off,
> still holding the umbrella aloft.

11 WATERGATE

> 2 Old Black Men sit on a porch.

Friend: How longs it been?

Guard: Long.

Friend: 20 years?

Guard: More than that.

Friend: Sure, 20 years ago Wilbert was born and it was before Wilbert.

Guard: 20 years ago I was a good-looking man.

Friend: You aint ugly or nothing.

Guard: Uh-huhn.

(Rest)

Back then in the day I could see in the dark practically.

Friend: Like a possum.

Guard: Yeah. And I walked around—I was working my rounds—

Friend: I heard this story before.

Guard: You got something better to say?

Friend: I think Alberta's gonna gimmie some time of day.

Guard: Alberta?

Friend: You heard me.

Guard: She aint gonna give you no kinda time of day.

Friend: She been smiling at me.

Guard: She been smiling at everybody. On account of the new teeth she got, not on account of no time she gonna give you.

Friend: Woulda been sweet.

Guard: Thats yr whole problem. Here I am talking about History— Capital H—and not just talking about it like you talk about something you seen on the tv. What I strolled up to on that night in that Watergate building, what I discovered, turned the whole nation upside down and all you talking about is getting some time with Alberta.

Friend: Forget Alberta. I got Clara on my mind now.

Guard: You can have Georgia on yr mind for all I care, but you aint getting none. Most you can get with that worm you got tween yr legs is a fish.

> Friend catches a fish.

Guard: He's too small to eat, give him a chance to grow.

Friend: Yeah.

> The Friend throws the fish back in.

12 SHOW ME THE WEAPONS OF MASS DESTRUCTION

> Mother crochets, Father eyeballs a girlie magazine,
> Sonny watches tv.

Father: Look at them things she's got, huh?

Mother: Theyre fakes.

Father: Yeah but still.

> Mother looks at the magazine.

Mother: That *girl* is Larry Carlton.

Father: The guy who used to mow our lawn?

Mother: Yep. He got a sex change.

Father: He mowed our lawn for 12 years. Wow—they did a good job.

Mother: The rhododendron hasnt been the same since he left. I think its in mourning.

Father: In mourning? Its a plant.

Mother: So I'll shut up. Look—on the tv. Theyre about to show us weapons of mass destruction.

> The Family eagerly watches tv. Upstage, with great ceremony,
> a Man unveils a great pile of nothing.

Sonny: Daddy, whats a hypocrite?

Father: Mother?

Mother: A hypocrite is someone who says one thing and does something else.

Sonny: Like the president.

Father: Sonny!   **Mother:** Oh dear.

> Mother begins to weep.

Father: Theyre not coming to get him. Dont cry, Mother. If they were coming to get him, they woulda been here already.

> Slow fade. As the lights go down
> the Family grows increasingly nervous.

13 IN THE AIR OVER LOS ANGELES

> 2 Businessmen in first-class.

Harold: Look, theres my house.

Joe: Impressive.

Captain (*From the cockpit*): We'll be on the ground in about 10 minutes. Thanks for choosing us and we hope to see you next time. Flight attendants please prepare for landing.

Harold: Its been nice getting to know you, Joe.

Joe: Call me Joey.

Harold: Joey, I feel like Ive made a friend.

Joe: Likewise.

Harold: You think?

Joe: I can see yr house from the air, thats something.

Harold: If you could see my wife from the air would that be something?

Joe: She'd be big.

Harold: She is big. Spiritually.

Joe: Right.

Stewardess: Tray tables up, please.

Harold: Ever cheat?

Joe: At cards?

Harold: On yr wife.

Joe: Im not married.

Stewardess: Seat backs and foot rests up, please.

Harold: But if you were, wouldja?

Joe: If the South had won the war, would I be sitting in first-class right now?

Harold: I dont follow you, Joey.

Joe: Too many ifs, Harold, too many ifs.

14 THE KINGDOM OF THIS WORLD

> A golden folding chair or maybe just a folding chair
> with a sign that says: "Golden" on it. A Woman enters and sits.
> She has the air of a superior being. She is also very very old.
> She is the Kingdom. As she speaks she does needlework:
> something allowing her to work with great precision
> and create long elaborate gestures—
> but it should be clear that she is sewing something.

Kingdom: Might as well get started. Dont have as much time as before. When the world was young! Youve heard that phrase before Im sure. Its a lie—yes—one of the lies. Yes. The world was never young. Not "young" in our sense of the word, no the world was never *unknowing*. And I should know, because Im one of the old ones. Oh, put away yr swords there! Its just a remark. God, you cant even make a remark these days without them reaching for their swords. And if you dont shout out quickly enough, say if you say the right thing but in the wrong way, I mean, in such a way that it sounds like the wrong thing, and they mishear you and you dont see them draw their swords—say yr reading a book or preparing a very important genetic experiment which requires both eyes on the petri dish—. Do you know that those twins joined at the head are still alive? Grown adults. Still joined. They must have some amazing thoughts, those 2. Incredible isnt it? Although—well dont mean to speak against the New Order, but, I wanna say, but I wont say. It wouldnt be smart. Things are dangerous these days. What with the Swordsmen running about. Say yr speaking and eating yr supper. Say you just speak yr mind, and yr mind has wrong things in it and so there you go, youve said something wrong and you dont have time to apologize, you dont have time to take it back, take it back and call off the Swordsmen, and before you know it—its yr head on yr platter and yr still going on automatic like those headless chickens and, so, yr still eating, and you—reach down with yr fork and knife to eat yr next bite, and yr head is on the platter and so you cut into yr own head, and taste yr own flesh.

The lights begin to fade.

Kingdom: The lights will go out before I finish. I used to run this place. All of it. Everyone knew my name.
(Rest)
When I was a child, God came to me: "Now?" or "Later?" God asked. "Now," I said. And he unfolded to me the kingdom of this world. And, let me tell you, it was good.

The speech should continue less and less audibly, perhaps continuing long enough to reach underneath the end of the 365th play, as the lights fade. For the full text of Kingdom's speech, see Appendix A, which has, unfortunately, been cut out by the Swordsmen.

14 (Again) HOMECOMING FOREVER

Lights up slowly as the Homecoming Queen waves.
Lights peak, then begin a slow fade.

Homecoming Queen: I thought this was "Homecoming Forever." Forever is, like, at least another 5 minutes, right?

Her smile is very bright, but her days are numbered.
Her whole life is about this moment and, after its all over,
she's going to seed.

15 THE GREAT WAVE OFF KANAGAWA

A Line of People stretch stageleft to stageright.
They do a wave like theyre saying hi, then a wave
like at a sports game. The Great Wave comes onstage,
perhaps we see a projection of Hokusai's painting,
The Great Wave Off Kanagawa.

The Great Wave: Im The Great Wave Off Kanagawa as painted by Hokusai himself. Im big and wet and misunderstood. Scholars say, in the original painting, that the frightening tentacles of the wave put the world in peril. But as I look at the painting and see myself, I see myself only waving. I am only saying hello and goodbye. Take it from me, The Great Wave himself, no matter what the scholars say. Also, to my mind, the painting is not about the wave at all. The painting is really about Mt. Fuji's ability to remain calm and immobile in the background especially with all the waving chaos of the world in its face.

> Wavers smile and keep waving. Lights out.

16 BLOOM

> A Man sits in a chair. He's thin and white and wearing glasses.

Penelope: Bloom!
Bloom: I cannot.
Penelope: But the people—

> Penelope opens the door, we hear the roar of the sea.

Penelope: —the people, they insist.

> The roar of the sea turns into applause. Bloom—
> pulled by the applause as a flower is pulled by the sun—turns,
> moving toward the door. For a moment, the applause morphs
> into some classical choir music. Onward moves Bloom.
> As he reaches the doorway, the sound turns back into
> applause, and then back into the sound of the sea.
> The whole effect is wondrous and a little sad.
> As Bloom cranes his neck toward the sound, a bucket of water
> comes splashing indoors, soaking his face.

17 GOD'S EYE IS ON THE SPARROW

> 2 people—a Believer and a Nonbeliever.

Believer: What you got there, you nonbeliever you?
Nonbeliever: None of yr business.
Believer: Lemmie see. Come on. *(Sees)* Fall on yr knees!
Nonbeliever: Get up, fraud.
Believer: Its the Dove of Peace!
Nonbeliever: You think?
Believer: Believe!

Nonbeliever: Im an atheist.

Believer: Believe!

Nonbeliever: I think its just a sparrow. It fell from the nest up there.

Believer: Oh.

Nonbeliever: Gimmie a boost, I'll put it back.

Believer: Yr going to re-nest the fallen sparrow?

Nonbeliever: Gimmie a boost, and I'll give it a try.

> Believer gives Nonbeliever a boost. Nonbeliever re-nests
> the fallen Sparrow. The Sparrow's Parents, Father
> with a Pipe and Mother Wearing an Apron, welcome him back.
> The Sparrow grows into a fine young man and leads our country
> into a future where, instead of being a nation of fat thieves,
> we are a nation of true and guiding lights. While this happens,
> a Gospel Choir, or maybe just a Gospel Singer, appears.
> They sing a version of "His Eye Is on the Sparrow."
> Maybe all this is too much to ask for. Maybe they just re-nest
> the Sparrow and theres a nice light change.

18 FATHER COMES HOME FROM THE WARS (Part 8)

> Mother stares out toward the audience into space.
> Father enters dragging an enormous bloody sword.

Father: Im home.

Mother: At last.

Father: Yes.

(Rest)

Mother: Where were you?

Father: The wars.

Mother: And then?

Father: Lost.

Mother: Oh.

Father: Where are the children?

Mother: Grown up and moved away.

Father: Oh.

> Sounds of the sea in the near distance.

19 **REMEMBER JUNETEENTH**

>   Writer and a Woman sit. Writer turns to the Woman.

Writer: Who are you?

Woman: The character for yr next play.

Writer
Woman

Woman: That was a joke. Yr not laughing.

Writer: Who are you?

Woman: Im yr biggest fan.

Writer: Yr in my house. You just walked in and I dont know you.

Woman: Im yr biggest fan.

Writer
Woman

>   At that very moment, the stage is flooded
> with recently freed slaves. Hundreds of thousands of people,
> most of African descent, but others, from other slave systems.
>   They run joyously, toward freedom.

Woman: Who the heck are they?

Writer: Theyre freed slaves. Today's Juneteenth and theyre free.
Like me.

Woman: Wow. Can I have yr autograph?

Writer: No. Not today.

Woman: Oh, ok. Do you think theyll let me join them?

Writer: Feel free.

>   After a moment, the Woman feels free. She happily joins with
> the Juneteenth crowd. A version of this is always happening.
>   Everywhere and forever.

20 **QUIVER**

>   A Woman with an enormous bow (the bow and arrow kind)
>   selects and shoots arrow after arrow.
>   Finally, her Servant creeps up behind her.

Servant: Madam?

The Woman is still drawing bows and aiming and shooting.

Woman: What is it?

Servant: Yr quiver is empty.

Woman: Ah. Well. No matter.

Servant: But, madam—

> Another Servant rushes in with a target struck with a 100 perfect bull's-eyes (or with a tomato red pincushion with hundreds of steel-headed pins in it).

2nd Servant: She's a perfect shot—all bull's-eyes—unlike any seen anywhere.

Woman: Tell the king. And tie my servant to the target.

Servant: Have mercy.

Woman: Mercy?

Servant: Please?

Woman: Not today.

> The Servant allows himself to be tied to the target.

21 PAPER TOMATOES

> A Strongman strides in. Sits on a crate. Immediately People come in and throw wads of paper at him. This goes on for quite some time. Then they leave. He sits there.

Strongman
Strongman

(Rest)

> He uses all his strength to hold back his tears.

22 BACK IN THE DAY

> 2 Workers come in cleaning up the paper wads.

1st: Back in the day they used to throw real tomatoes.

2nd: Get outa here!

1st: No really.

2nd: Real tomatoes? Get outa here.

1st: Im telling you. Real tomatoes and—if you hung around after it was all over, the Strongman let loose and blubbered like a baby.

2nd: Who the fuck are you, huh?

1st: Im just telling you.

2nd: Telling me, telling me what? That there was *real* tomatoes and that the Strongman blubbered?!? Huh? Yr trying to ruin things, huh? Things aint bad enough, you gotta make them worse.

1st: Im just telling you how it was.

2nd: And Im gonna tell you how it is.

> The 2nd Worker begins beating the 1st savagely.
> The 1st Worker is caught off-guard, protects himself
> as best he can, but it is clear that the 2nd Worker wont stop
> until the 1st is dead.

23 ARE WE THERE YET?

> A Lady and Gentleman sit in chairs. A Servant on either side
> holds a candelabra. A Musician Servant enters with a violin
> (or a sign that says: "Violin" and a recording of some violin
> music like Paganini). 4 more Servants enter. 2 carry covered
> plates, the other 2 tuck napkins under the Lady
> and Gentleman's chins, then feed them.

Gentleman: Hmmm?

Lady: Hmm.

Gentleman: Nice enough?

Lady: Hm.

Gentleman: Hm?

Lady: Of course its nice.

Gentleman
Lady

Gentleman: Yr not happy.

Lady: Dont be silly.

Gentleman: Yr not happy I can tell. "Hmm. Hm." I can tell yr not happy.

Lady
Lady

(Rest)

Lady: Different food.
1st Feeding Servant: Yes, Lady.
Lady: The Gentleman too.
2nd Feeding Servant: Yes, Lady.
Lady: And more light and different music.
Musician Servant: Horns?
Lady: Whatever.

> All Servants exit in a hurry. The Lady and Gentleman
> are left in quiet, foodless, darkness.

Gentleman: Would you like me to go too?
Lady: Not at all.
Gentleman: What then?
Lady: Just be quiet. And hold my hand.

> They sit there quietly holding hands. It lasts for a moment
> before the Servants rush in again with the food, lights, music.
> As they get going again the lights fade.

24 HAT TRICK

> A Woman walks onstage. She carries a hatbox.
> She glances around as if she's afraid of being followed
> or caught or seen. She opens the hatbox and removes the hat
> with great care. It could be a baseball hat or a woolen hat.
> She places the hat on her head. She breaks into a smile.
> Suddenly a Mob runs onstage. They are a bloodthirsty bunch.
> They stop and stare.

Mob
Woman
Mob

Mob: Nice hat.

> The Woman shrinks from them.

Mob: Nice hat.
Woman: Have pity.

They surround her. She removes her hat and offers it to them.
They are satisfied. They smile and breathe and one by one
try on the hat—grabbing it from each other when its their turn.
The Woman, when the coast is clear, runs off.

25 INTERFERENCE

A young Woman walks in and turns on a flashlight.

Great Father *(From offstage)*: Hows the coast?
Woman: The coast is clear.
Great Father: You sure?
Woman: Come on in, Great Father.
Great Father: Have you checked the corners?

The Woman stands there, then goes offstage. In a quick moment
she returns leading the Great Father. He's old but sprightly.
She places him near the flashlight.

Great Father: My chair.
Woman: I'll get it.

She goes off and returns with a milk carton. He sits on it.

Woman: Warm yrself.
Great Father: You call this a fire?
Woman: Its all we have.
Great Father: Its not even warm!
Woman: Lower yr voice.
Great Father: I will not lower my voice! I will—

Suddenly the lights go up very bright. Fun dance music is heard
and a swarm of Chorus Boys and Girls dance across the stage
as if they are from the final big number
of a very successful Broadway musical.
They dont even notice the Woman and Great Father.
But the Woman and Great Father notice them.
The Chorus is gone as fast as they came.

Woman
Great Father

(Rest)

Woman: What was that?
Great Father: Interference. It happens. You all right?

(Rest)

Woman: No.

> Lights fade.

26 MORE INTERFERENCE

> Chorus Boys and Girls from yesterday's play
> come onstage. Theyre trying out for a musical
> so theyve all got numbers pinned to their chests.
> There is a Dancemaster with a whip and an Elegant Ballerina
> with a clipboard. Both walk around,
> sometimes conferring with each other.

Dancemaster: 5-6-7-8!

> The Chorus Boys and Girls dance wildly.
> This should resemble salmon spawning.
> The Great Father and Woman walk in. The have walked
> a long way. They are weary. They walk straight through
> the dance routine, oblivious to it, ruining it.
> 2 of the Audience Members, who sit downfront,
> begin yelling at each other.

1st Audience Member: I thought you said you paid the bill.
2nd Audience Member: Fuck you!
1st Audience Member: Fuck you? I'll show you fuck you.

> She raises her fist.

2nd Audience Member: Not in public, huh?

(Rest)

> The Great Father and the Woman have moved on.
> The Dancers continue dancing, and then are eliminated,
> one by one. The Audience now sits onstage, facing out.

1st Audience Member: Whew.

2nd Audience Member: That was close.

1st Audience Member: Wheres the snacks?

2nd Audience Member: Right here. That was close huh?

1st Audience Member: Very.

2nd Audience Member: Love me?

1st Audience Member: Always.

> They eat and watch, looking out at us as if watching tv.
> The Dancers dance glamorously behind them.

27 BUCK

> A Man with a sign that says: "Buck." He looks as if he just needs
> directions, or that he needs to return some gadget that he paid
> a lot of money for, which is broken now soon after purchase.
> He approaches several different People, each pointing him to
> another. He walks from one to the next. After a moment he is
> moving, darting, scurrying from one to the next. The Scholars
> come toward us and explain things:

1st Scholar:
Ever notice how,
in this country especially,
the buck gets passed?
Its his fault
no his,
not mine,
speak to that one,
not me.
And so on.

2nd Scholar: Theres a tale about a buck, you know, a wild male
deer. This buck smelled a sweet scent and, searching for the
source of this scent, ran around in the woods, running himself
to death only to discover, with his last breath, that the scented
sought-after thing was himself.

> The Man continues scurrying to and fro as lights fade.

28 MY USED TO BE

Man: Here we were back in the day.
Dealer: That really you?
Man: Who else?
Dealer: How much you want for it?
Man: Just some applause.
Dealer: "Just"? I'll give ya 200 bucks.
Man: Nope. Applause.
Dealer: I could get locked up—
Man: I'll go elsewhere.
Dealer: Wait. Gimmieuhminute.
(Rest)
How loud you want it?
Man: You got 5 folks back there. I see them. I want 5 folks worth.
All 2-handed, of course.

(Rest)

Dealer: 4 folks.
Man: 5 or I walk.

Dealer
Dealer

(Rest)

Dealer: Come on out.

> The Folks come out and begin applauding for the Man,
> who drinks it in like water from the desert.

29 3 USES OF GRAVITY

Number 1

> 1st Man and 1st Woman, each with a feather.

1st Woman: Ready, set—go!

> They drop their feathers and cheer them on
> as the feathers race to the floor.

Number 2

> 2nd Woman sits in her own world.
> 2nd Man circles her—moon around the sun.
> She doesnt notice him. He trips, falls horribly. Gets up.

2nd Man: Im in love.

2nd Woman: Im with a guy and he's better-looking than you. He's got more than 2 dollars and he's got a car, but you can keep looking at me like you been, cause it makes me feel pretty.

Number 3

> 3rd Woman and 3rd Man sit solemnly.

3rd Woman: Weve been together for so long.

3rd Man: And we'll be together forever.

3rd Woman: Even though its over. We're over.

> They laugh sadly.
> Lights out.

30 $1 FOR GAS

> Poorman with a gas can.

Poorman: You got a dollar for gas?

> The Poorman shall repeat this question as many times as he can manage with total sincerity, until 2 Women come along.

Poorman: You got a dollar?

Moneybags: You got a ride?

Poorman: Im working on the ride. I figure I'll get the gas hooked up and then I'll get the ride together. You got a dollar for gas?

Moneybags: Give him a roll.

Sidekick: Maybe he dont take pennies.

Moneybags: He takes pennies. He's poor. You take pennies?

Poorman: Yeah, I guess.

Moneybags: Give him a roll.

Sidekick gives Poorman a roll of a 100 pennies.
Poorman tips his hat and runs off.

Sidekick: He'll just spend it on drugs.

Moneybags: Maybe he needs drugs. Hell, maybe I need drugs. The way things are these days.

Offstage, Poorman parlays his roll of pennies into a million bucks and lives an offstage version of the American Dream.

July

1 WESTWARD HO

A Man walks along. He is frightened of his surroundings but still he walks. He drops balled-up paper, very deliberately, as he goes. He exits. Birds swoop down and read his papers, then eat them. They fly away. The Man comes back.

Man *(To God)*: I left bits of paper to mark my path. Paper instead of bread crumbs. I thought you said they didnt eat paper.

A Stranger comes in.

Stranger: Walk this way, I think.

They walk off in the wrong direction.
Dont worry, it could just be part of the plan.

2 THE ELECTROCUTIONER'S DAUGHTER

A Man wearing a striped shirt, his hands are tied. He speaks slowly. He's got a lot to say but he's taking his time.

Man: . . . Just as well, he thought. Just as well. That he had no sense of smell. Just as well. Born with it. Or. Without it. Born without it more accurate. In all his years of living he hadnt found anyone who knew what it was called. He asked his doctor. His doctor was—not what he would call competent. He was a Northerner, not a Yankee exactly but . . .

From offstage left comes a cane—the hook-em-offstage kind.
It creeps up during the above. It skips around the Man.
Pulls. No luck.
Daughter comes out. She's a scrawny gal
wearing a cotton print dress and a black hood.

Daughter: Come on.

Man: Is it my time?

Daughter: Nope. Its just supper.

Man: My last supper?

Daughter: Nope. Not by my paperwork.

Man: Oh. Wheres—my electrocutioner?

Daughter: Pop? Pops eating his supper. You can eat with him. I got a place set for you.

Man
Daughter

(Rest)

Daughter: Its suppertime. Come on.

She hooks him like Bo Peep would and hauls him off.

3 THEIR BETTERS

A Group of Kin, hopeless and lonely, huddles together.
A Man strides in. He sings his lines sounding kinda like
Paul Robeson, enchanting the people.

Man: Ive been to the mountaintop where the grass is green and full, and the air is clean and cool and thin. Let us go and live there, My Kin!

Kin
Kin

Kin:
Youve only been to the hilltop!
You aint never been to no mountain.
All you know is hills!
You been to hilltops, we'll grant you that,
but to think that mountaintops

and hilltops
is one and the same
and to come down here and
enchant us with the talking of it.
No wonder we're as bad off as we are!

Kin
Man

Man: The hills I know are large. I took them for their betters.
Where are the mountains?

The Kin point in many directions and then their pointing resolves
itself into a single direction, full of purpose and promise.
The Man rips his clothing, tears his hair. After he's spent his
anger and pain, he gets up and then purposefully walks
in the direction theyre pointing.

4 THE KING'S HEAD

A Large Crowd—each person wears a number, folded,
not visible. Every so often one of them peeks through a curtain.

572: What are you?
613: In the 600s.
312: Yr lucky. They started at one.
1636: Its random. Its all at random.
719: 1-2-3-4-5-6-7-8: random?
1636: 1-2-3-4-5-6-7-8-397: random.

(Rest)

572: Random or not, whatever it is, it looks bad.

A great shout offstage, sound of the chopping block
and cheers.

613: Is he dead?
572: Looks that way.
1636: All I ever was, was his bowler. He loved bowling.

A Child comes in carrying a burlap bag.

Child: 1636.

1636: My turn?

Child: No, sir. His head, sir. For you, sir.

1636: His head?!?! My God!

Child: It was his will, sir.

312: Take it. It was his will.

613: Its said to have magical powers.

572: Turn folks into stone, it can.

1636: Fiddlesticks.

Child: Enjoy it, sir. It was his will, sir.

> 1636 takes the burlap bag and hugs it close.
> Another sound of a chopping block. More cheers.

5 BOWLING

> A Woman, Sadie, with a bowling ball bag, walks past 1636,
> who holds the king's head in the burlap bag.

1636: Where are you going?

Sadie: Bowling.

1636: Dressed like that?!

1636
1636

(Rest)

Sadie: I won a trophy last year, remember?

1636: Has that Daniel proposed yet?

Sadie: He will. Tonight, maybe. Sometimes its hard to tell.

1636: Youll be his trophy wife.

Sadie: Theres worse things, Pop, hmmm?
(Rest)
Come with me if you like.

1636: I'd rather stick straight pins under my fingernails, thanks.

Sadie: Pop?

1636: Sadie?

Sadie: Whats gonna become of you, Pop?

1636: I'll be pathetically executed in front of a drooling crowd.

Sadie: Yr a professional bowler, Pop. You think theyd really assemble a crowd for you?

1636: If I did something heinous.

Sadie: More heinous than bowling?

> He reaches into the burlap bag and pulls out the head.
> Sadie looks at it. She stands very still for a beat, then exits.

1636: You were supposed to turn to stone! Sadie?! Sadie?!

> Lights out.

6 TREASURE

> 3 Soldiers with sticks for spears. A Leader.

Leader: Give me the map.

> A Soldier gives him the map.

Leader: Its blank.

1st Soldier: The Sun, sir.

Leader: Its hot.

2nd Soldier: And very bright, sir.

Leader: This map is nothing but a blank page! Where are the words and—the whatnots—the squiggly lines and—you know what Im talking about.

2nd Soldier: The Sun—she took them, sir.

Leader
Leader

Leader: Big yellow bitch.
(Rest)
I suppose she wants me to visit her? Spend some time with her. Get my words and line squiggles back, huh?

1st Soldier: She is a terrible power, sir.

2nd Soldier: Melt you in an instant.

3rd Soldier: Or blind you.

Leader: Which way is west?

> They point.

Leader: Make camp. I wont be long.

> He strides off with great confidence.

7 SCATTER (A Musical Melodrama)

> Swelling music plays. The Songstress, Ginger,
> and the Band Leader, Mac, play their scene. Its in black and white.
> The Songstress says her lines kind of like Judy Garland would.
> The Band Leader sounds like Humphrey Bogart.

Ginger: Ive lost my voice, cant you see? Im no better than a bird in a cage who thought she could sing—sing her way out, but didnt know until it was too late, and now theres no way out. No way at all. In good times the bars are far apart, in bad times theyre close, but Im telling you, oh, all the world's a cage, Mac, cant you see?!

Mac: Its those jingles, Ginger. Theyre killing you. Singing crappy songsll kill the best of songbirds, sweetheart. But you need to live. And you need to eat to live. If you only had a dime in the world youd still be the world to me, Ginger.

Ginger: Oh, Mac.

Mac: Oh, Ginger.

Ginger: I need more than good songs, Mac. I need to be free and I—I cant have freedom in this world, baby. Not in this world.

> She rises to go.

Mac: Where are you going?

> She runs out, locking him in.

Mac: Where are you going? Ginger dont go! I love you! Please!

> Sound of a car roaring off. Then crashing horribly.
> Mac buries his face in his hands as the music swells.

8 IS THERE A KIND OF TORTURE WHERE THEY LEAVE THE LIGHTS ON ALL THE TIME?

Scene 1: A Day

> Naked lightbulb, very bright, hangs from the ceiling.
> Man stares at it. Woman reads a magazine.

Man
Woman
Lightbulb

(Rest)

Man: Is there a kind of torture where they leave the lights on all
the time?

Woman: Yes. Its called "Los Angeles."

Man: Dont be such a sourpuss.

(Rest)

Woman: You staring at it, youll go blind. You go blind, folksll
think you play with yrself.

> A horn sounds. The day ends. Lightbulb goes out.

Man: Quitting time.

Woman: Yep.

Man: End of another day.

Woman: Thank God.

> They stare straight ahead.

Scene 2: Another Day

> Man stares at bulb.
> Woman eagerly unwraps a brown paper magazine.

Man: Youd think itd go out.

Woman: Go out where?

Man: The bulb.

Woman: The bulb what?—

Man: Nothing.

Woman: It wont give you a tan. If thats what you want, and you
figure by looking at it like you do, itll give you a tan faster than
it would if say—if you werent looking.

Man
Man

Woman: Hubba hubba. Look at that huh?

> The horn sounds. Bulb out.

Woman: Thank God.

> The day ends. They stare straight ahead.

Scene 3: A Year Later

The Man has a long beard.
The Woman unwraps a brown paper package.

Woman: Im never gonna be lonely again.

Man: Its brighter than it was a year ago.

Woman: Yr gonna be blind and need a dog and a red-tipped cane. But me—Im not gonna be lonesome, nawsir. Ive got a friend, 6 feet tall, muscular, with all his manly parts. And friendly, thats the main bit, very friendly, if you know what I mean. Heh-heh-heh-shit.

She collapses in tears.
The horn blows.
The lights get so bright that we have to look away, eventually,
and then the show is over.

9 THE PRESIDENT'S PUPPETS

A Small Man with hand puppets.

President: This is me. Here I am. Im the president of the United States of America. Lower case "p" for "president" cause Im not acting in an official capacity right now. Im not acting. Im just being. Im just being me. Im just being me being here. Im just being here with my puppets.

Presidential fanfare plays on kazoos.

President: And Im good. And everywhere I go I look—oh heres the bad guy! Boom boom zing—oh there, he's dead! And the bad guy's henchmen—boom boom—theyre dead, and Im the champ! Yeah! Im the champ!

He goes on playing like this forever. Maybe we see him
in the background, or hear him from offstage, etc.,
throughout the rest of the plays.

10 2 WRITERS DIGGING BACH

> 2 Writers: a woman who could be mistaken for
> Suzan-Lori Parks (but not) and a Man who could be mistaken for
> William Faulkner (but not), both digging the same hole.
> They take turns passing the shovel back and forth.
> There is some Bach music playing:
> Cello Suites by Pablo Casals.

Simone: How far we gotta dig you think?

Walter: To get back?

Simone: Pretty far, right?

Walter: Yeah. Hard work, digging.

Simone: Mmm. The heat makes it worse.

Walter: I got a pretty good sunburn. Red neck.

Simone: Me, its my face that peels. Especially around the nose.

Walter: Yeah.

Simone: But they say sweating's good for you.

Walter: Gimmie a cloudy day any day of the week. Gray skies dont have to make you blue. Gray skies are candy.

(Rest)

Simone: Its my turn to dig.

> She digs. He sings with the music.

Simone: Youve got a nice voice.

Walter: Yr just being nice.

Simone: Maybe. My people we dig too. Dig?

Walter: Is that a poem?

Simone: Maybe.

Walter: Sounds like one of them haikus on the ear.

Simone: Not much in life that beats digging a hole, huh?

Walter: I'll drink to that *(He drinks)* Drink?

Simone: Hot enough for me in here already.

> He laughs uproariously. She laughs too.
> They pause and listen to the Bach and smile.

Walter: My turn.

> She hands the shovel to him.

11 I CANT HELP THE MOOD IM IN, BUT RIGHT NOW IM THINKING THAT THE NARCISSISM OF WHITE AMERICA KNOWS NO BOUNDS

> 2 people of any race or gender:
> the Other is thinking or daydreaming even.
> White watches.

White: You thinking of me?

Other: No.

White: How bout now?

Other: How bout now, what?

White: You thinking of me?

Other: No.

White: How bout now?

Other: Lay off, huh?

White
Other

White: Whatcha thinking about?

Other: None of yr business.

White: Why not?

Other: Im not thinking about you, ok? I'm thinking about—other things.

White: What about when you woke up this morning: the sun through the dusty blinds, yr warm partner at yr side and—me in yr head, right?

Other
White

> The Other smiles.

Other: Tell you what. See this light? Ima turn out this light and we're gonna be in the dark in a minute. And if yr here when I turn the light back on—well, then its gonna be me and you in a room with the light on, you understand what Im saying?

White: —Not really.

Other: You will.

> The Other turns out the light.

12 ANTAEUS

> Several people at the depot, one with several suitcases.

Papa: You cant leave, darlin.

Darlin: I can leave. Just you watch me.

Junior: Mother, you were born and raised here.

Papa: This land is yr land! Its what gives you yr strength.

Darlin: You can have my strength.

Sue: What about yr family?

Darlin: You can have my family.

Papa: Darlin, how could you say that?

Darlin: I curse my family and all theyve done.

Junior: Mother, I take that personal now.

Sue: Leave, go on. Yr gonna speak yr mind, I'll speak my mind. Leave.

Junior: Sue, hush.

Sue: She's an old witch.

Papa
Darlin
Junior
Sue

Papa: You leave and I'll get a new wife. A younger gal with perky doodads.

> Sound of the foghorn.

Darlin: Theres my boat.

> Darlin gets up to go. They all fling themselves on her, grabbing an arm, a leg, a purse corner, a dress hem. They see it as futile, and as some music comes up—something like the Carter Family—they release their holds slowly and with great sadness. Their hands still hover around Darlin though, and she, free, does not move, but just stands there with her bags in hand about to take the first step.

13 AN INTERMISSION

Many people onstage—more than listed in the speaking parts—
milling about, watching. The lights come up on them.

Donor: Intermission.

Friend: Right.

Star: Do you get it so far?

Star's Assistant: Its very—postmodern.

Star: Right.

Academic: What should we do now?

Administrator: Nothing.

Academic: But its the intermission. Lets get a coffee.

Friend: Wheres the toilet?

Star: We cant do anything. Its intermission—isnt that the time
when we dont do anything?

Star's Assistant: Im not sure. I'll double check.

Star: If you see the writer, dont tell her I didnt get it.

Star's Assistant: Yr covered.

Donor: Were you in that movie?

Star: Yeah. Shhhh.

Donor: Shhhh?

Star: My assistant will explain.

Star's Assistant: Its the intermission, she's not allowed to do anything.

Academic: Really? Oh. Quiet, everybody! And stand still!

Stage Manager: Do whatever you want. Really. Feel free.

What follows is 2 minutes of the actors doing
whatever they want, after which time
the Stage Manager comes back in.

Stage Manager: 5 minutes.

5 more minutes of whatever they want.

Stage Manager: Places!

The actors mill about as they did at the top
of the play. The lights go out.

14 FAITH, HOPE AND CHARITY

> 3 Old People (Faith, Hope, Charity), or old-looking people,
> sit on a short bench downstage. They pass a set of teeth
> (dentures) back and forth. As one puts the teeth in, she smiles,
> as if taking a picture with the other 2.

Faith: Pity we cant all smile toothy all at the same time.

Hope: We could but—

Faith: Pass the teeth.

Charity: Im not done with them.

Hope: Yr hogging them!

Charity: I am not. It takes me longer to get them in, so—

Hope: Yr hogging them!

Faith: My turn.

Hope: Over my dead and wrinkled body!

> They dont fight over them but just reach until one gives them up.

Faith: Pity we cant all smile toothy all at the same time.

Hope: We could but—

Charity: Theres a shortage.

> They continue passing the teeth and smiling as the lights fade.

15 4 DIRECTIONS

> 4 People enter, each with a compass. They fiddle
> with their compasses. As they find North, East, South and West,
> they speak the directions and walk off in that direction
> as far as they can for as long as they can. In theory,
> the One Who Walks North, for example, may be walking North
> for the rest of her life. In practice, however, the world being
> as it is and friction being a reality, the One Who Walks North
> may, say, hit a wall, walking into it, her head against the bricks,
> her feet treading, everything going nowhere.
> She would become exhausted at that point or
> maybe just disgusted and bored with it and quit.
> Another walker, the One Who Walks East, perhaps,
> should he reach a cliff, he should stop.
> No, suicide is not necessary here. And so on.
> Thanks for listening. Thanks for playing this far.
> Here are 4 directions. There are many more.

16 A PLAY ABOUT A UNIFORM

> A Man walks in. He's wearing a uniform. It can be any sort of uniform or a made-up uniform. It should be dark with some gold braid—a military suit, or a bandleader suit. He's been at work all day.

Man: Honey!
Honey *(Offstage)*: Yr home!
Man: Yeah.
Honey *(Offstage)*: Early.
Man: Yeah.
Honey *(Offstage)*: Very—early.
Man: Yeah.
Honey *(Offstage)*: I didnt hear the car.
Man: I walked.
Honey *(Offstage)*: That doesnt sound like you.

Man
Man

(Rest)

Man: Wheres my valet?
Honey *(Offstage)*: In here. I'll bring it out.
Man: Now.

> Honey hurries out. She's dressed in lingerie and is putting on a robe and lipstick. She stands in front of him, adjusting her hair, perfecting her lipstick.

Honey: Be my mirror. How do I look?
Man: Good. My—
Honey: Yr valet. Coming up.

> She gives him a kiss. This surprises him. She hurries out of the room and returns with a valet, that is, a self-standing coat rack. When he sees the valet, he relaxes. He takes off his shoes, then coat, then pants. He just wears his modest boxers and plain socks. He takes out a brush and brushes down his uniform.

Honey: You hungry?
Man: No.
Honey: Thinking?

Man: No.

Honey: Angry? Sad? Fed up? Let down?

Man: I thought youd sold the valet. When I walked in here and didnt see it, I thought youd sold it. In one of yr—garage sales.

Honey: I dont have—garage sales anymore—

Man: "And she'll sell the uniform next," I thought. "First the valet, then the uniform."

Honey: Did they salute you? They didnt, did they? I told you they wouldnt. But it coulda been worse. Next time you wear it out there, they might throw stones. Someonell hit you right between the eyes and then youll be dead in the middle of the street. And I'll hear on the news that one of you died, but they wont say which one.

> Man rummages, he finds more gold braid.

Man: I forgot to wear all my braid. I'll put on more braid. Give it a good brushdown. Spit-polish the shoes. Theyll salute me and if not me, then at least the uniform, you betcha.

> The Wife lies on the floor. She makes the shape of a cross.
> A Soldier Boy comes in from the bedroom.
> He is putting on his clothes. He sees her and gets on top of her.
> Theyre very still.

Man: I thought you didnt like soldiers.

Soldier Boy: She dont, pal. Its the uniform she likes, aint it, Honey?

> Man continues to brush uniform. Lights out.

17 THE PLANE ON THE RUNWAY AT 6 A.M.

> Bach Cello Suite #1 (Pablo Casals) plays.
> The Stewardess silently performs the safety instructions:

> She smiles.
> She shows where the exits are.
> With hand signals she shows us how to:
> "Locate yr exits. The nearest exit is often behind you.
> Some exits have inflatable slides."
> She shows us the lights along the floor.
> She shows the seat belt and how it works.
> She shows the air mask. How it will drop from the ceiling
> automatically should there be a loss of cabin pressure.

She shows the elastic strap, the baggie. She illustrates
how we should put ours on first, then assist any small children.
She shows the flotation device (the life vest),
and where in the seat it is hidden, and the tabs you pull
to inflate it (once you exit the aircraft). If it fails to inflate,
you can inflate it manually by blowing into the tubes.
No smoking on this plane, please!
No cell phones allowed in flight!
Refreshments will be served soon! And a movie too!
Bye for now!

All of this was presented without words. Once the Stewardess
has gone through the sequence, she is joined by 5 other Flight
Attendants. They perform the sequence again.
This should not be a sendup, but—with all the respect
of a life's calling, a great and important service, performed daily
at 30 thousand feet. Let the Cello Suite guide the mood.
Once the Flight Attendants have reviewed the sequence,
the Passengers stand and repeat the sequence.
It should be a beautiful series of gestures. Not at all diminished
by the number of Passengers. Some with small children,
some who are weary, some who are afraid to fly today.

18 A PLAY FOR THE WRITER CAROL SHIELDS

Carol Shields: Hi. Im Carol Shields. Ima writer. Some of you who
are familiar with my work may find that last statement odd.
"She *reaches*," you may be thinking. "She's not a writer anymore,
honey. She's dead. Carol Shields, the writer, died today. I read it
in the paper just this morning on the way to the airport," you
may be saying, but only in a whisper and only to yr spouse. And
he'll look at you—he'll give you that look—that perplexed look
that he has. He doesnt look at anyone or anything else with that
look. He made up that look for you, you think, for those times
when yr talking to him and he's actually listening, because he's a
good husband. He's listening, but, well, you know, he's thinking
of something else—
(Rest)
Im probably talking too much.
(Rest)
Ima writer and—well!—Ive come all this way and forget my pen
and paper.

A Woman and Man walk in. They sit downstage left.
They make themselves comfortable, then sit still.

(Rest)

Carol Shields: Thats the tricky thing about being dead—they say you cant take it with you. Well, you *can*, but if you happen to forget it, as one does—even writers, even *real* writers—sometimes we do—we forget it, and walk out of the house without a thing to write with—.
(Rest)
I walked out of the house without a thing to write with.

Carol Shields
Carol Shields
Carol Shields

Woman: My sweater! I lost my sweater!

Man: Maybe its back at the house.

Woman: No, I had it in the car. And in that line to get through security, when we were in that long line? I had it then too. Did you see how they looked at me when I went through security? They thought I was a terrorist.

Man: You dont have time to be a terrorist.

Woman: My sweater! The one you brought me back from Scotland.

Man: I'll get you another sweater.

Woman: When you got it for me you said it was a one of a kind.

Man: I'll get you another one. Another one of a kind.

Woman: It pulled my whole wardrobe together. Oh, honey, my sweater. It matched my pants.

> The Woman looks fearful. The Man lovingly pats her hand.
> Carol Shields walks toward them with great tenderness.
> They notice her watching, and smile at her—the kind of smile
> that strangers in an airport smile at each other,
> nothing more than that.
> Carol Shields, the writer, died today.
> She noticed things that most of us overlook.

19 A PLAY FOR BARRY WHITE

> 2 People: one in black, the Mourner;
> the other in blue and green, the World.

Mourner: Oh, Im the Mourner and yr the World.

World: Yes, Im the World and yr the Mourner.

Mourner: Right.

World
World

Mourner: Whatcha doing?
World: Turning.
Mourner: Right.
(Rest)
Barry White died.

World
Mourner

Mourner: Stop.
World: Nope.
Mourner: Just for a second. Barry White was—
World: I know who Barry White was.

Mourner
World
Mourner
World

> The Mourner bursts into tears. Real tears.
> And the World keeps turning.

20 WELCOME TO NASHVILLE

> 2 People contemplate the Great Enormity
> (a.k.a. the That that is All That) as represented in,
> say, a palm-sized rock.

1st: Who made that?
2nd: That.
1st: That?
2nd: Yep.
1st: Yeah?
2nd: Yep.
1st: Dang.
2nd: Welcome to Nashville.

> Lights out, and fast!

21 AS IDI AMIN LIES IN A COMA IN SAUDI ARABIA

3 African Women dressed in modest black suits
sit on a simple bench. The entire look is sparse,
with the excellent simplicity of a documentary.
They sit with their heads bowed—not trying to look anywhere
but the floor. A Black Man in a white doctor's coat comes
onstage. He stands there, moving his mouth.
Speaking without talking. The Women crane their necks to hear.

Doctor
Women
Doctor
Women

As the Doctor exits, one Woman reaches out, pleading for more
(or better) information concerning her beloved Idi,
dictator-husband. She receives none. She crumbles,
collapsing to the floor, the sadness creeping into
her through her outstretched hand.
The 2 other Women look upon her with compassion,
but do not rush to her.

1st Wife: She does not know Idi as we know Idi.
2nd Wife: She's young.
1st Wife: And his crimes are old.

2 other Wives continue to watch for news in the area
of the Doctor's recent exit.

22 MOTHERS AND DAUGHTERS AND FATHERS AND SONS

2 Women sit. One is very Old, one Younger.
The Younger one keeps glancing offstage.

Older: Yr sweating it.
Younger: Im not sweating it.
Older: In my day we didnt even glance.
Younger: Im not glancing. Who is glancing? Not me.
Older: In my day we didnt even sit and wait.

The Younger abruptly stands.

Younger: Whose sitting? Not me.

Older: Im sitting. Im sitting because Im old. But Im not waiting.

Younger: Im waiting.

Older: In my day we didnt—

Younger: Do you want a beating? Keep it up and I'll give you a costly beating. A beating so costly even I couldnt buy it. Yes. I'll beat you in yr secret female places so he wont notice.

Older
Younger

(Rest)

Older: (In my day we didn't speak (with such volume.))

(Rest)

Younger: Theyre coming. Fast.

> Just then 2 Men run in screaming—a great life-in-danger kind of terror. They huddle behind the Women, then, as their terror gets closer, they exit screaming. The Younger watches them go.

Older: In my day our feet didnt follow them and neither did our eyes.

> A Man comes in, sword drawn.

Man: Which way?

> The Younger lowers her eyes. The Older points, and the Man follows after the terrified Men, sword drawn.

23 EL SILENCIO GRANDE

> A large Man onstage. He's been there since the beginning of time, or at least since the beginning of the plays, or at least for a few minutes. He's wearing a small nametag. He stands arms akimbo. 2 Tourists enter.

1: Lookie.

2: Read it for me, honey.

1: "El Silencio Grande."

2: He's big. Excuse me, sir, could we take our picture with you?

El Silencio Grande
El Silencio Grande

1: He probably doesnt speak English.
2: This country used to be—
1: Dont get started—we're on vacation.
2: He needs to know—. He—. We—.
1: Hon?
2: What?
1: Let it go, hon. Let it go.

> The Tourists age 100 years. Nurses come in
> with wheelchairs and wheel them away.
> El Silencio Grande remains.

24 OUR 2ND ANNIVERSARY

> 2 People, Man and Wife of 2 years,
> open a bottle of champagne and share romantic slurps.

Wife: We're 2 years married.
Husband: Yes. Toast.

> They toast.

Wife
Husband

Husband: When we get old—
Wife: God willing.
Husband: Yes.
Wife: Toast.

> They toast.

Wife: What will we be like?
Husband: My thoughts exactly.
Wife: Toast.

> They toast.

Husband: When we get old—
Wife: We'll be—older—I imagine.

They laugh, get more comfortable.

Husband: Older and wiser.
Wife: Better but grayer.
Husband: And together.
Wife: Toast.

They toast.

Husband: Imagine. We're in our 80s or 90s, slow-walking seniors. I want to love you until yr all shriveled up like a prune. I'll love you the most then. What do you think?
Wife: Yummy.

They toast.

25 AJAX BIG AND LITTLE

A Large Man and a Small Man. A Servant holds an antenna. The Large Man directs the Servant to move about for better reception. The Small Man eats courses of an enormous meal, then weighs himself. He calls a Servant, who brings in more food, then he keeps eating.

Ajax the Big: Remember when it started.
Ajax the Little: We didnt think it would last.
Ajax the Big: And now Im reduced to listening.
Ajax the Little: At least yr big.
Ajax the Big: You never served did you?
Servant: No, sir, but I have served those who served.
Ajax the Little: Thats more than some.
Servant: I thank you.
Ajax the Big: Yr gonna pop if you keep eating.
Ajax the Little: Im hungry and Im small.
Ajax the Big: Suit yrself.

A horrible noise—tragic and terrifying—is heard from offstage. All look up.

Ajax the Big: What in the name of Zeus was that?
Servant: The new shipment of dead.
Ajax the Big: Were we so—noisy?

Servant: During the tail end of history, they get noisier with each passing year, so Im told.

Ajax the Big & Ajax the Little: Ah.

26 SUGAR (For Nina Simone and Celia Cruz)

A Group of Singers sings call-and-response.

Singers:
Here lies one
she sang sweet.
A million roses
at her feet.
Still we can hear her
sing!

A bowl of sugar cubes is passed around and tasted.
A rose is passed around and smelled. 2 Girls walk by.

Girl: This morning I woke up and I knew just what Im gonna do with my life.

Friend: Last week you wanted to race a NASCAR.

Girl: Forget that. Now, Im gonna be a singer. Like Nina Simone.

Friend: Like Nina who?

Girl: Or, if not like Nina Simone, Im gonna be like Celia Cruz.

Friend: Like who like who?

Girl: Shit. I dont know why I even give you my time of day, yr so ignorant.

They walk on as the ceremony continues in the background.

27 MR. BACH AND MR. GOULD

J. S. Bach, Glenn Gould and J. S. Bach's sassy Interpreter.
Gould has a boombox and several worn CDs.

Gould: Listen to this part here.

They listen to Gould playing The Well-Tempered Clavier.
Bach whispers something to his Interpreter.

Interpreter: He says it sounds familiar. Vaguely.

Gould: I'll take that as a high compliment. Critics called it masterful. I like to think I at least got the spirit of the thing, sir.

>   Bach whispers to his Interpreter.

Interpreter: Mr. Bach is exhausted.

Gould: One more, please, sir, one more.

Interpreter: Mr. Bach would like to go home.

Gould: On this one, it sounds like Ive got 4 hands!!

Interpreter: Mr. Bach is frightened.

Gould: Listen! 4 hands! Like an Indian god!

Interpreter: Frightened by yr—enthusiasm.

Gould: Dont be ridiculous.

>   Bach begins to cry like an old dead man would.

Gould
Bach

(Rest)

Gould: Tears of joy? Right?

> Gould turns up the volume. Horribly loud. Earplugs are lowered
> from the ceiling. The Interpreter grabs plugs and inserts them
> gently into Mr. Bach's ears. Having safely plugged Mr. Bach,
> she hurriedly earplugs herself. Gould is approaching ecstasy.

28 RUBY

> A Younger Woman and 2 Older (much older) Folk.
> The Younger Woman has an enormous magnifying glass.
> She picks up a speck of something. Examines it.

Old One: What is it?

Younger Woman: I havent got anything.

Old One: I can hear you—turning yr magnifier this way and that.

Other Old One: I can hear yr jaws. SLOBBERING!

Old One: Mother can hear—the sounds of anticipation.

Younger Woman: I dont have anything, Im telling you!

Other Old One: I can hear—

Younger Woman: Thats it! Im leaving! OUTA HERE, you hear! And there wont be nobody to bury you and there wont be nobody to make sure you get the pine box and the plot *not* near the coloreds and—that Cadillac you want to take you to the plot! HA! Kiss that Cadillac goodbye!

> The Younger Woman works to catch her breath. When she regains her composure the Old One gently kisses the wind (eyes closed like a lover's first kiss) and waves gently.

Younger Woman
Younger Woman
Younger Woman

(Rest)

Younger Woman: I found a ruby.
Old One: Ruby?
Other Old One: Ruby.
Old One: Hand it over.

> The Younger Woman hands the ruby to the Old One. He smells it and nods, then passes it to the Other Old One, who smells it and eats it. The Old One smiles and rubs his knees. The Younger Woman sighs.

Younger Woman: I dont know why I bother.
Old One: We're all youve got.

29 WILD WEST

> From every direction imaginable come running the Good Citizens of the Western Prairie. Theyre plain-dressed country folk. Theyre all dusty. They line up across the stage, watching something that is offstage left and right.

Ma: You seen what I seen?
Pa: Good Lord!
Unc: Think theyll fight?
Jr.: Think theyll fight? This is the Wild West! Course theyll fight!
Sis: With guns lets hope.

Good Citizens
Good Citizens
Good Citizens

> Theyre hoping.

Lil Sis: Only one of emll walk away alive.
Jr. X: Bloodshed over a heifer. Aint right.
Jr. Y & Jr. Z: The pot's calling the kettle black.
Neighbor: Shh! Theyre trading their insults.

Good Citizens
Gunslingers

(Rest)

Gunslingers *(Offstage)***:** Bang!
Sis: Lets go see them die up close!

> Good Citizens run offstage.

30 THE LEGEND OF WILGEFORTIS

> The King of Portugal, the most disgusting man imaginable,
> is surrounded by several Servants with trays of food.

King: SNACK!

> A Servant rushes up to the King. He grabs food,
> stuffs it in his mouth, swallowing without chewing.
> The food further soils his already-soiled Kingly attire.

King: SNACK!

> Another Servant, more food.

King: SNACK!

> Servant with Bag approaches.

King: What the hell is it?
Servant with Bag: Brown Bag Surprise, sire.

> King reaches in—gobbles up whatever.

King: I like it. You live.
Servant with Bag: Thank you, sire.

> A Herald enters with bowed head.

Herald: A suitor for yr 7th daughter.
King: My 7th. Christ-on-the-cross, what time is it?

> Servants grab watches and
> answer with several vastly different times.

King: Someone give me the time in *this* kingdom.
Timely Servant: Half past noon, sire.
King: Not yet 5? Good. Send in the suitor.

> The Herald goes.

King: SNACK!

> Eating continues.
> The Herald and the Prince of Galveston appear.

Herald: The Prince of Galveston.
Prince: I am the Prince of Galveston.
King: I am the King of Portugal and several other places. My full list of titles is available upon request.
Prince: I am familiar with yr kingdoms and yr daughters. 6 beauties I missed marrying because Ive been at sea for so long. Yr 7th daughter will be my wife.
King: You want to marry Wilgefortis?
Prince: I am the Prince of Galveston.
King: Isnt Galveston a part of Texas?
Prince: As Portugal is part of the world, sire, but very much its own kingdom.
King: Yr by the sea—as I recall from my geography.
Prince: Exactly.
King: Time!

> Again, many different times are stated—
> then the time for Portugal is given.

King: Good. Still early yet.
Prince: Yr daughter—
King: My daughter is at her loom. Would you like to see her?

Prince: Im sure her portrait does her justice.

King: But you would like to see Wilgefortis in the flesh?

Prince: I do not doubt the skill of the king's portrait painters.

King: I am a practical father. I insist.

Prince: I defer to yr insistence.

King: Time!

> Correct time.

King: Glass!

> Spy glass is rushed in.

King: Hurry.

> The King hands the spy glass to the Prince, who looks offstage.

Prince: Oh dear.

King: What?

Prince: Yr daughter—the girl at the loom—uh—

King: Has a beard. What of it? Keeps her warm in the winter and itll keep you warm too. She's very well-shaped, yes?

Prince: My parents, sire, with all respect my parents and my lineage—

King: We shave her in the morning—it forms a slight shadow by 5, but—it seems to be more shadowy today.

> The Prince tries to leave as quietly as possible.

King: Christ-on-the-cross, man, she'll have a handsome dowry.

Prince: With all respect.

> He sneaks off.

King
Wilgefortis
Kingdom

(Rest)

King: My 7th daughter, the bearded Wilgefortis, have her shaved.

Servant: Yes, sire.

King: And that Prince. Catch him. And crucify him.

Servant: Yes, sire.

King: SNACK!

All rush at him with food. He gobbles up everything
in his reach as the lights fade.

31 BEHIND THE VEIL OF THE GODDESS

2 or 3 Veilers enter. They carry a curtain or a sheet
and stretch it long. They stand on a downstage-to-upstage line
so that while the sheet is stretched it doesnt obscure anything
onstage. 2 sets of actors enter: 2 Women in Contemporary
Dress stageright and 2 Women in Ancient Dress stageleft.
The Veilers move as the actors move, obscuring
the Ancient Women from the Contemporary Women,
while allowing us to see whoever is speaking.
The action of the veil movement is beautiful and precise,
much like the movement of a matador's cape.

Contemporary Women

1: I woke up this morning and I wanted a child.

2: Really?

1: Crazy, right?

2: Natural. And crazy too.

1: The thought came out of nowhere.

2: Its not like you want to flip off the president—I mean, you
might want that—anybody with sense might wanna do that, but,
what I mean is—yr a woman, you want a kid. Welcome to the club.

1: I guess I'll have to call Joe.

Ancient Women

1: Was it sent to the world?

2: Yes, maam.

1: How is it faring?

2: Well enough. It survived the journey and the mother is quite
fond of it.

1: Will it live long?

2: Dont you want to know what kind it is? What sex, what race,
what nationality, what religion?

1: No.

2: Whats this?

1: Another one. Hide it like the others and erase the trail so he
wont find them and eat them.

2: One day, madam, I fear he will find them. And yr hiding place, yr little blue planet—
1: Will be destroyed. Heres another. And another. Hurry!

Contemporary Women

1 on the phone with Joe while 2 watches.

1: I wouldnt ask you, Joe, if I wasnt serious about it.

2

2

1: No, Joe, no, theres nobody here. Im alone.
2: I bet he'll tell you to go to a sperm bank.
1: Joe, of course I love you. No theres no one here.

1

2

2 leaves.

1: Remember how yr always saying you wanted a family? With me? Well, heres our chance, right?

Lights fade.

August

1 LIMOUSINE

An endless Line of Prisoners (a loop of people walking from stageright to stageleft and then going backstage and coming onstage again). All hold a chain or are even more elaborately shackled. 2 people at either end of the stage talk to each other as the Prisoners pass by. One counts them with a Clicker, the other ticks them off on a Clipboard. The Prisoners shuffle by. Silently.

Clicker: I used to work in a factory.
Clipboard: Me too.
Clicker: Whatd you make?
Clipboard: Limousines.

Clicker: Really?

Clipboard: Limousines. Posh. Long, shiny and black mostly. Interior new leather and soft as butter. Hand-stitching. Finest crystal glasses in there. For champagne. Posh. Im telling you. Posh all the way.

Clicker: You make them from start to finish?

Clipboard: No, so yr thinking my job wasnt all that? Go on, kick me in the nuts, you bitch's bastard.

Clicker: Im just asking.

Clipboard: Go on, bite off my dick then swallow it, and turn my jewels to shit, go on.

Clipboard
Clicker

Clipboard: Whatd you make. In yr factory?

Clicker: In my factory?

Clipboard: Yeah.

Clicker: Me?

Clipboard: Yeah.

Clicker: Hell. I made hell.

> The Prisoners keep trudging by.

2 CLOTH PRAYER

> A Group of People performs a series of 4 movements:
> 1. They come together.
> 2. They show great dismay.
> 3. One holds a cloth aloft.
> 4. They retreat from each other.
> The movements have been going on forever.
> At first they perform the first 3 movements in the dark. And, as
> the lights come up, all we see is
> movement 4: "They retreat from each other."

(Rest)

> Then they perform the first 3 movements
> in strict numerical sequence. During movement 3
> we get our first good look at the cloth.
> They see us looking.

– So small!
– Last time it was larger.
– It was the size of a generous blanket! Large enough for us all.
– Is this the prayer they spoke of?
– Not big enough.
– Much too small.
– We can do better elsewhere, dont you think?

Performers
Prayer

> Movement 4: They retreat from each other.
> They perform the movements in sequence.
> This time the cloth prayer has shrunk to the size of
> a postage stamp.
> They see us looking.

– Turn the lights off.
– Yes. Turn the lights off.

> The lights fade to black as the movements continue.

3 LUCKY

> A Row of People on a park bench reading newspapers—
> papers not all from this country, ok?
> One Man gets up, dropping his newspaper on the ground.
> A Homeless Man comes in, shits on the paper then leaves.
> The small pile of shit is right in front of the bench.
> Another Group of People come walking in from all directions.
> Theyre at a cocktail party. A Man steps in the shit.

Man: Shit.
Woman: Lucky.
Man: Lucky?
Woman: Yeah, stepping in shit is lucky.
Man: Not where I come from. Im the president of a big important company. And I just came from there. Where I come from, stepping in shit is stupid. And smelly. And unlucky.
Woman: I guess that means the party's over.
Man: I'd say so.

The party stops. The Woman pulls out a gun, shooting the Man dead. Then she looks up into the sky.

Woman: One less!

The party starts up again. At first it sounds like a record turned on with the needle in the middle of a groove.

4 DECOY

A Woman sits looking into the far distance. She sees what she thinks she's been waiting for her entire life. She waves enormously. A Man runs in with a bucket of water. Splashes her in the face.

Woman: What the fuck?
Man: You waved.
Woman: Not at you.
Man: No? Oh. I'll leave.

The Man leaves. The Woman waits. Suddenly the stage fills with Wipers—a troupe to wipe the stage clean and dry. They do a very good job.

Woman: Who sent you?
Head Wiper: He did.
2nd Wiper: The least he could do, he said.
3rd Wiper: All clear!

They exit in an elaborately organized fashion. The Woman waits. She waves. No one comes. She fixes her hair. The Man enters again, this time with a gorgeously wrapped package.

Man: For you.
Woman: Get lost.
Man: Im lost already.
(Rest)
Did you like the Wipers?
Woman: Yes. Thanks.

Just then, the Other Woman runs onstage. She is dressed much like the first Woman, enough to be taken for her at a distance by someone who wears glasses but has misplaced them. The Other Woman sets up a chair, waits, looks, waves.

Woman
Other Woman

(Rest)

Man: Dont mind her. She's just a decoy.
Woman: You talking to me?
Man: Yes, Im talking to you.
(Rest)
You gonna open the box?
Woman: Is it for me?
Man: Of course its for you.
Woman: It doesnt have my name on it.
Man: Look on the card. It says "Sarah" plain as day.
Woman: My name's Joan.
Other Woman: Im Sarah.

Man
Woman
Other Woman
Man

(Rest)

Man: Excuse me.

> He exits, then runs back in with another bucket of water.
> He splashes the Other Woman, then stands by her, waiting.
> Lights fade.

5 EPIC BIO-PIC

Act 1: The Beginning

Woman: Something smells. God!
Man: I farted.
Woman: I thought that was a car backfiring! Christ-on-the-cross!
Man: Christ-on-the-cross yrself.

Act 2003: The Middle Bit

Woman: This makes me look fat, doesn't it?
Man: Yeah.

Woman: What?!?!?!
Man: Dont be silly. You look great.

Man
Woman

Woman: I want to try something. Skydiving. Or race car driving.
Maybe we should climb Everest.
(Rest)
Or have another kid. My skin is losing its elasticity. My ass is
wide and my middle. Look at my middle. God, this is a bad town
to grow old in.
Man: Did you take yr medicine?
Woman: I took my medicine and I took yr medicine.
Man: Have a cookie.
Woman: You think?

She looks at the cookie. Nibbles at it.

Woman: Did we pay our electric bill? When I think of where
electricity comes from—like nuclear power or dams that have
ruined natural rivers—I—I dont know what to think. Makes me
wanna sit in the dark. Its not Ben Franklin running around in
the rain with his kite anymore, is it? Things are more complicated.
More *advanced*, so lets just turn the lights out.
Man: We cant yet.
Woman: When?
Man: Soon.

Act 3175: The End

Woman: No more?
Man: Thats it.
Woman: We're dead?
Man: Yep.
Woman: There were so many—
Man: —things I wanted to do.
Woman: Dont I get my own—
Man: —lines anymore?
Woman: Guess not.
Man: You can be alive again. If you want.
Woman: How?
Man: See that line? You stand there and you wait.

Woman: Yr kidding. Come on, yr kidding.

Man: We can turn the lights out now.

Lights out.

6 EMPTY BUCKET

An empty bucket. 3 Women watch. A Waterbearer comes in and sets down a bucketful of water, then transfers water from the full bucket to the empty one with a thimble.

1st Woman: Pour it! Why doesnt he pour it? With that thimble itll take forever. Pour it, I tell you!

2nd Woman: Yr raising yr voice, like a woman whose privates are for sale.

1st Woman: Pour it! Pour it!

3rd Woman: Shout all you want. The waterbearer's blind, deaf and dumb.

1st Woman: I'll beat him with my fists.

3rd Woman: And spend the rest of yr life in prison? Oh no, you wont.

2nd Woman: In my day we didnt shout or threaten.

The Women watch the Waterbearer.

Scene: Years Before

The Waterbearer, much younger, but still working with that thimble, transfers water and cries himself a river.

3rd Woman *(Younger)*: Mummy?

1st Woman: What?

3rd Woman: Mummy? Why is he crying, Mummy?

1st Woman: Mummy's tired, child.

2nd Woman: Yr Mummy's a woman who sells her privates in the street.

3rd Woman
3rd Woman

3rd Woman: Grandmummy?

2nd Woman: What?

3rd Woman: Where does he get the water?

2nd Woman: I dunno, child.

Waterbearer: I cry into the bucket. I carry the sadness of the world.

1st Woman: Do something for Mummy, child. Take this knife and cut out his tongue, stab in his eyes and poke his eardrums hard. I wont have him talking that kind of trash in my country.

> 1st Woman gives 3rd Woman a very large and very sharp knife.
> 3rd Woman runs at the Waterbearer, who,
> seeing that she is going to mind her mother for once,
> takes off screaming, with the 3rd Woman in hot pursuit.

7 ALL'S NOT ALL WELL

Memory:
All the world's indeed a project
and you and me are deep up in it.
We come we go we come we go,
trying to know a little more
than we come in the room with.

When I was a kid, this kid
across the hall told me
I didnt have a father cause, hell,
she aint never seen him.
How could I not, as a child of my mother
and as a child of the world, not have a dad?
This didnt make no kind of sense to her,
so she took it upon herself to kick my ass
once a week like clockwork,
cause she hadnt never seen
her father, and her moms told her
she didnt have one,
that she was her mother's sole creation—
that her mother'd made her solo.

> A Mother and a Child look at a glossy catalogue:

Mother: Pick one. He'll be yr dad.

Child: Yeah?

Mother: We'll call him up and he'll come over, I guess.

Child: Some dont come over.

Mother: Wheres it say that?

Child: Here.

Mother: Dont be nuts. You call them up, you pay them, theyll come over. After work or whatever. Theyll bring things. Candies. Dolls. And a pony on yr birthday.

Child: And flowers for you.

Mother: I guess.

Child: And for yr—whadayacallit—yr anniversary—he'll bring you—

Mother: Shut up.

Mother
Child

Mother: Pick one. Just pick one.

Child: I cant decide.

Mother: Close yr eyes. Now, I'll flip the pages and spin the book and you pick.

>   She does so. The Child giggles. She even spins
>   the Child around as if theyre playing Pin the Tail on the Donkey
>   or Smash the Piñata.

Mother: Now pick!

>   The Child picks. The Mother is pleased and hugs the giggling
>   Child close. They both regard the photo. Then the Mother
>   picks up the phone and dials.

Mother: Here comes Daddy!

8 NET

>   A Man walks in with a Woman.
>   She has a net over her head and shoulders.

Man: Ive found her.

Mother: God be praised.

Granny: Go get the dress.

Mother: I'll go get the dress.

>   The Mother goes.

Father: Whats wrong with her, then?

Grandpa: Yes, whats wrong with her?

Man: Nothings wrong with her.

Father: She'll never do.

Mother *(From offstage)*: Whats wrong with her?

Man: Nothings wrong with her!

Father: She's got a fucking net on her head, doesnt she?

Granny: A net on her head!

Grandpa: A net on her head!

Father: A net on her head and shoulders!

> The Mother returns with the dress.

Mother: Well, Im not putting the dress away. Thats 48 stairs Ive just climbed. Up and down.

Man
Family

(Rest)

Woman: I ran. I ran far. Not far enough, I guess.

> Lights out fast.

9 A PLAY FOR SARAH KANE AND THE ROYAL COURT THEATRE

> A Young Woman lounges on a chaise lounge.
> The Other Woman, slightly older, watches her.
> A ways off, an Older Man and an Older Woman sit
> at a cloth-covered table. A bottle of wine and 2 glasses.
> The Stage Manager walks on.

Stage Manager: 5 minutes, Miss Kane, 5 minutes.

Older Woman: Its never been so hot as this. Today we're setting a record.

Older Man: Ive never seen so many folks in shower shoes.

Older Woman: Flip-flops, theyre called.

Older Man: Are they?

Older Woman: Thats what little Tina calls them: "flip-flops."

Older Man: She ought to know.

Older Woman: Yr drinking.

Older Man: God yes.

Stage Manager: Places, Miss Kane. Places.

Miss Kane puts something that looks like a rope
around her neck.

Other Woman: Yr not going on tonight.
Kane: I dunno.
Other Woman: Youve put yr rope on.
Kane: Have I?
Other Woman: If you had it to do all over again, would you?

Kane
Kane

(Rest)

Other Woman: Im trying to say I miss you. I dont know how.
Kane: You know that film *Citizen Kane*? Its very—seminal. You
seen it?
Other Woman: Ive seen it, like 3 times, but I dont really get it.
Stage Manager: Miss Kane? Yr on.
Kane: Im on.
Other Woman: On what?

Other Woman
Kane

(Rest)

Other Woman: How are you these days?
Kane: Better. Worse. Yr troubles follow you.
Other Woman: Yeah?
Kane: No matter where you go. Yr troubles know. Yr address.
Other Woman: Yes.

Older Man begins singing: "Well I guess it doesnt matter
anymore . . ." Older Woman is deeply embarrassed.

Kane: Fan me, huh?

The Other Woman fans her.

Other Woman: No sweat, kid. God bless you and no sweat.

10 DAVID HAMPTON DAYDREAMING

(I met John Guare on a Monday and then, the very next day,
I met David Hampton, the man whose exploits were said
to have inspired Guare's *Six Degrees of Separation*.
Dear Mr. Hampton died recently.)
A woman, Mrs. Hampton, washes dishes in a bucket.
Her son, David, dries the dishes. Most are cracked and broken.
Mother and son work for a moment at a good pace,
then David stops, holding a cup or plate suspended in the air.

David Hampton
David Hampton

Mrs. Hampton: Wipe. Wipe, son.

David Hampton
David Hampton

Mrs. Hampton: Yr daydreaming.
David Hampton: I was born—on a gold, burnished throne.
Mrs. Hampton: No. You were born in Buffalo. Wipe.

He wipes.

David Hampton: Im going to *be famous*. Do you mind?
Mrs. Hampton: Youll have to get yr father's permission. Here he
comes now.

David Hampton and Mrs. Hampton continue washing
and wiping. Mr. Hampton comes in. He totes a sign on a stick.
Its a road sign reading: "Be Famous—235 Miles,"
and an arrow pointing the way.

Mr. Hampton: What a day I had. What a day, what a day. My back
my arms my legs. A million times I wished for a bag of see-ment.
And a million times I praised God that see-ment is scarce.
Woulda mixed it up with my spit and stuck my sign in it, I woulda.
But see-ment is scarce. Scarcer than life and so I thanked God
for giving me gainful employment as a sign holder. Come rub my
shoulders, Mother. David, son, come rub my feet.

They rub his shoulders and feet. He closes his eyes and groans.
David Hampton looks at the sign. Its direction is difficult to
ascertain. Sneaking away, he crawls off on his belly
in the direction that the sign's arrow is pointing.

David Hampton: Im going to *be famous*.

Mr. Hampton: Wrong direction, son.

Mrs. Hampton: Tell him all you want. He wont believe you.

11 *TOPDOG* CLOSED AND OPENED

One man, the Barker, comes onstage guiding the Show.
The Show's mouth gapes open. The Barker forces it closed.
The Show struggles to keep its mouth closed. This aint so easy.

Barker: The Show is closed! An historical fact: On 11 August
2002, *Topdog/Underdog* closed in New York City. Some say this
partially accounts for at least 3 of the following 4 events: 1.
A remarkable coincidence—On the streets of London the play's
director and writer both, but separately, run into the same
famous actress, Miss Angela Bassett. 2. A Happening—During
the London run of the play, England experiences a heat wave,
and records 100 degrees fahrenheit for the first time in recorded
history. 3. An event of great and long-lasting sadness—Gregory
Hines dies. And 4. On 11 August 2003—A year to the day it
closed in New York—*Topdog/Underdog* opens in London!

The Barker cracks the whip. No response from the Show.
He then pries the Show's mouth open.
The Barker works with great difficulty.

Barker: The Show is open!

The Barker stands there panting, working to catch his breath,
as the Show stands there with his mouth gaping open.
At last, the Barker catches his breath and leads
the Show offstage.

12 NOW GREGORY HINES IS DEAD

A Man enters followed by his Shadow. As the Man speaks his
Shadow stands in the left corner trying to mouth the words.

Man:
When I am dead and buried in my grave,
when I am dead and buried in the good cold ground.

When all is said and theyre putting me away,
when all you reading folks done read,
how this life of mine, this dance, done killed me dead,
will you stomp and shake a leg for me?
On my brave brave grave,
so we'll all say yr sad Im good and gone,
sad you alone are left to pay
for all our living's shame.
When I am dead and buried in my grave.

When I am dead and buried in my grave,
will you all take all them clothes I used to wear
and burn them
in a heap?
You dug my hole way too deep—
howmy ever gonna get back to you
howmy ever gonna get back?
You dont live in the house you used to,
yr living with that somebody new,
the one with the yellow dog and the yellow car,
making hot hootchie-koo.

> The Man exits. The Shadow stands looking at his script,
> turning the page over and over, then trying to read
> his next move from his palms,
> but completely unsure of what to do next.

13 THE TROUBLE OF THE FAMILY IN WINTER

> The Shadow from the previous play lingers onstage.
> He becomes the Trouble.

Shadow
Shadow

> A gushing wind and other sounds of a blizzardy winter.
> A family comes in: Mother, Father, several Children,
> all bitter cold and bundled against the elements.
> Its as if theyve entered their cabin or cave.

Father: The cold!

Mother: Not in here, though.

Kid 1: Can we—

Kid 2: —eat now—

Kid 3: —Mother pretty—

Kids: —please!

Mother: Fatherll make a fire.

Father: As fast as I can.

> He grabs sticks and rubs 2 together.
> Mother notices the Shadow.

Mother
Shadow
Mother

Mother: Children? Huddle.

Father: Hud—?

Mother: *Now.*

> The Children obediently huddle. They do it slowly and calmly
> with no sense of alarm. Not because theyre unafraid,
> but because they are resigned to the fact that some day
> theyll fall victim to something.

Father: What is it?

Mother: Him.

Father: He's nothing.

Mother: He's a Trouble.

Father: But he's not *our* Trouble, is he?

Mother
Trouble

(Rest)

Mother: I dunno.

Father: He's not.

Mother: Yr not sure. I can tell yr not sure.

Father: Im sure.

Mother: Yr sure?

Father: —Yes.

Mother
Father

(Rest)

Mother: Im gonna keep my eye on him, just the same.

Father: What else am I supposed to do? What else is anyone supposed to do? I have a family. I am the father of a family. That means something to me.
(Rest)
Theyre huddling. But theyre not huddling scared.
(Rest)
Kids?
Kids: Yes, Father?
Father: You scared?
Kids: No, Father!
Father: I am the father. Of a family. I do my job.

> The fire comes brilliantly to life.
> The Kids gather round, warming themselves.
> The Father rummages through his raggedy,
> not-quite-thawed-out bag of belongings. He finds a flask,
> holds it over the fire, then sits down to drink.
> The Mother holds her hand out for a swig. He gives it over,
> and she drinks for a long long time. She finishes
> and wipes her mouth. There is still plenty left for the Father though.
> The Children have fallen asleep.

Mother: He's not our Trouble. All our Troubles look like us.
Father: Not really.
Mother: They was like us to the life and you know it.
Father: I murdered them all. In their beds. One got away, though he was the baby. He grew up. Took his time doing it too. He grew up and went away.

Mother
Trouble

Mother: Huddle.

> The Trouble huddles. Mother pets him.

Mother: He's still a child!

14 BACK IN L.A.

> 2 folks: 1 Earthling and 1 Spaceling in a space suit
> with a fishbowl for a helmet or, you know,
> just do the best you can with the budget youve got.

Earthling: Ever been up?

Spaceling: Nope. I aint been up but I have been down.

Earthling: Not up?

Spaceling: Nope, not up, not yet, but Im gonna.

Earthling: Whatcha waiting on?

Spaceling: Im what you could call one of them pro-cras-tin-a-tors. I got the suit on, but, all I do is think about going up all the time, but, aint got to it yet, I guess.

Earthling: But yr English is so good. I mean, I wouldnt of taken you for a procrastinator, not with English like youve got. A communist maybe, but—

Spaceling: Cause of this suit?

Earthling: Yeah.

Spaceling: Not a communist. But am a pro-crast-in-ator. Bad. Yep. I got it. Bad.

Earthling
Spaceling

(Rest)

Earthling: Mars is the closest its ever been to the earth in 400 years.

Spaceling: For true?

Earthling: I heard it on the radio.

Spaceling: Shit. Well, Im off then.

Spaceling reads the following stage direction:

Spaceling: I leap into the air, flying effortlessly to Mars. I get there, colonize the planet, bring back slaves who, in their superiority, after 400 years, overrun the earth and dominate.

Spaceling
Earthling

(Rest)

Spaceling: What do you think?

Earthling: No one's ever gonna go for that.

Spaceling: Yeah. Oh well.

(Rest)

This is L.A. The land of "limited ability."

Earthling: Dont be such a buzzkill. Look at all the movie stars.

Spaceling: Yeah. Pretty.

They do some heavy-duty gawking and then, à la Stephen Hawking, look up, at outerspace.

15 VASE

> A pretty vase on a pedestal. A Woman is seated.
> A Man paces.

Man: Im at my limit.

Woman: Just a bit more.

Man: Im at my limit. Please.

Woman: Whats that?

Man: A vase.

Woman: Yr favorite vase?

Man: Not really.

Woman: Says here its yr favorite.

Man
Woman

(Rest)

> The Woman picks up the vase. She drops it to the ground,
> it breaks. The Man stops pacing. The Woman rings a bell.
> Another Man comes in. He looks at the vase,
> picks through the pieces. He finds small,
> fortune cookie–like paper among the shards.

Another Man *(Reading)*: "Things, at last, are coming together!"

> The Man and Woman rush toward each other and hug. Hard.
> The hug becomes a struggle.

16 BLACKOUT

> The stage is completely dark.

Voice:
New York, New York
went black today
black out
no power
(but black power? Maybe.)
Something about a loop
in Lake Erie. Other folks
sitting around

cursing Canada
saying its all somehow
Canada's fault.
But me,
Im blaming Idi.
Idi Amin.
Cause when he was living
he was into the most notorious shit:
feeding folks to alligators
while they was still living
having 1000 babies with his 1000 wives.
Im stretching the truth a bit, but, hey,
you need to get the picture
even in the dark,
like once
when one of his wives, when she back-talked him,
he cut her up and ate her.
Black power? Go figure.
(Rest)
Can we have the lights on now?

Another Voice: Tomorrow.

Voice: Ok.

Another Voice: Idi Amin's just died!

> The stage fills with Wailing Voices.
> The Wailing reaches a crescendo. Then stops.
> The stage stays dark.

Voice:
Energy going.
Out the door.
Good or bad? No matter.
Energy going.
Out the door.

17 CRIME AND PUNISHMENT

> The Guilty Man makes an hysterically impassioned plea
> before the judges. He has been stating his case for some time.
> Hundreds of years most likely, but its only just now
> caught the eyes and ears of the media,
> cause right now theres something that can be called a lull
> in the war. Anyway—

Guilty Man: Yes yes I am guilty. There is nothing I can do that will undo my deed, nothing I can say to the injured party or parties, for I readily admit that I have injured a large number, a countless number. Countless beyond measure. But I was only—doing my job. Cant any of you understand? All you people—you all and yr families have jobs. You must understand. Perhaps some distant connection—in a quadrangle or a cul-de-sac, unspoken of in polite company—but known all the same, perhaps one of those quadrangles is in a—

> A loud bell goes off.

Head Judge: Time!

President: At last!

Guard: The condemned and his counterpart will be seated!

> A Mass of Judges scribble things as the Condemned
> sits on his haunches with his head bowed low.
> His Counterpart whispers gently to him and pats his head.

Counterpart: ((You did the best you could. But you started to cry. They hate that. But you couldnt help it. You should of mentioned Copernicus or the 4th veil or the presence of perspiration on the upper lip of the Virgin. We rehearsed that stuff. Instead you mention the Family. Ah, but what can you do. They dont allow do-overs.))

Head Judge: Time!

> The Judges stop scribbling.

Head Judge: Show.

> The Judges show their scores. A slew of numbers on cards.

Head Judge: Next!

18 A YARN FROM THE SKEIN OF (UN)HAPPINESS

> The Skeinster comes on holding a skein of red yarn.
> A Daughter and Mother come on.

Daughter: She's late.

Skeinster: She's what?!

Daughter: Late.

Mother: All we can do is wait.

Daughter: And hope for the best.

> A Woman walks up slowly. For a long time,
> while she's moving toward them, she's still in the far distance.

Daughter: She's coming. Look sharp.

> The Woman walks up. She gives the Daughter
> a sign that reads: "Happiness."
> Then the Woman pulls the yarn and walks off with the yarn trailing.
> The Mother, seeing the yarn trailing, begins talking
> as if on automatic, as if the yarn's movement is her start button.

Mother: I have a daughter. A great beauty. Cheeks like fresh-bloomed roses. Hair glossy as a raven's wing. She took after her father, the milkman. Her father was my first husband. Dont worry, its all happy. My 2nd husband—was allowed 2 at a time under the new rules—Carter, his name was, oh, he was a big and burly brute. A hunter by trade. He'd stay out all night. Come home with enough meat for the day. Eat it all, most of it, by himself. I prefer vegetables. My daughter likes cake. Bonita her name is. Ah! When she walks, the sky showers diamonds down!

> The Other Woman runs on, very late. Her sign says: "Un."
> She stands there catching her breath,
> then moves to stand next to the Daughter.
> Together their signs read: "Unhappiness."

Mother: Hhhhh.

Other Woman: Sorry.

Daughter: It was going so well.

Skeinster: But what can you do?

Mother: It was just getting good.

Other Woman: Im sorry. Traffic.

Mother: We were going to have a happy ending.

Daughter: I was just beginning to enjoy myself.

Other Woman: Dont make a big deal out of it, K? Late happens.

Mother & Daughter: Right.

Mother
Skeinster
Daughter
Other Woman

(Rest)

> Somewhere the Woman is still holding the end
> of the skein of red yarn. She is still walking,
> and so the red skein of yarn is still unrolling.
> Mother looks at the yarn unrolling. She touches the yarn,
> like a woman would touch a clothesline thats been hanging
> in the backyard since before she moved in,
> and now that she's moving out—after her divorce
> from a husband who has found love with another—
> "I'll never be happy like this again," she's thinking. But—.

Mother: We dont call my daughter Bonita anymore.
(Rest)
Thats the *Reader's Digest* version of our story.

19 MASON JAR GENIE

> Master rubs a lamp and makes a wish.

Master: I want a ham sandwich.

Master
Steward

Master: Where the hell's my ham sandwich?
Steward: Not here yet.
Master: Where the hell's my genie?
Steward: I dunno.
Master: Try the copper-colored lamp with the inlaid turquoise and the purple shiny tassels. And, if thats a no-go, try every lamp in the universe.
Steward: As you wish.

> Slowly fade to black.
> Slowly fade up. Many eons have passed.

Master: Yr not my genie, yr my steward. Wheres my genie?
Steward: Ive tried all the lamps.
Master: Rub them again and harder.
Steward: My hands are already raw.
Master: Rub the lamps or I'll beat you.

Steward
Steward

Master: Did you rub the mason jar?

Steward: I did not rub the mason jar.

Master: Go rub the mason jar.

Steward: I wont.

Master: You wont and I'll beat you. You wont and I'll beat yr wife. And yr daughters. And I'll take yr keys.

> Steward exits quickly.

(Rest)

> A Black Man comes in.

Mason Jar Genie: What.

Master: "What"? Im yr master.

Mason Jar Genie
Mason Jar Genie

(Rest)

Mason Jar Genie: What master? Shit. Do you see a master? I dont see a master. You want a piece of me or what, Master? What?! What?!?!?!?!

Master: Lights out!

> The lights go out.

Mason Jar Genie: Lights on!

> They come on again.

Mason Jar Genie: Lights go out when I say so. Yr turn in the mason jar, Master! Get stepping or Ima fuck you up like only a genie can fuck you up.

> The Master runs offstage in complete terror. Complete terror, given the events of our day, may be hard to do, but, you know, think of the worst and do yr best.
> The Steward comes on with the mason jar.
> The Master is inside.

Mason Jar Genie: Is the "master" in there?

Steward: Yep. Hungry?

Mason Jar Genie: I want a ham sandwich.

Steward: Very well, sir.

> Steward goes to fetch the food. Mason Jar Genie finds the tv-remote in the folds of the couch and, as the lights dim, changes channels with a mood approaching joy.

20 HOUSE OF CARDS

> A Woman comes in. She takes out a deck of playing cards and begins building a house of cards. A Man comes in. He has a brown paper bag.

Man: Ive brought a head of cabbage. Its in here somewhere. Its purple. Yll love it. Im not sure about the taste—but yll love the color.

Woman: Shhh. Theyre listening. Theyre listening even though I paid them not to listen.

Man: (((Here I am with a brown paper bag of groceries, which includes one stunning head of purple cabbage!)))

Woman: Can we live here, you think?

Man: Dont see why not.

Woman: Because you think we can or because you think we dont have nowhere else to go?

Man: This land is my land! Land where our fathers died! Of the people, by the people and etcetera. Purple mountains majesty!

Woman: Simmer down or Mrs. Jackson will report you for— artificial patriotism.

Man
Woman

(Rest)

Man: At least weve got this cabbage.

Woman: I paid them not to listen but someone else paid them more. I know that in my gut. Theres no winning in this country. It frightens me to think about whats really going on, so I just look at everything with my peripheral vision and keep my eyes mostly to myself. I dont want people thinking I am not with the program. We are slowly being bamboozled. The rich have set up a series of smoke screens and we're just in the mist of it. Theres no way out but in.

(Rest)

Man: Have some cabbage.
Woman: I bet you work for them.
Man: Have some cabbage. Come on. Enjoy.

> The Man takes a bite from the cabbage.
> The Woman continues to build the house of cards.
> It gets quite grand. They lacquer it and live in it.
> It survives the rains and the mudslides. It makes the cover
> of *House Beautiful*. Their children sell it for a pretty penny.
>   In short, life goes on, and it goes on pretty well
> when you compare the existence of the average American Joe
> to the existence of the Average Joe in a less-fortunate country.
> Still in all, the Woman's worries, while mostly forgotten,
> were very well-founded.

21 BEAR

> A Woman and a Man sit in chairs.
> She has been falling a great long while.

Woman: I dunno. I feel very—insignificant. Ive been writing—"plays" I call them. I have, what my dad would call, the "audacity" to call them *plays*.
(Rest)
Shits. Theyre shits. 365 shits.

(Rest)

Man: Rhymes with "tits."
Woman: Also rhymes with "asshole."
Man: You should see someone—
Woman: I am seeing someone—else.
Man: I see.

Coming from outside, a great vicious, ferocious ROAR is heard.

Man: What the fuck was that?!
Woman: A bear.
Man: A bear? Yr telling me a bear escaped from the zoo!? We're in the fucking city for Christ's sake!
Woman: Go see.

The Man puts on his jacket and goes outside.
Almost immediately more ROARS, and then the Man's
screaming as the Bear eats him alive.

Woman
Woman

(Rest)

The Other Guy enters, from the kitchen with 2 cold ones.

Other Guy: What was that?
Woman: What?
Other Guy: Sounded like—I dunno—a *bear*.
Woman: Maybe.
Other Guy: Hope these are cold enough.

Woman pops hers open. They toast.

Woman: Cheers.

They drink.

22 A SEARCH FOR THE MEANING OF LIFE

Get as many people who, in a hands-and-knees position,
can be crammed onto the stage.
Have them slowly enter from one side, crawling.
Theyre all looking for something.
For awhile they pack the stage.
One raises her hand gesturing: "Ah! Ive found it! No. False alarm."
They go back to crawling. They creep and crawl
in a very methodical fashion, falling off the stage like a million
lemmings. And after a time the stage will be empty again.

23 LUCKY FELLA

A young Lucky Fella comes in with a shopping bag.
He changes his clothes for a hot date: snazzy threads,
very cool, but from another era. He styles and profiles.

Lucky Fella: Whats yr name, baby? Whats yr name, whats yr sign?
(Rest)
How bout you and me go—you know.
(Rest)
Yeah, I got a job, baby. Lemmie hip you to how much I bring home a week.
(Rest)
A girl like you deserves the best. Here I am.
(Rest)
Ah, yr too beautiful, baby. I bet yr a model or something, am I right?

> An elderly fella, Pop, comes in, crawling on hands and knees.
> He's looking for the people from yesterday's play.

Pop: Im old. I crawl slow.

(Rest)

Lucky Fella: You gotta go, Pop.
Pop: Im going. I just. There was a crowd here, just a minute ago. They crawled in from outside. Through the living room and up the stairs and down the hall. You see them?
Lucky Fella: Pop. Turn around and get out. Get out my room, Pop. Im—
Pop: Yr talking to yrself.
Lucky Fella: Im practicing my lines.
Pop: In my day we didnt learn lines for girls. We were just ourselves. For better or for worse, and we wore our hearts on our sleeves. A girl knew what she was getting into. And there was plenty of bases back then, and most of us only went to 1st before we got married, and if a fella needed to bust a nut he went to the house of ill-repute.
Lucky Fella: Pop.
Pop: They came this way.
Lucky Fella: Go home, Pop.
Pop: I know you seen them!
Lucky Fella: Yeah. But yr too late, huh?
Pop: Im *hungry* is what I am.

> Lucky Fella turns back to his mirror.
> Pop is still crawling around, looking, and eating whatever
> he finds along the way.

Pop: There were a dozen of them at least. All honest-looking people. Crawling. Were looking for the—the something or other, they said.

Lucky Fella: Whats yr name whats yr sign?

Pop: I didnt believe them at first. I tried to keep up. They came this way I tell you. Right through yr room.

Pop exits crawling.

Lucky Fella: The light coming off yr smile, its like *magic*, Im telling you.

He smiles awhile.

24 YR DREAMING, NATHANIEL

The Entire Group from the play for August 22 crawls back onstage. This time they crawl from right to left. As they crawl, very slowly along, a young man, Nathaniel, talks to a Woman.

Nathaniel: Im gonna have a son someday. That son's gonna have a *room*. A nice room in a nice house.

Woman: Yr dreaming, Nathaniel.

Nathaniel: What if I am.

Woman: Dreaming is against the Laws: "You shall not create a false situation—"

Nathaniel: "—out of thin air, i.e., when you have not a dime in either yr pocket or the bank . . ." I know the Laws.

Woman: Weve got to keep looking.

They continue searching along with the others.

Nathaniel: My son'll have—*good looks*! Why not. And with good looks comes, of course, *a way with the ladies*—

Woman: Why are you telling me this?

Nathaniel: Cause we could get married maybe?

Woman: Yr dreaming, Nathaniel.

She crawls around, with the others, very methodically and with great purpose. Nathaniel stops. People crawl over him and onward. He is alone onstage. He looks around. Lost and alone, he hurries to rejoin the group.

25 UNFIT TO PRINT

Scene 1

A Man and Woman. He's in a suit. She's in a white dress or pantsuit. Theyre standing before the Preacher. Its their wedding. "You may kiss the bride," the Preacher says, but we dont hear it.

Woman
Kiss
Man

The Servant comes in and throws rice.
The Man and Woman walk upstage to 2 chairs.
The Servant presents them with a bottle of wine
and a tv-remote. They sit and watch tv.
He is excited about the Big Game. She is bored, then cries.
He gallantly changes the channel.

Woman: My hero!

They cuddle sweetly. The Servant comes crawling in.
She picks up a bit of rice, eats hungrily.
Her Kids appear like young birds with their mouths gaping
and necks straining. She feeds the rice to them
instead of eating herself.

Scene 2

The Woman from the last scene and a Cop.
The Cop rubs the Woman's fingers in the inkpot,
about to fingerprint her. He hesitates and she stands there
with inky fingers.

Cop: You kill him?

Woman: Yeah. I aint gonna lie. Things were nice, but they went sour.

Cop: Jeez. Why do I waste my time?

Woman: Because thats how things are done in this country.

Cop: If we were somewheres else I wouldnt be wasting my time.

Woman: But we're not somewheres else, are we? We're not somewheres else and you know what else? Im guilty but Im gonna get off. Scot-free. Get off scot-free and sell my memoirs for millions and be on all the talk shows. Yr gonna see me on tv and wish you were me.

Cop
Cop

> The Cop turns in his badge and his gun, quits his job.

Woman: Hey, the ink on my fingers is drying! Hey!

Scene 3

> The Cop and a Co-Worker on the subway.

Co-Worker: Where you all going?
Cop: Home.
Co-Worker: Shit.
Cop: No shit.
Co-Worker: Home?
Cop: You deaf?
Co-Worker: Shit. Whered you get that kind of money?!

> The Cop tells the Co-Worker, but the roar of the train
> obscures his words from us.

26 FROM *THE ABSOLUTELY TRUE ADVENTURES OF AFRODITE JACKSON-JONES* (For Stephanie)

Wanda X: It was 1976, but I was *not* feeling it. Do you know where Im coming from? Everybody was feeling bicentennial and walking around in some jive-ass version of red, white and blue. The dudes sporting blue leisure suits, most of my friends had at least one wrap-around dress with the flag on it. My little sister, Shandra, she walked around like a different 1776 historical personage every week: Betsy Ross, Ben Franklin, Molly Pitcher, Crispus Attucks, George Washington, she was the little drummer boy, she was the unknown soldier.

Rufus: You gonna drink yr drink?

Wanda X: Not yet. You neither. I aint done with the foundation. Talking about 1976 cause this part of the world thought it was happening. Me in chemistry class bored as hell. So I got to mixing up some of Grandpa's recipe. Mixing it was easy, but waiting for it to ferment all these years, thats been hard.

> She takes a drink of her recipe.

Wanda X: Rufus. Drink.

He drinks.

Rufus: Now what?
Wanda X: We wait.

They wait.

Rufus: Lemmie knock you off yr feet with a kiss.
Wanda X: You cant kiss for shit.
Rufus: Ive been practicing. Look.
Wanda X: Thats nerdy.
Rufus: Yeah.
Wanda X: I dont feel so good.
Rufus: Me neither. Whats that stuff you mixed?
Wanda X: I was following the recipe from Grandpa's book. Guess I—

Funk music is heard. Loud and proud. The 2 kids transform into Afrodite Jackson-Jones and Natural Man.

Natural Man: What the hell?
Afrodite: We superheros!
Natural Man: Lets get on the corner and show off our threads.
Afrodite: Please. We gotta go fight crime, brother. Come on.
Afrodite & Natural Man: PEACE AND POWER TO THE PEOPLE!

They fly off to save the world. Forever. A little girl comes on dressed as Betsy Ross.

Betsy Ross: To be continued . . .

27 MORE MONEY THAN GOD

Suit, a man wearing a 3-piece suit with lots and lots of pockets, comes onstage. Methodically, he empties his coin-filled pockets and neatly stacks and arranges the money.
Herb and Harriet reading through a stack of newspapers.

Herb: He's a big man. He's a big, big man. His daddy was a big, big man, but he's bigger.
Harriet: No shit.
Herb: No shit.

(Rest)

Harriet: How much money do you think God has?

Herb: Plenty.

Harriet: More than Father?

Herb: Father who?

> Suit continues emptying pockets and arranging money.

Herb: He wants you to work.

Harriet: I told him no.

Herb: Me too. I barely let the words clear his throat before I said no. Came calling. Stood in the doorway. He wants to turn me into a—

> Suit continues with money, turns pockets inside out.

Herb: He wants to turn me into what he is. No way.

> Suit takes a string from his pocket. The string leads
> from the bottom of his pocket to an unknown destination
> offstage. He pulls the string. Once. Twice. A 3rd time, yanking it.
> Slave comes on, the other end of the rope around his neck.

Suit: Count.

> Slave starts counting money in a wonderfully methodical
> and rhythmic fashion.

Suit: Im a big man. Im a big, big man. My daddy was a big man too. But me, Im bigger than he.

(Rest)

Slave: You know something? God dont gotta dime. I mean, whats God need with money?

Suit: Whassat?

Slave: Nothing.

> Suit leans back to rest. Slave continues counting.

Herb: He said Im gonna pay you anyhow, and I'll give the money to yr wife.

Harriet: Yr wife?

Herb: You, I guess.

Harriet: He's fucking with us.

Herb: Theres worse things, arent there?

Herb

Harriet

Harriet: Yes, theres worse things.

Herb: Hear the counting?

Harriet: Yeah.

Herb: Dont worry. Theres worse things.

> Slave tries to pocket a coin. Suit sees, yanks the rope.
> Slave puts coin back in pile, his counting continues.

28 A PLAY ABOUT SUIT

Suit: I need my own play.
(Rest)
I need my own play.

> He pulls a string. Slave walks in and flops, belly down,
> flat on the ground, prostrating.

Suit: You come when I call. Suit likes that.

Slave: You didnt call, Mr. Suit.

Suit: I pulled yr string. Isnt that the same thing?

Suit
Slave

(Rest)

Slave: An eclipse! Look!

> Suit looks.

Suit: Ah! Im blind.

> He pulls another string. A Chorus of Slaves comes in
> and leads him around. They feed him, read to him, etc.
> That is, they assist him in his blindness.

Slave: I was free, living my life, doing a host of beautiful things, and I had the respect of my community. "Come with me," he said. "I'll make you big cause I am big," he said, "I got pockets full of money. I got a fancy car, I got a garage for 2, I got the mortgage due, I got—"

Suit: This is my play! Im not blind anymore. Scram!

> The Chorus of Slaves scrams. Suit pulls a string and Slave runs
> to his side. He flops and prostrates as before.

Suit: Thats more like it.

Slave: What do we do now, Mr. Suit?

Suit: Nothing. We wont do nothing. We wont do nothing because we dont gotta. And when we do do something, itll be what I say. Because this is my play.

(Rest)

Slave, take my picture.

> Suit gets ready for his picture.
> Slave does something shady to the flashbulb.
> He takes Suit's picture. Very bright flash.

Suit: Ah! Im blind.

> Slave turns out the lights.

29 LIVE FREE OR DIE

> People come onstage holding hands like in Red Rover,
> lining up from upstage to downstage. They are the Furies.
> The Mythical Murderess approaches from stageleft—
> hands bloody, looking guilty, just walking.
> When she sees the Furies, she walks more quickly,
> but straight toward them. Her speed increases
> as her distance diminishes. She throws her body at them,
> trying to break their ranks. She almost does.
> We see it in slow motion, like a sprinter through a tape,
> every muscle strained to cross the finish line, but then the tape,
> instead of breaking, holds her by the hands.
> They remain extended like this.
> She pulls away as they pull her back. Lights out.

30 HOLEY MOLEY

> A Woman stands at the door. A Man eats cherry tomatoes
> from a small, green, plastic basket.

Man: These are good, very good. You could win a ribbon in the county fair if youd just believe in yrself. Yumm. You hear me? Yummmmm.

Woman: The hole. Its out there.

Man: Its always out there. Close the door and come sit down. Ive got an idea.

Woman: Its turned onto its side.

Man: Tomato pie. Youd win a blue ribbon in the novelty section sure as Im sitting here.

Woman: Its calling to me.

Man: Dont be silly.

Woman: It wants me to cross the threshold.

Man: Look! The holey mole!

Woman: Outside?

Man: Inside.

Woman: Holey Moley! Where?

Man: Its small, come see.

> The Woman comes to look. He points to nothing. She smiles.
> He smiles too.

31 | THE KING AND I

> 2 Men with buckets scrub the floor.

The Knight: 'Tis an affront, sire—

The King: Peace.

The Knight: An affront against Nature.

The King: Or could it be—Nature's design? There is Springtime and there is Winter. When the Winter showeth herself in her black barren branches, and hills thick with snow, and lakes frozen over, we do not say: "Winter affronts Nature—"

The Knight: Yes, sire.

The King: We say she *is* Nature.

The Knight: And we welcome her.

The King: Yes.

The Knight: But I cannot welcome this. You are king. You have lands that stretch from here to that far horizon and back again. You have subjects. You have armies. You have gold. You have a queen unmatched in her grace and beauty. You have children. You have a crown.

The King: Had. I had all that and more. But my fortune visits Hades' lair. We shall wait out this Winter. Time will tell. And in the meantime, for the time and circumstances are very mean, we'll scrub.

> The King scrubs with noble vigor.
> His strokes are strong and even. The Knight follows suit.

1 A PLAY FOR THE PEOPLE

Lots of people are lounging about. Perhaps in recliners
or lawnchairs with some drinks and sunglasses.
Perhaps playing dice or cards or gossiping on cell phones.
The Great Poetess with her Amanuensis strides in.

Great Poetess: I will write a play for the people.

Amanuensis *(Writing)*: I will write—

Great Poetess: Dont write that down, silly. And dont write that down either.

(Rest)

Where are all the people?

Amanuensis: Here are the people.

Great Poetess: There are the people?

Amanuensis: Not so loud—theyll hear.

Great Poetess: (((There are the people?)))

Amanuensis: (((These are the people.)))

Great Poetess: The people, it seems, are not what they used to be.

Amanuensis: There are other peoples, Great Poetess, who still retain the more subdued characteristics.

Great Poetess: Let us go then, you and I.

They stride off into the sunset. Someone wins in a dice game.
The shouts of joy catch the eye of the Great Poetess.
She stops.

Great Poetess: Write that down. You never know.

Her Amanuensis writes.

Great Poetess: What is it? I can feel you about to ask me something. Dont be shy.

Amanuensis: I'd like my own play.

Great Poetess: We'll give the Amanuensis her own play.

The Great Poetess snaps her fingers and the lights go out.

2 HER AMANUENSIS

Great Poetess: This play is called "Her Amanuensis."

> The Great Poetess lies on her side on the ground.
> Her Amanuensis stands with a book and a pencil.

Great Poetess: Read it back to me. A day's labor. Read it back.

Amanuensis: The entirety?

Great Poetess: Begin. I'll tell you when to stop. If you see my eyes close, dont stop. But go to the bottom of the page and write: "She shut her eyes." If my break should become deep, dont stop yr reading, but write beneath: "She fell into a deep sleep."

Amanuensis: If you should snore?

Great Poetess: If the Great Poetess should snore—

(Rest)

I fear for this world. Do you?

Amanuensis: Fear for this world, maam?

Great Poetess: Mmmmmmm.

Amanuensis: I fear for the next world. Not this one. This one was built to pass away, and so its flaws will pass with it. But the next world, the one where we are all headed, where we are all headed with all our flaws—

Great Poetess: Maybe we'll lose them in transit.

Amanuensis: That would be a blessing.

(Rest)

Great Poetess: If I should fall asleep and you see me sleeping, dont stop yr reading, but write: "She sleeps and tunnels underneath the surface of the ground, digging her way towards the Great Lake." And should, while yr reading, if I should die, chart every aspect of my decomposition. The loss of body heat. The soft warm flesh turned cold and hard and the weight beyond its living pounds. The rigor mortis, the disintegration, how death turns the color. The stench. Watch closely. Write down everything. When the ants and flies visit me, and when the flies' eggs hatch their maggots to feed upon me, and, unlike in life, when they are not shooed away, Im theirs now. And soon, quite literally, one of them. My rotting body will be my final text, and you will be my pen.

(Rest)

Begin!

3 A ROUND FOR GLENN GOULD

First, Parts 1–3 are performed one right after another.
Then theyre performed simultaneously,
creating a cacophony of sound.

1st Part: Master's Part

Master: Saddle my horse! You heard me! I said saddle it!
Mistress: And then, play me a ditty! On the tuba, for God's sake, not the viola, you fool!
Master: Good help is hard to find.
Mistress: I know where theres good help. Shall I call them?
Master: Do. Quickly.
Mistress: Ring ring ring ring. Theres no answer. Ring ring ring ring.
Master: Keep trying!

2nd Part: Mower's Part

Head Mower: Build the wall, keep going.
Brick Layer: Higher?
Head Mower: Higher! Higher! Higher!
The Chorus of Phony Polled Constituents: We feel so much safer already. It will keep us from them, and them from us. We feel so much better and safer already.

3rd Part: Joan Crawford Is Remembered

Joan Crawford: Sing! You heard me! Sing! If you do nothing else, sing the song and bring a light to this gray desolate life! Oh, life instead of death, because yr voice can do that, Sonny.

Sonny sings the last piece of the Puccini aria, "Nessun Dorma,"
the bit right at the climax.
After each Part has been performed separately,
the round begins. It grows steadily, gets loud, then gets quiet,
down to a mumble, before it stops or peters out.

2 Women

Woman: Its like Glenn Gould said once.
Other Woman: Whatd he say?
Woman: You know Glenn Gould?

Other Woman: He played piano.

Woman: Right.

Other Woman: I put his Goldberg Variations on my iPod. Its all I listen to on the bad days. Whatd he say?

Woman: He said, "For every hour Im around people, I gotta spend 50 hours by myself."

Other Woman
Woman

Other Woman: Deep.

Woman: Very deep.

> They lean back in their lawnchairs and relax.
> The round starts up again, picking up volume and intensity.
> It could continue as long as you like,
> perhaps continuing underneath other plays
> as the evening of theater progresses.

4 TOO CLOSE

> A Writer Woman with a clear plastic bag.
> She blows her nose on a tissue, balls it up,
> then drops the tissue into her bag.
> She coughs into a paper napkin, examines the phlegm.
> She is concerned. She balls up the napkin and tosses it
> into the bag. Then she takes paper from her pockets,
> lots of folded, tiny sheets (not sheets, but slips,
> slips the size of fortune cookies with many words,
> some of them as full as sheets of paper).
> She unfolds some of the slips, reads them,
> then slowly places them into the bag. She sneezes into a tissue,
> puts the tissue in the bag; coughs into a napkin,
> throws the napkin into the bag; she puts
> a slip of paper into the bag.

Writer Woman: You start thinking after awhile about the ones that got away. Not the ones you wrote. But the ones you didnt write. Like the eggs that passed out of yr body without becoming babies. Or sperm, if yr a guy. Imagine if each one became somebody. Time is limited, I know, even in a work of this length. So Ive jotted down the un-included ones and put them in this plastic bag.

September

Upstage left. An Old Man and Old Woman appear.
They stare suspiciously at the Writer Woman.
They speak in "talk." (For more info regarding "talk,"
see S. Epatha Merkerson or *Fucking A*).

Old Man: Crack nevah? *(That her?)*
Old Woman: Neintah. *(Not sure.)*
Old Man: Watah. Watah. *(Ask her. Ask her.)*
Old Woman: Not me, Charlie. Qua deevah sha-na woah-ho! *(Not me, Daddy. She looks like a real bitch!)*
Old Man: Pah!
Writer Woman: Pah yrself!

Lights down on Old Man and Old Woman.

Writer Woman: A mother and father. Mine. Yeah. We werent very close.

5 FATHER COMES HOME FROM THE WARS (Part 9)

Several Fathers, men in army suits or uniforms, are sitting in a row:
a Soldier, a Sailor, a Janitor with a broom, a Security Guard
with a badge and a gun, a Mechanic with an oily rag
and a wrench, a Businessman with a suit and a briefcase,
maybe an Astronaut even. They are all young-looking:
fresh-faced, and firm-limbed; but very, very old-acting
in the most typical of ways: forgetful, passive, paranoid, sad,
weak, infirm, angry. The Mechanic wipes his head.
The Security Guard peers worriedly at the audience.
The Janitor sweeps. The Businessman opens his briefcase,
realizes its empty, and closes it
The Soldier and Sailor are having a conversation:

Soldier: "Father's Home—Comes from the Wars."
Sailor: You got the title wrong.
Soldier: Did not.
Sailor: Did too.
Soldier: You got water in yr ears. You wanna step outside?
Sailor: You got the title wrong. Im just trying to—
Soldier: What the hell is it, then?
Sailor: I dont know. But "Father's Home—Comes from the Wars" it aint.

(Rest)

Janitor: They put me in the doghouse. Thats not a lie. Do you know how hard it was? A man my size, living in a house so small. And in the backyard.

Mechanic: Least they didnt put you on the junk pile. Thats where they put me. Cause I'd cost them an arm and a leg to fix. So they junked me. After that, I turned to junk. Drugs, you know. Thats what I did. Lots of drugs. What else could I do?

Security Guard: Look! The war!

> They strain their necks downstage to get a better look.

Businessman: Its something, isnt it?

Soldier: Its bloody.

Businessman: Cant have a war without blood.

Janitor: Why have a war at all?

Businessman: Clean-up. Theres money in the clean-up.

Sailor: Its closer than it was yesterday. I can feel the heat from the fire on my face.

> They all lean in their chairs slightly, like heliotropism,
> when flowers crane and strain
> and turn beautifully toward the sun.
> Theres the sound of a high-pitched whine underneath,
> like the barely audible (but sustained) screeching of fingernails
> on a blackboard. The lights grow very bright and then pop out.

6 INTO THIS WILD ABYSS

> A man, Grant, comes in, wearing a heavy coat,
> hat, gloves, boots. A woman, Kitty, sits by the phone.

Grant *(Instead of: "Hi, honey, I'm home," he says)*: Its hell out there.

Grant
Kitty

Grant: You hear me? I said its hell out there.

Kitty: Its hell in here.

> Grant walks to the fire. He warms his hands, his ass.

Kitty: Fire's not good enough.

Grant: How come?

Kitty: I was cold all day.

Grant: Put more wood on when yr cold.

> He takes a log, adding it to the fire, which blazes brightly.
> Or, if the "fire" is just a pile of wood, quiet, and nonflaming,
> we would hear the dull sound of wood against wood.

Grant: Its simple.

Kitty: I dont like it simple.

Grant: Ah.

> He reaches into his coat's many outer and inner pockets,
> removing an impressive selection of guns, knives, grenades,
> molotov cocktails, slingshots, and a spoon. He neatly sets up
> his weapons on the floor. He removes his boots,
> placing them neatly. The knife from his boot too.
> He takes off his coat. Underneath he is heavily armed
> with a great length of ammunition, a double shoulder holster,
> and several grenades, like apples, hidden in his shirt.
> He removes all these, laying them in a line, so that the line
> of arms and weapons, etc., is one continuous line.
> If the playing space is too small, then the line can turn
> into a circle, encircling Grant and Kitty.
> Kitty, who has been watching Grant unload his weapons,
> sneaks nervous glances at the telephone.
> Finished unloading, Grant takes out a tin of Brasso polish.
> He gets busy polishing and cleaning his goods.

Kitty: You sell anything today?

Grant: No. You?

Kitty: Very funny.

Grant: Phone been ringing off the hook, right? Yr sitting there
sweating it out, hoping it dont ring while old Grant's here, right?
If it do, no need to sweat. I'll just leave. I'll just step out into the
hall or something.

Kitty: The hall?

Grant: I'll step out into the parking lot. I'll put my rifle over my
shoulder and walk back and forth, up and down memory lane.

Kitty: The phone didnt ring all day.

> Grant picks up the spoon, cleans it with great care,
> then sets it down again.

Grant: Not once?

Kitty: One wrong number.

Grant: You sure?

Kitty: Im sure.

Grant: You used to be able to turn wrong numbers into right ones.

Kitty
Grant
Kitty
Grant

(Rest)

Kitty: Whats the spoon for?

(Rest)

Grant: Their eyes.

> He mimes the scooping out of their eyes.
> Kitty's impressed, in spite of herself.

7 THE HANDSOME LEAD

> A man, the Handsome Lead, walks onstage as if he's lost.
> He finds an "X" centerstage, checks that the X matches
> the X on his map, then stands on the X confidently.
> Just as he does this, lounge music begins to play.
> The Lovelies, a chorus of lovely women, come onstage
> and mingle about.
> The Handsome Lead speaks to the audience:

Handsome Lead: Hi. Im the Handsome Lead.

The Lovelies: Hi.

Handsome Lead: Its good to be good-looking.

> The Lovelies continue to circulate as if thats their job.
> They dont approach him, they just walk around looking lovely.
> Again, he's very pleased with himself.
> He checks his map to the X on the floor
> and rocks back and forth on his heels. Suddenly another man
> comes in, lost like the first. Like the first, he finds the X,
> checks the X, then checks the man on the X.

New Lead: My turn.
(Rest)
Scram.

> The Handsome Lead leaves. The New Lead takes his place.

The Lovelies: Bye.
(Rest)
Hi.

> The world continues turning.

8 TRIGGER

Woman: BANG!
Man: We used to make love.

> Violin music comes on. Maybe Paganini.
> The Woman mimes playing the violin to the violin music.
> The Man pulls a silk scarf from his pocket,
> weeps copiously into it, then becomes worried,
> for the silk scarves are endless, like a magic trick.

9 INTO TEMPTATION

> A Man watches a Woman get dressed. He's kinda mousy
> and wears boxer shorts. She's kinda mousy too.
> She wears a full-length slip. She looks at her watch,
> heaves a sigh. She puts on a sexy dress, pantyhose,
> and high-heeled shoes.
> She sighs again, then smears on lipstick.

Man
Woman

> The Woman continues getting dressed: heavy ugly winter coat,
> crappy woolen hat, scarf, and mittens.
> She goes to look out the window, sighs again.
> She takes off her shoes and puts on socks,
> then stomps into a pair of heavy, winter, rubber boots.
> She's ready to go. She sits down.
> (The next 2 lines have the same number of syllables.
> Let that inform their delivery.)

Man: Where are you going?
Woman: Into Temptation.

> She gets up, goes to the door, stands alone.

Man: Will you be home in time for supper?
Woman: I dont know.

> She walks out. He waits and worries.

10 SOU'WESTER

> Dawn. A Mother sleeps. A Child wakes, goes to the Mother,
> and nudges her. She sleepily shoos him away. The Child sighs.
> The Child looks in bowls for food,
> he scrapes out yesterday's leftovers with his fingers.

Child: Mother, the ants got into the food again. Theres not much
left. Mother?

> The Child nudges Mother again. Again she shoos him away.
> Another sigh. An army of ants, all wearing sou'westers, races in,
> and, hoisting the Child high, carts him off to their lair.
> The Mother wakes and watches, but its all so strange,
> she's sure she must be dreaming.

11 THE BURDEN OF HISTORY

> A Woman with a bucket washes clothes on a rub board.
> Other Women and Men are gathered in the background.
> A Man, snappily dressed, comes in. He carries a suitcase.
> The Woman sees him. He counts time. They sing
> (just talk it if you wanna):

Woman:
The burden of history.
He's coming back again,
walking up and down my streets
in the shape of a man.

Chorus:
Oh, no.
Whatcha gonna do?
This town aint big enough for him and for you.

Woman:
The burden of history.
In on the noon train,
he got his meanness for his passage,
he *knows* my slave name.

Chorus:
Oh, no.
Where you gonna go?
Betcha dont even own
yr own house no more.

Woman:
The burden of histree.
Calls me up, calls me down,
put yr best dress on, girl,
we gonna go paint the town.

Chorus:
Oh, no.
Stay with the one you know.
Dont need to go scratch up nobody's floor.

Woman:
The burden of histree.
Is laying in my bed,
his feet way over the edge
Im pillowing his head.

Chorus:
Oh, no.
We seen this game before.
Send him out yr house, girl,
cause you dont know whats in store.

Woman:
The burden of histree.
He's walking on down the road,
I got his baby in my belly,
and he's got nice nice nice clothes.

Chorus:
Oh, no.
Better close yr door.
Close yr book on him, girl.
He wont come back no more.

The Man snaps his fingers, counting time.

Woman:
The burden of history.
He's coming back again,
walking up and down my streets
in the shape of a man.

> The Woman goes back to work. Lights out.

12 MAKE ME A PALLET

> Mother Rena lying in bed. A Kid looks underneath his pallet,
> taking out a sou'wester—a yellow raincoat
> and hood ensemble. He puts it on, sits and waits.
> Joe comes in, he's dressed like a Gloucester fisherman—
> also in a yellow rain ensemble—
> shaking out the raindrops from his coat.

Joe: Raining cats and dogs, I tell ya! Rena, the Kid ready?
Rena: Kid?
Kid: Yes, Mother. Im ready.
Rena: Oh, dont: "Yes, Mother" me like that. Here, I'll get up—
just for you.

> She gets out of bed. She's wearing a ballerina costume
> and is somewhat past her prime.

Rena: Give Mama a kiss, Kid.
Kid: Its wet out there, huh, Joe?
Joe: So wet we'll have to go in the boat.
Rena: Kiss me, Kid. There.
(Rest)
You hungry?
Kid: I ate.
Joe: We're late.

Rena
Joe

Rena: I wish he didnt have to go.
Joe: Dont be silly.
Rena: He's so small—and its raining.
Joe: He's wearing a sou'wester.

Kid: Plus, its yellow.

Rena
Joe

> Once again the stage is mobbed by strange ants
> in yellow sou'westers, or maybe just the characters onstage
> are mobbed. Just remember that the yellow ants were there
> once and ran off with a small child (see the play for September 10).
> And the ants are thankful that civilization came when it did,
> even though the food is all genetically engineered these days,
> and we never get to visit with each other like we used to
> cause everything is so—fast.

Rena: Whats he gonna be when he grows up?

Kid: An astronaut!

Joe: A drunk. A drunk, most likely.

Rena: Whatever you be, be good, huh? Listen to everything Joe tells you. I'll light candles for you—so—make sure you send a bird back to tell me you got there. Candles cost money.

Kid: I'll send 2 birds, but theyll be space birds from outerspace, so theyll come in the house wearing helmets and theyll talk with their hands and theyll fog up the glass.

Joe: Lets hit the road, Kid!

> They go without ceremony. Rena sits.
> She smokes or picks up the tv-clicker and changes channels.
> A New Kid comes in, sits beside her.

Rena: Another one?

New Kid: They said you had space.

Rena: I guess.

> The New Kid sits close to Rena and shares her cigarette
> and her tv-clicker.

13 THE FACE OF THE DEEP

> A Woman sits on a bench. She wears a mask.
> Any sort of mask except a gas mask.
> Perhaps a kid's Halloween mask.
> Perhaps a Greek theater mask.
> She has a huge shopping bag with her. A Man comes in.
> Also masked. Also with a shopping bag.

Man: Bus come yet?

Woman: Just missed it.

Man: You too?

Woman: Im having a lucky day.

Man: Lucky?

Woman: Long story.

> Suddenly seized by panic,
> they both rummage through their bags, choose another mask,
> replace the one theyre wearing with one theyve chosen.
> They relax.

Woman: The fallout. Its raining heavy today.

Man: I dont mind. Makes me feel like weve got weather. Remember when the fog would roll in?

Woman: Before my time.

Man: It was beautiful, the fog. Like little gray stars—

Woman: I know what fog is. I know what fog looks like. Ive completed my studies.

Man: Of course.

Woman: I'm not out of the loop.

> They sit in silence. An Escapee runs in. He is maskless.
> He is running from someone. He silently begs for the Man
> and Woman's help. No response. He grabs ahold of the bench
> on which theyre sitting. As they give him evil looks,
> he shrinks away. A Hunter comes in. Also maskless.
> The Escapee claws the floor. The Hunter shoots him dead
> and drags him away. As he is dragged away,
> marbles spill from his pockets and litter the ground.
> Upstage, someone walking by slips on the marbles.

14 A PRAYER FOR JOHNNY CASH

> A longish bench with people, almost enough to fill it.
> All dressed in black. A woman, Lavinia, comes in.
> She speaks to a Man nearest to her on the bench.

Lavinia: Is there room on the mourning bench?

Man: IS THERE ROOM ON THE MOURNING BENCH?

> *The people do their best to make room on the bench.
> Someone stands and weeps copiously.

Lots of mournful shuffling of feet and behinds and folks,
as they all pack up their belongings and trundle down the bench.
Lavinia gets a place. The bench is now pretty full.
Everyone sits there sadly.

Lavinia: Johnny Cash passed.
Man: June, too. Mother June, too.

The Mourners
The Mourners
The Mourners

A New Man comes in, dressed in black.
He carries a small suitcase filled with all he owns.
He holds a cheap, small, paper posy bouquet.

New Man: Is there—
Lavinia: IS THERE—
New Man: —any way that youll say something kind to me,
Lavinia? Im begging.
Lavinia: IS THERE ROOM ON THE MOURNING BENCH?

Lavinia
New Man

New Man: Lavinia, Im on my knees.

Repeat from * with exact sounds and movements as before.
The bench should be too crowded now.
People are squeezed together.
Those on the end struggle to stay on.
Another man comes in. He speaks silently to the New Man.
The New Man yells silently. The weary Mourners make room
on the bench even though there is no room.

15 KISSING BOOTH

2 Women: Doll, dolled-up; and Moll, dressed plainly.
Moll holds a sign: "Kisses: $£?¥ 2,000."

Doll: I aint in the mood for it today.
Moll: You sick?
Doll: Im not sick.

Moll presses her hand roughly to Doll's forehead.

Moll: You aint sick.

Doll: I didnt say I was.

Moll: Open yr mouth. Come on, theyll be here in a minute.

Doll: Aaah.

Moll: Looks alright.

Doll: Feels alright too. I just dont wanna—

Moll: Remember when you had that "problem" and I had to go 2 days in a row, cause Trini went to see that castle with that "prince" and ended up getting "married"? Who did double-time then, huh?

Doll: I feel like—I dunno. I need a vacation.

Moll: We got the 15th regiment coming today. Theyve been in the valley for—for a long time.

Doll: Trini said she wants to come back to work.

Moll: *Trini.*

Doll: You would have weekends off.

Moll: *Trini.*

Doll: She likes their tongues.

Moll: Fucking Trini. Fuck her. She likes their tongues. Fuck her. And no I aint going to kiss for you today, so get yr plastic lips ready. All Trini talks is big time. Fuck her. Like we could say what day we wanna do what. Yeah, right. We go by *their* schedule. Not vice versa.

Doll: I didnt ask you to go for me.

Moll: You were about to.

Doll gets her plastic lips ready: she takes a square of saran wrap and covers her lips and mouth. A plexiglas wall comes up to her neck, so that the Kissers can see her whole naked body, but only touch her lips.

Doll: What would Mom be thinking, you think?

Moll: What would Mom be thinking about what?

(Rest)

Doll: She would—disapprove.

Moll: Turn on the charm, Doll, here they come.

Doll sits pretty. Moll rings her bell. She begins her spiel as the lights fade.

Moll: Kisses! Kisses! Best that money can buy! First-date kisses, honeymoon kisses, shy kisses, one-night-stand kisses, kisses of all sorts. You name the style, Moll and Doll will deliver. Lips only, though, and no tongues please! Sweet kisses, honey sweet, right here, folks!

16 THATS THE DOPE TALKING

Woman: Here.
Man: What are these?
Woman: Videos. —I mean DVDs.
Man: Theyre late. You gotta see the Late Lady.
Woman: Come on.
Man: Sorry.
Woman: Its 2 minutes after midnight. Come on.
Man: We got signs posted all over. We got a strict policy.
Woman: Its fast—yr watch is fast—its just 1 minute after midnight.
Man: Sorry.
Woman: Come on, man.
Man: Go see the Late Lady! She's waving at you—go see her.
Woman: I wanna see *you*.

Man
Woman

(Rest)

Man: Thats the dope talking.
Woman: It sounded good, though, right? I mean for a second—for a millisecond, for a fucking nanosecond, before you even, I mean, for a beat, in the silence between me saying and you knowing, from *whence it came*—it sounded good, right?
Man: Right.
Woman: And now?
Man: And now yr later, lady.
Woman: Right.

> The Woman walks off and gets in a line full of gray, drab people.
> Her clothes actually change from fresh and new
> and bright clothes to dull and gray clothes.
> She gets in line to see the Late Lady.
> The line stretches twice around the globe.

17 DRAG

A Woman trudges onstage. Behind her she drags
an enormous bundle by a thick rope.
The bundle need not be really heavy, but it should be large,
and with her sweat and effort
she should make us feel its weight.
She drags the bundle from stageright to stageleft.
This takes a long time. A Man comes in. He sits downstage right
on the floor and plays solitaire. He hears/sees her,
watching without watching.

Man: Drag, huh?
Woman: Not—at—all.

Almost stageleft, she stops. She rests, wipes the bundle clean,
then sits on it. Quite completely. As if it were her favorite red
meditation cushion and she were in a place
where enlightenment were as attainable as a cup of coffee.
Flowers spring from the bundle, birds sing,
and some of our favorite people—Bobby Kennedy,
Martin Luther King, Jr., and Mahatma Gandhi—
come back from the dead. Beautiful music plays.
The Man, watching all the while, gets it,
smiles, goes back to his cards.

18 PROUST'S COOKIE

Cookie sits on a park bench, waiting. After a moment,
A Man comes up, looks over Cookie.

Man: Are you he?
Cookie: "It" actually. I am "it."
Man: I dont feel comfortable calling you an "it."
Cookie: Im a cookie. Just a delightful afternoon snack. Cookies
are "its." Cookies are not "he's." Cookies are not "she's." Unless
we were speaking German. Or French.
Man: Parlez-vous Français?
Cookie: Seulement un peu, monsieur.
Man: Ah, dommage.
Cookie: Not really. The fact that I speak *anything*, is this close to
miraculous, me being a cookie, I mean.
Man: Of course, cookies dont speak.

September

Cookie: Ive never met another one that does.

Man
Cookie

Man: Do I have to pay you? I'll pay you.

> The Man gives Cookie money.

Cookie: Yr a writer.
Man: Aspiring.
Cookie: Good luck.
Man: Thanks.

> The Man prepares himself, maybe prays to the 4 directions, lights a candle, takes a deep breath, maybe washes his hands, and does other things, you know, things writers do to prepare.
> Then he sits there.

Man: Where should I—?
Cookie: Anywhere.
Man: Is there a best spot?
Cookie: Anywhere is good.
Man: Anywhere?
Cookie: Yeah. Make it a place you like. Dont worry about me. Im just the cookie.
(Rest)
Go for it.

> The Man sits gingerly on th bench next to Cookie.
> He nibbles Cookie's neck.

Man
Cookie
Man
Cookie

> The Man takes a cigarette from behind his ear. Smokes.

Cookie: Well? Anything?
Man: Not yet.
Cookie: Now?
Man: Nope. Nothing.
Cookie: I inspired Proust. I was the cookie that inspired Proust. He nibbled a cookie and got the whole idea for his *Remembrance of Things Past*. Remember? Well, Im the cookie he nibbled.

September

Man: Have you inspired others?

Cookie: —.

Man: Have you inspired others?

Cookie: —Well, sure—.

Man: Maybe yr just not *my* cookie.

Cookie: Take another nibble.

Man: I really dont have all that much time. Im sorta on my lunchbreak—

Cookie: But my *reputation*.

Man: I wont tell anybody, dont worry.
(Rest)
Well. Goodbye.

Cookie: Goodbye.

> They shake hands. Man leaves.
> Cookie remembers the past and worries for the future.
> Another Man comes in as the lights fade.

19 LICKETY-SPLIT

> A Man onstage. Just standing there.
> A Woman runs in zigzagging around, and then,
> sorta like a freight train coming into the station,
> sorta like a honeybee finding a flower, she runs up to him.

Woman: Hi.

Man: Hi.

> She moves to him, licking him up and down and all over,
> licking like a thirsty dog at a water bowl,
> licking him like she wants to lick his color off,
> licking him like she's liking licking him, and, yeah, oh yeah,
> she's enjoying it. So is he. Then, she stops, catches her breath,
> maybe wipes her mouth with the back of her hand.
> He's standing there thinking that Romance with a capital R
> is coming toward him. But she runs offstage, running pell-mell,
> just leaving him there.

(Rest)

Man: Oh. Darn.

> Lights out.

20 BUDDY

Scene 1

> An Old Woman sits by the fire. She's knitting
> and she's got the radio on. She gets up
> and pours a cup of hot tea. She sits back down.
> She sings while she works. A Young Man comes in the room.
> He wears a hoodie and a bandanna over the lower part
> of his face. Or maybe a stocking over his face.
> He sneaks up behind her. He carries a gun.

Old Woman
Robber

> She turns to look at him. She looks him up and down.

Old Woman: Its over there.
Robber: Where?
Old Woman: Under that doily.
Robber: Cool.

> The Old Woman gets back to her knitting. He lifts the doily,
> sees a shoe box, goes to lift it.

Robber: Shit.
Old Woman: Thats what my Benjamin Franklin said, my husband.
Took him and 8 of his closest friends to lift it.
Robber: I can lift it. Maybe.
Old Woman: Do you know why we called him Benjamin Franklin?
That wasnt the name his mother gave him. His mother called
him "Woops." He was a mistake. We all are mistakes, I think.
Our kind is but chance. Deep down, Im sure of that. On the
surface, of course, its different, but Im not talking about the
surface. Im talking about the deep down.
Robber: Im gonna shoot the lock.
Old Woman: Whatever.
Robber: Shut up.
Old Woman: Why waste bullets? You may need them later—later
this evening, or tomorrow, or the day after that when yr on the
run, holding out in cheap motels with a 2-faced obliging woman.
She spread her legs quick but when the going gets rough, she
might turn on you. Yeah, you may need yr bullets then. Now
theres no need. I have a key. Its under that doily.

Robber: Cool.

> He gets the key, opens the shoe box. The shoe box is full of
> money and jewels. He stuffs his pockets, shirt,
> puts jewels around his neck, etc.

Robber: Shit, bitch, yr loaded!

Old Woman: He was struck by lightning. He was working in a
baseball field. It wasnt raining when he started, but when it
started raining he kept working. Everyone ran for cover. Not
Woops. "Ima take my chances," he said. KABLAMM!
(Rest)
"Kablamm!" said the lightning. Woops was Benjamin Franklin
after that.

Robber: Thank you for yr—hospitality, but I gotta split.

Old Woman: Of course. Wait.

Robber: What?

Old Woman: Something about—yr voice, yr face in the dim light,
and yr voice.

Robber: What about it?

Old Woman
Robber
Old Woman
Robber

(Rest)

Old Woman: *Buddy!*

> She gets up and hugs his legs.
> He just stands there looking at her.

Scene 2

> A foxy woman, Mamma, wearing a slip and smoking.
> As Buddy unloads the jewelry, she looks it over.

Buddy: She thinks Im Buddy.

Mamma: You done good, kid. You done real good. Keep doing this
good and I'll have my pension—and—you and me we'll get a
house by the seaside.

Buddy: "Buddy" she called me.

Mamma: This shit's gotta be real. It could be costume but—shit—
the workmanship—its the real shit, kid.

September

Buddy: She held on to my legs—

Mamma: You was late, and I was like, I guess the kid got popped. I was *interested* in you tonight. I missed you, but at least yr back in one piece and—you done very good.

Buddy: For a whole hour it felt like; she was clutching my legs.

Mamma: Sounds very moving.

Buddy: It was.

Mamma: Yr getting a promotion, kid. Of course I'll have to get the ok from the Powers That Be, but—

Buddy: I wanna be Buddy.

Mamma
Buddy

(Rest)

Mamma: Who is Buddy?

Buddy: Her brother.

Mamma: So be her brother Buddy. I dont give a fuck. You see me giving a fuck? Be Brother Buddy. Be her brother Buddy and maybe youll get capped while yr at it, but you wont see me giving a flying fuck.

> He pounces on Mamma, strangling her with his hands.
> This should be a stylized murder. Quick and sharp.
> He stacks up the jewelry and money. Then he lights a fire,
> warming his hands and thinking of his next move.

Scene 3

> The Old Woman sits and knits. Buddy cleans his gun.

Old Woman: I was wondering where you were. All these years. And look at you. I went and got old, but you, you stayed young.

Buddy
Old Woman

(Rest)

Buddy: Its good to be home.

> She keeps knitting. He keeps cleaning his gun as the lights fade.

21 BUDDY STARRING IN "WE NEVER CLOSE"

> Buddy is led onstage by the Old Woman. His mouth is open.
> She gets up on her stool. Then she puts a sign around his neck.
> The sign reads: "We Never Close."
> She sits on a campstool with her knitting.

Old Woman: It was his idea. Does that look like the idea of an old woman? No. Buddy's idea. Buddy's idea all the way. Wanted to earn his own keep. "I'm loaded!" I said, but he wanted to work. Hardheaded. That's what he is. So now look at him. Standing there, his mouth open for a whole year almost. There are little insects and things that have taken up residence between his teeth.

> Buddy's mouth slowly sags, almost shut.
> The Old Woman gets up slowly. As his mouth almost shuts,
> she slaps his face and he opens it up again. Wide!

Old Woman: We never close!
(Rest)
Want to earn yr keep? So earn it. Huh.

22 BUDDY STARRING IN "YOU CANT TAKE IT WITH YOU"

Scene 1

> Buddy in a security guard uniform.
> Several people with shopping bags—shopping.
> Shoplifter steals clothes. Buddy apprehends him. Wild applause.

Scene 2

> Buddy at home, drinking. Booze. The Old Woman knits.

Buddy: Ima nobody, I should just admit it.
Old Woman: Yr not a nobody. Yr Buddy. There are kids on the front stoop right now whove traveled all the way from Milwaukee to get yr autograph.
Buddy: Ima security guard, has-been nobody.
Old Woman: Those kids from Tokyo. What about them? All the way from Tokyo to see Buddy.

Buddy grabs his chest. He's having a heart attack.
The Old Woman, not noticing, keeps talking.

Old Woman: Who did they get to host the Thanksgiving Day Parade for 3 years in a row? Buddy. There are guys with more money, but you have the love of the people, Buddy. You have the love of the population. The world is crazy about Buddy. And—oh God.

She runs to him, cradling his head.

Buddy: Remember when I was a hood? Just a 2-bit hood with nothing going for me except the way I scared people—made them sweat when I had my gun aimed on them. I was nothing. I wanted to be something, I wanted to be something so much— oh, I wanted the world!

Old Woman: Youve had it all along, Buddy.

Buddy: Have I? I guess—I have—had the world. All along.

He dies. She cries. Melodramatic music plays.

23 ALL THINGS BEING EQUAL

One Person with a big gold crown comes onstage. She's a queen. She waves to the people. As she does so, Another Person with a big gold crown comes in, and then Another, and Others, until the stage is packed with people wearing big gold crowns. Theyre packed-up like sardines. They struggle to maintain their composure. During this play there is a light that fades up high quickly, then fades out very quickly, sort of like a slow flashbulb. The Crowned People crowd the stage. Some are smiling and waving, others dont look happy (no overacting please). Some are just doing their best to stay on the stage without falling off into the pit.

24 PLAY (Condemned Version)

Scene 1

A woman Writer sits in a chair, typing on a laptop computer.

Writer: She picks up a silver slinky and plays with it.

> She picks up a silver slinky and plays with it.

Writer: Although it doesnt have to be silver. It could be blue or pink or green neon.

> She puts down the computer and picks up a notebook.

Writer: Writer puts down the computer and picks up a notebook. The portal in the back of her head has fully dilated. The play has begun.

> She laughs.

Writer: Ha ha ha ha.

> She plays with the slinky.

Writer: Yr out of yr mind.

Scene 2

> A Man wearing prison stripes sits in a chair.
> The Writer sits on the floor writing with her computer.

Writer: You cant stay here.
X-Con: Why not?

Writer
X-Con

Writer: Because Im working.
X-Con: I dont need you to entertain me. I'll just sit here.
Writer: I got a brother in prison.
X-Con: Not any more you dont.

Writer
X-Con

X-Con: Im yr brother.
Writer: No yr not. This sucks. It was getting good and then you came in here and—sat there—and Im gonna go to the next scene, k?
X-Con: Am I in it?

> Lights fade.

Scene 3

Writer: Yr an X-Con.

X-Con: Not really. Not *technically*. Technically Im still a convict. Because—

Writer: Once a convict always a convict.

X-Con: Because—long and the short of it—well—they didnt let me out. I sort of let myself out.

Writer: Where are you going with this?

X-Con: The door was open. It was the strangest thing. Open door. So I just walked through it. And kept walking. No one followed me. No one shot at me. The alarm system didnt, you know, *trigger*.

Writer: I'll bet they were having a problem with overcrowding.

X-Con: Could be. But—

Writer: But what?

X-Con: To let me out—well. Im a killer.

Writer: Ive put you in my play. It wont be *you*, itll be—someone like you—but not so like you that anyone will know, k?

X-Con: Ive killed. A lot of people.

Writer: I wont put that in.

X-Con: You can if you want. I'd be flattered.

Writer
X-Con

Writer: Maybe in the play—youll kill someone.

X-Con: Maybe.

Writer: Maybe youll kill me.

X-Con: You think?

Writer: It was just an idea.

X-Con: I could kill you. I could kill somebody else—I could kill you and somebody else—anybody really—it doesnt matter.

Writer: My pen ran out of ink.

> X-Con hands her his pen.

X-Con: I was in the GED program.

Writer: You graduate?

> X-Con slowly shakes his head no.

Writer: I dunno.

X-Con: You gonna rat me out.

Writer: I dont like you being my brother.

X-Con: I could be yr dad, but youd have to get someone older for that, right?

Writer: Yeah.

X-Con: In yr play, make me good-looking, though. I always wanted to be good-looking.

Writer
Writer

X-Con: Whatcha doing?

Writer: Writing.

X-Con: Can I see?

Writer: She shows the books.

X-Con: I cant read.

Writer: Dont sweat it. I'll teach you. But not now.

Writer
Writer

Writer: I wonder what happens at the end. Ima go there now. This is the condensed version after all.

Scene 12

Writer: Writer has a butcher knife in her chest.

(Rest)

X-Con: The end?

Writer: Maybe.

X-Con: What about me?

Writer: You split.

X-Con: Into multiple personalities?

Writer: No.

X-Con: Cause that would be cool.

Writer: Maybe.

X-Con: Do I get a speech before I go? Like I stand and explain the roots of my rage and how—or maybe—I didnt kill you. Maybe you killed yrself.

Writer: Or maybe someone else, yr friend or—

X-Con: Or yr brother. Yr *real* brother.

Writer: That could work.

X-Con: Remember those letters I sent you from the joint?

Writer: One each day for 12 years. How could I forget? Theyre under my bed all catalogued.

X-Con: I got Joey to write them for me. I did—favors for him. I seen yr picture on CNN when youd just won—

Writer: A prize.

X-Con: Yeah and I wanted to write you. I ordered all yr books and had Joey read them to me and—they all ended so violent.

Writer: "24 September 1991. Dear Miss Writer, Why do all yr plays end so violent? Have you ever been to prison?"

X-Con: My first letter to you.

Writer: Yeah.

Scene 13

Woman: X-Con is on the floor with a butcher knife in his chest. The End.

The End.

24 (Again) PERFECT

> A Woman sits in a chair with a thick pad of writing paper and a pen or pencil. Another woman, the Timer, sits with an hourglass or stopwatch.

Timer: Ready?

Woman: Yep. I mean, I think so—yes. I think.

Timer: And—

Woman: Question?

Timer: What?

Woman: Whats the question?

Timer: Aaahhh.

> The Timer starts the watch or hourglass, then leaves.
> The Woman, after a beat, writes furiously, hesitates,
> becomes discouraged, rips paper from the pad, balling it up
> in a wad and guiltily stuffing it in her pockets.
> This continues until her pockets, blouse, shoes,
> socks are all full of crossed-out, imperfect, balled-up answers.
> She is reduced to throwing her balled papers onto the floor,

at first stuffing them under her chair, then sitting on them,
then just throwing the imperfect answers on the floor.
Maybe she throws some out the window. The more she writes
the more dissatisfied she becomes with what she has written,
and the whole activity becomes really frantic and desperate.
Perhaps her pencil lead breaks and she has to resharpen it.
Perhaps her pen runs out of ink and she, after massaging it,
throws it into the now-massive paper pile, then digs through her
purse for a new pen. She writes, crosses-out, balls-up paper,
throws paper, faster and faster. Balling-up with left or right
hands, sometimes both. Her hair comes out of its hairclip.
There is sweat under her armpits and on her upper lip.
Last piece of paper. Still not good enough.
Balled-up and thrown-down, just as
the Timer comes back in calling:

Timer: Time!

Timer
Woman
Timer
Woman

The Timer looks at all the balled-up papers.
The Woman looks as if she's about to be put to death.
The Timer gathers up as many balled-up papers
as she can hold. She gathers them slowly,
as if she's picking up children. When her arms are filled,
she approaches the Woman, who cringes as if she'll be struck.
The Timer gives the Woman a kiss on the forehead.

Timer: Perfect.

The Timer goes. The Woman starts making a slow smile—
a smile that will take her the rest of her life to finish.

25 REEL

2 Men. Both with elaborate fishing poles
and dressed in waist-high rubber fishing pants,
or fishing caps with vests. Theyve cast out.
Theyve been waiting for a bite for a long time. Suddenly:

Lucky: Woah!

Less: Looks like you got something.

Sure enough Lucky's line is taut.
He grabs it up and begins the difficult process of reeling it in.

Lucky: Its a big one!

Less: Goddamn!

Lucky: They dont call me Lucky for nothing, Im telling you.

Less: 5-pounder, I'll bet!

Lucky: 10-pounder more like. Get the camera.

Less: How bout the video?

Lucky: Woah! He's a bigun.

Less: Im getting the video!

Lucky: Ima put him on my wall above my desk.

Less: First you walk into the boss's office with him in yr arms and just stand there. "Smell this!" you say.

Lucky: "I'm Lucky, goddamn it!" I'll tell him.

Less: Dont let him get away.

Lucky: Not a chance! Not a chance!

Less: Old man and the sea, thats you.

Lucky: Wait till I show Gloria.

Less: Now yr talking.

Lucky: I'll ring her doorbell and just, like, just *stand* there.

Less: She wont be slamming the door in yr face tonight!

Lucky: Fish, fish, make a wish, jump into my frying dish!

Less: Here he comes, I see him. Keep coming, boy, keep coming on!

Lucky walks backward, reeling in his fish. Then we see his "fish":
a Man dressed exactly like him, with Lucky's hook
and line deep in his jacket. The "fish," a.k.a. Lucky 2,
is also reeling in a fish (his fish is offstage, and out of sight).
Lucky, walking backward, reels Lucky 2 onstage,
as he himself exits and Lucky 2 takes his place.
Less, strangely oblivious to the slight change in companionship,
keeps on fishing.

Lucky 2: Im Lucky 2.

Less: Keep it coming, man, keep reeling him in, show him whos got the balls!

The men continue enjoying themselves, it is, after all,
their only day off all month. The lights fade.

26 A PLAY FOR GEORGE PLIMPTON (and John Ritter)

2 men. One very dapper, the other in t-shirt and jeans:
George Plimpton and John Ritter. George Plimpton
does a crossword puzzle in pencil.
John Ritter plays with a yo-yo.

George Plimpton: "Handel's handle"?

John Ritter: Hallelujah?

George Plimpton: Good. "That falling feeling"?

John Ritter: Death.

George Plimpton: 7 letters.

John Ritter: —. —. Deathly.

George Plimpton: No.
(Rest)
She's writing a play for me.

John Ritter: For you?

George Plimpton: Yes. Right now. As we speak. She's writing a play
for me. I can feel her scratching it out.

John Ritter: You are—?

George Plimpton: George Plimpton.

John Ritter: Right.

George Plimpton: *The Paris Review.*
(Rest)
Dont say you havent heard of *The Paris Review.*

John Ritter: Oh, sure. —. Surely.

George Plimpton: I was *The Paris Review*'s big cheese.

John Ritter: —. Lovely.

George Plimpton
George Plimpton

George Plimpton: I hope it wont be, you know, too, you know, out
there, you know, too abstract.

John Ritter: What? Death?

George Plimpton: The play. The play she's writing for me. Ima fan as
much as anybody of experimentation, but, if people cant *follow*
it, then—whats the use, dont you see?

John Ritter
George Plimpton
John Ritter
George Plimpton

George Plimpton: You seem unhappy.

John Ritter: Not at all.

George Plimpton: Unburden yrself.

John Ritter: Not on yr life.

John Ritter

John Ritter

John Ritter: She's not writing a play about me! Is there "A Play for John Ritter"?! No!

George Plimpton: "John—Ritter," did you say? Any relation to Thelma Ritter?

John Ritter: Wahhh.

George Plimpton: Dont cry.

(Rest)

Three's Company! Right? You were the guy—

John Ritter: Thats right.

George Plimpton: Maybe she'll put you in my play. Im probably better known, but—perhaps she'll put you in—parenthetically. I saw her—at a book fair in Los Angeles. She was sitting in the corner and playing a guitar. We waved across the room at each other. She seemed pleasant enough.

John Ritter: Parenthetically?

George Plimpton: Its better than nothing.

(Rest)

John Ritter: I thought people like you did crosswords in pen.

George Plimpton: Sometimes.

John Ritter: "That falling feeling"—7 letters: "vertigo."

George Plimpton: Ah. Thanks.

John Ritter

George Plimpton

John Ritter: You really think she would put me in parenthetically.

George Plimpton: I would be proud to have you along. Youd make my play feel a little less highbrow.

John Ritter: Thats a left-handed compliment.

George Plimpton: Not at all. Hey, you were great in that movie—*Sling Blade.*

John Ritter: Gee. Thanks.

John Ritter: And, ok, I love yr magazine. I just didnt want to gush. I mean, you were acting like you were clueless as to who I was, so why should I admit to knowing you, right?
George Plimpton: No worries, Mr. Ritter.

> George Plimpton licks his pencil tip and continues
> with his crossword. John Ritter continues with his yo-yo
> as the lights fade.

27 SELLING OUT

> Several people standing around. They all look suspicious.
> Copper walks in, as nonchalant as possible,
> but you know he's jonesing.

Copper: Psssst.
Joyce: What?
Copper: You got inny?
Joyce: Inny what?
Copper: —. You know.
Joyce: In this day and age you gotta be specific.
Copper: Scripts. You got any scripts?
Joyce: —. —. Nope.
Copper: Shit.
Joyce: Try Charley. The guy with the flowery hat.

> Copper gestures, showing his profound gratitude.
> Joyce gestures, showing his gratitude for Copper's gesture.
> Copper approaches Charley.

Copper: Charley?
Charley: Whats happening, my man?
Copper: You got inny?—
Charley: SCRIPTS?
Copper: Not so loud, man.
Charley: What are you, a critic?
Copper: You got inny?

Charley: Im sold out, man.

Copper: Bullshit.

Charley: I been selling out every day, man, no bullshit. See my hands? Empty. See my briefcase? Full to the brim with scripts usually, right? Empty too. See my pockets?

Copper: Come on, man. Im in a tight spot.

Charley: Im turning my pockets inside out. Just for you. You see inny scripts, man?

Copper: Shit.

Charley: I been selling out, Im telling you. Joyce, over there. He dont never sell out. Always got something. He's like Joyce in that respect.

Copper: He *is* Joyce.

Charley: —Carol Oates, man. Joyce Carol Oates. Always got something, she does. Joyce is like Joyce Carol Oates.

Copper: He said he was out.

Charley: He's the only one whos got anything. Dont waste yr time on the others. Ask Joyce again. Go head, man. The man in the flower hat dont lie.

> Copper makes a gesture of slight thanks to Charley, who just shoves Copper away. Copper wanders around then ends up with Joyce again.

Copper: How much?

Joyce: 400.

Copper: Steep.

Joyce: Tough.

Copper: 400?

Joyce: 500.

Copper: Motherfucker.

Joyce: Inflation, man. I didnt invent it.

Copper
Copper
Copper

> A Woman and Man walk through talking loudly.

Woman: YES IT IS.

Man: NO ITS NOT.

Woman: YES IT IS.

Man: NO ITS NOT.

Woman: WANNA BET?

September

Man: NOT ON YOU. YR ALWAYS LOSING.

> They go.

Joyce: You could use *that*.
Copper: Fuck *that*. Heres yr 5.
Joyce: Heres yr script.

> Joyce hands Copper an index card.
> Copper stands there reading the very small print.
> Copper starts giggling.

Copper: Its a comedy.
Joyce: Move along, man, move along.

> Copper makes a gesture of great and undying thanks.
> Joyce returns the gesture in its exact reverse.

28 SPLITSVILLE

> Lights up on 3 situations:
> 1. A Man and Woman hold hands.
> 2. A Woman holds a covered plate. Her Butler stands nearby.
> 3. A Ballerina in a tutu.
>
> Drumroll and 3 actions happen simultaneously:
> 1. The Handholding Couple yank their hands apart.
> 2. The Butler lifts the cover from the plate,
> revealing a banana split.
> 3. The Ballerina does the splits.
>
> Fanfare and lights out.

29 THE WORST

> 2 Men. One with a big plate full of food,
> the other with an empty plate. Full Plate eats all his food quickly,
> leaves one thing on the plate.

Empty Plate: What is that?
Full Plate: What?

Empty Plate: That there. On yr plate.

Full Plate: This is a wurst.

Empty Plate: Ah.

Empty Plate
Full Plate

(Rest)

Empty Plate: It is NOT the worst when we can say, "This is the worst."

Full Plate: "Wurst" not "worst" and this isnt *the* wurst, its just *a* wurst.

Empty Plate: Even so.

Full Plate: Yes, even so.

Empty Plate: You gonna eat it?

Full Plate: No.

Empty Plate: May I?

Full Plate: Help yrself.

> Empty Plate eats with great delicacy. Long before he's through, the lights fade out, the play ends, and the audience grows old and moves on into a precarious retirement.

30 GOODBYE NEW YORK

> A Woman and Man with suitcases. An Old Man sits in a chair.

Woman: Goodbye, New York!

Man: Yes, New York, Goodbye!

> They stand in the doorway's threshold.

Man
Woman

(Rest)

Man: He's not even looking at us.

Woman: He's sad.

Old Man: Im not sad.

Woman: Well, yr ignoring us.

Old Man: Its not because Im sad.

Woman: Angry then.

Old Man: Ive never been ANGRY IN MY ENTIRE LIFE!

(Rest)

Man: Come on, lets go. I just wanted—well, I didnt want to make a scene.

Old Man: Maybe in the 70s and maybe in the olden-day riots. Maybe then. Maybe then I was angry. But not never over the likes of you, was I angry. No, sir.

Woman: Now you see here, we are not "the likes" of anybody.

Man: Come on, honey—theres no need—

Woman: He's insulting us and I wont stand for it. Why, every day, people leave and arrive and he's—sitting there angry—

Old Man: Im not.

Woman: —grumpy and sad—

Man: We'll miss our plane, dear.

Woman: Ive put in 15 years here. 15 good years.

Man: And I was *born* here. Surely we deserve a decent sendoff, but—

Old Man: You want me to *cry*. To *weep*. To *snivel*. You want me to become a sniveler for you, huh? To have every meal I eat from here on out wetted with tears that I cry for you? Youd like it if I tore my hair out or pulled at my clothing. A howl would suit you, wouldnt it? Or maybe a swoon? Put my hand to my head: "I cant live a day without them, I'll go dark without their lights, the country is lopsided with them on that other coast." The land of endless *sunshine* and palm trees and peaceful oceans and fake tits. Pah! I spit in yr ocean. Give me a life of concrete and ratholes and crowded subway trains. Give me a life of skyscrapers! I'll never go on vacation! I'm singing, see? Sing-Sing singing. So get lost before I start dancing.

Woman
Man
Old Man

> The Woman and Man approach the Old Man.
> The Woman gently kisses his cheek. The Man gives
> the Old Man a kind, firm handshake.
> And, then, all of them together take a deep breath.
> The Old Man stays put as the Woman and Man go.

October

1 HERE WAIT

> A Man comes onstage. He spray-paints a white line and
> the words: "Here Wait." As he paints, Another Man comes on,
> holding up a sign, showing us whats being painted.
> They sit and wait.
> A Group of People comes jogging up—about 8 people,
> 2 abreast. They see the line.

Leader: Here wait!

> They jog in place, waiting.
> The Painter and Sign Holder trade smiles. Lights out.

2 SCALES

> The 1st Scale is led onstage: a woman with eyes covered
> by a blindfold. Her Handler stands her in position,
> takes out a pitch pipe, plays middle C for her. The 1st Scale
> sings a C major scale, beginning at middle C.
> The 1st Scale continues singing her scale as the Handler brings
> in the 2nd Scale Woman. The Handler places her in position
> and gives the pitch. The 2nd Scale sings the E major scale,
> beginning at E above middle C.
> The 3rd Scale Woman is brought in, positioned and pitched.
> The 3rd Scale sings the G major scale, beginning at G
> above middle C.
> All the Scales sing their scales independently. They continue
> singing as the Handler brings in a Man, who wears
> a prison uniform and shackles. The Handler positions him.

Handler: Guilty?

Prisoner: No.

Handler: What then?

Prisoner: Innocent.

Handler: Ah.

Prisoner: No one believes me. Yr my last hope. Youve got to believe me.

Handler: You, you *look* guilty.

Prisoner: Thats just the way I look. All these years in here. A man's face takes on the guilty look. Its contagious. Its in the walls. Its in the air and in the water. You breathe in guilty every day.

October

344 Suzan-Lori Parks

Handler: I'll do what I can.

Prisoner: Theyre putting me to death tomorrow!

Handler: Eye for an eye.

Prisoner: But I didnt eye anybody!

Handler: Tell you what Im gonna do.

> The Handler talks on and on with impressive,
> elaborate gestures. But, as the Scales sing louder and louder,
> we cant hear a word he's saying.
> The Prisoner puts his hands over his eyes, then his ears.

3 BOOK OF LIFE

> A Man and Woman are curled up together under a blanket.
> Very cozy.

Woman: How do you know?

Man: Know what?

Woman: How do you know what you know?

Man: When youve read 15 more years from the book of life, then youll know.

Woman: Mmm. Then I'll know what?

Man: For me to know and you not to know yet.

> The Woman giggles.

Man: You could write that down. It could be yr play for the day.

Woman: Mmm. Maybe.

> They cuddle and are warm and snug. Lights out.

4 WAITING FOR THE BARBARIANS

> 3 elegantly dressed people are assembled. They wait.

1: What, good people, are we waiting for?

2: The barbarians arrive today.

> 3 looks at her pocketwatch.

3: The barbarians, gentlemen, are late.

5 FOR SALE BY OWNER

> A Man, Woman and their Child all wear signs:
> "For Sale by Owner" around their necks. They stand waiting.
> Theyve been waiting for a long time.

Woman: Its slow.

Man: If only it hadnt of rained.

Woman: Yeah.

Child: What can you do.

Man: Thats the spirit, kid. "What can you do." Thats the spirit.

> They wait. People pass by. No one stops.
> Then Some People do come up—a New Man,
> Woman and 2 children, all wearing signs: "For Sale by Owner."

Woman: What, you blind?

New Woman: No—

New Man: We just thought—

Man: That you could stand here.

Woman: Cause yr blind. What is this, National Blind Day?!

Man: Honey, that ring yr wearing!

Woman: Must be my invisibility ring, dear!

New Woman: We're so sorry.

Woman: THIS IS OUR CORNER! WE WERE HERE FIRST,
AND DONT YOU EVER EVER FORGET IT!!!!

Family
New Family

(Rest)

> The New Family creeps away.

Woman: The nerve of some people.

Man: And they hardly spoke English.

Child: You shoulda cut them—quick slice across the face! To
teach them respect.

Man: Thats the spirit, kid! Thats the spirit!

> They continue waiting. They notice an umbrella that the New
> Family left behind. They open it up and huddle under it together.

6 COMME CI, COMME ÇA

A Woman stands, seething. A Man comes in
with a tall stack of plates. He sets them down gingerly.
He hands off the plates to the Woman, and she throws them
to the floor, breaking them—handoff/smash,
handoff/smash—very rhythmic.
Soon the unbroken pile is depleted. No more plates.

Woman: You know what I hate? *Mimes.* I hate mimes.
Man: Mimes? Yeah. Me too. I hate mimes too.
(Rest)
You feel better?

The Woman makes comme ci, comme ça gesture.

Woman: Shit—those were the good plates! Whyd you bring me the
good plates?!

The Man makes gesture that says: "Honey I do my best,
and, I guess I sorta fucked-up, but whats a pile of plates, right?
Good plates, bad plates, so what, right?"

7 VOTE BOOTH

A Woman in a voting booth. A Man peeks in.

Man: Voting for me?
Woman: No.
Man: Who for then?
Woman: None of yr beeswax, mister.
Man: Gimmie a hint.
Woman: Im calling the cops.

He snatches her voting card and hands her money.
She covets the money and lets him look.

Man: Yr voting for a loser.
Woman: Its early days yet.
Man: Its him, the loser, who gets yr vote, even though I have more
money, more votes, more women, more children, more fans, a
bigger dick, a better car.
(Rest)
Maybe not a bigger dick, ok.

Woman: The losers shall inherit the earth.
Man: Says who?
Woman: Says God.
Man: Dream on, lady.

> He reaches for the money. She puts it in her purse.

Man
Woman

(Rest)

Woman: Gimmie that. Im changing my vote. Im voting for you. Im tired of losing.

> She votes for him. He makes a macho-winner gesture.

8 PACKAGE

> A Woman comes in with a lovely brown paper package, obviously sent by mail from someone who loves her, like her mother or her father or her favorite aunt.
> 2 Others look on.

Package Woman
Package Woman

1st Other: *Package.*
2nd Other: Yeah.
1st Other: *Package.*
2nd Other: Yeah yeah yeah.
1st Other: I wanna package.
2nd Other: Oh yeah. Me too.
Package Woman: Wanna share?
2nd Other: Yeah!

> 1st Other nudges 2nd Other.

2nd Other: Naw—
1st Other: No thank you.
2nd Other: Yeah.

They keep staring at the package, salivating now,
but just from the habit of desire
and not from real desire anymore.

9 THE AIR OVER OMAHA

An American Man leads in 2 Non-Americans,
one man one woman.

American Man: Well, here you are.

Non-American Man: Weve arrived?

American Man: Yep.

Non-American Woman: So this is America.

American Man: Part of it anyway.

Non-American Man: Shall I kiss the ground?

Non-American Woman: The whole journey you were talking about how you would kiss the ground should we arrive in one piece, and here we are, so why do you ask me?

Non-American Man: I shall kiss the ground. The ground of America. America the Most Beautiful.

He kisses the ground.

Non-American Woman: Back home, he was the Master of All Ceremonies.

American Man: Well, that explains it.

Non-American Woman: Fanfare accompanied his every movement.

American Man: If I had a horn, I'd blow it.

Non-American Man: My lips dusted with the dirt from the ground of America.

He resumes kissing.

American Man: *Omaha*, if you wanna be specific.

Non-American Woman: He doesnt kiss me like that. Even on our wedding night. Its like he's a new man. Its like now, in America, he believes in foreplay.

American Man: Im blushing, maam.

Non-American Woman: Yr handsome face is as red as a beetroot.

Non-American Man: And the air over Omaha is sweet—and free!

Non-American Woman: If I werent falling in love all over again, I'd think this were just a cheap bit of Western propaganda!

Non-American Man
American Man
Non-American Woman

(Rest)

Non-American Man, Non-American Woman & American Man:
Hahahahahahahahahahaha.

> Non-American Man goes back to kissing.
> American Man sees the beauty of the Non-American Woman.
> Non-American Man sits up and takes several blissful
> perfect breaths.
> American Man kisses Non-American Woman delicately
> on the cheek. She smiles shyly, indicating that there is more,
> so much more, to come: a long run of old-fashioned American
> adultery, but not now, not in this moment, not just yet.

10 WONDERFUL, WONDERFUL

> 3 sick people (nothing over the top) sitting up in their beds
> with their covers pulled to their chins and sad looks
> on their faces. A Nurse sits with them, watching them.
> Then she checks the time.
> A Bag Stranger stands at the door. He holds a bag.

Nurse: Well look whos here! You come right in. I'll call time when
its time.

> The Bag Stranger takes toys from his bag. Cheap toys:
> a slinky, a sock puppet, a windup set of teeth,
> cheap 5-and-dime toys. He places one on each Patient's bed.
> The Patients play with the toys. Tentatively at first,
> but then with increasing joy and gusto, sickness takes a walk in
> the park, that is, it is nowhere in the room. Miracles happen:
> the blind see, the lame walk, the stupid president gets a lick
> of sense, it is not impossible, anyway.
> The Bag Stranger sits and watches the Patients,
> then he checks the time.

Bag Stranger: Wonderful, wonderful.

> The Nurse appears at the door. She rings a bell.

Nurse: Thats time.
1st Patient: Thats time.
2nd Patient: Thats time.
3rd Patient: Thats time.

The Bag Stranger collects his toys. He leaves.
Perhaps he bows gallantly just before exiting.
The Nurse retakes her seat.
Sickness returns from its walk, that is,
the Patients go back to being ill.

1st Patient: If we had a better health-care system, he would come visit us all the time.
2nd Patient: Yeah, and then everybody would get a puppy.
3rd Patient: I'd like a puppy.
2nd Patient: Shut up.

11 ANOTHER DEEP HOLE

2 people walk along.

– Woah!
– Yeah!
– You think?
– Could be.
– Measure it, man, measure it.

2nd measures the hole.

– Well?
– Yep.
– You sure?
– Oh yeah. Its another deep hole.
– All right.

1st puts up a sign: "Another Deep Hole."
They go.

12 ANALYSIS

- Another deep hole.
- Mmm.
- And you?—
- Fell in.
- Sorry to hear that.
- Mmm.
- Where are you now with it?
- The hole?
- Yeah. Where are you now with it?
- In it.
- Deep.
- Yep.

> Interludey music plays.
> Something from the soundtrack of the 70s,
> or something mushy and very recognizable, or maybe something
> deep like a cut from *Miles Davis in Stockholm*.

- In it deep?
- Yep.
- Mmm.
- I brought a sample.
- Of the hole?
- Yep.
- Wassit made of?
- The hole?
- Yeah.
- Space.
- Deep.

13 THE WILL OF THE WORLD'S WAY

> A Man and a Woman both facing East. It is Brahma time:
> the minutes between night and dawn. The air is fresh and clean.
> The dew is jeweling the spiderwebs. Everything is possible.
> Just then Dawn comes in—a loud man with a yellow shirt
> and sunglasses banging 2 pot lids together,
> making an enormous and awful racket. He walks and clangs.

His Steward walks just behind him.
As Dawn reaches the Man and Woman, he,
with his Steward's assistance, climbs over them.
Dawn's ascent and climb are fluid and without pause.
The clanging of the pot lids is continuous.
As Dawn finishes climbing over the Man and Woman,
the Steward begins blowing a whistle or horn.
The whole thing has the feeling of inevitability and also of rape.
Dawn and the Steward exit.
The sound of the pot lids fades quickly.

Woman: Another day.
Man: Another dollar.

14 NEEDING TO BE NEAR WHILE WANTING TO BE GONE

Man with Rope and another man called Pully.

Rope: Heres the rope. One end around my waist. The other end in yr hand.
Pully: How much do I get?
Rope: Lemmie lay it out first.
Pully: Lay it out.
Rope: You pull the rope. Not yank it, just pull it. You *ease* me away. Ever seen a dog straining to sniff something and you just wanna walk and the dog wants to sniff?? Sorta like that.
Pully: Whats the pay?
Rope: Here.
Pully: I got 10 mouths to feed.
Rope: Heres more. 10 mouths, huh?
Pully: Me and the Mrs. got carried away.

A Group of 2 or 3 People. They enter chattering.

Rope: Here they come. Go off somewhere. Its more effective if they dont see you.

Pully goes offstage. Rope stands with the Group chattering.

Group: You wanna stay for dinner?
Group: We can watch the game!
Group: We could shoot the shit!

Group: Itll be fun!
Rope: I'd love to stay.

> Pully pulls the rope and Rope is pulled away from the Group.
> He stretches his arms out toward them,
> as if wanting to be near. They do the same. It may sound silly
> but it is odd and almost painfully sad.
> Rope is pulled out of the range of physical contact.
> The Group and Rope still strain toward each other.
> The Group may move slightly in Rope's direction but, after a bit,
> they go back to chattering among themselves, while Rope, still
> reaching toward them with all his energy, is pulled neatly away.
> Maybe Pully appears, the Group may see him,
> some care, some dont.

15 EASY COME, EASY GO

> Joe stands onstage. Freddy comes strolling slowly in,
> like a pimp-daddy heading to church
> on a perfect Sunday morning.

Joe: Easy?
Freddy: *Easy.*

> They trade pounds and then create this elaborate
> and gorgeous gesture-groove of hip street-soul camaraderie.
> After theyre through with it, Freddy keeps walking, passing Joe,
> and heading offstage.

Joe: *Easy.*

16 ALL I CAN SAY IS THANK YOU

Writer: "All I can say is thank you."
Actor: Is that my line?
Writer: Yes. Do you like it?
Actor: "All I can say is thank you."
Writer: Do you like it?
Actor: Yes. Very much. What else do I say?
Writer: Thats all.

Actor: You dont like me. You dont think Im worthy. Ive gained weight. "He's gained weight," yr thinking.

Writer: Its not—

Actor: "All I can say is thank you." I would like to say more than that. Perhaps a list of those I'd like to thank. A long list. I'd be so very grateful. And at the end of the list, of course, "I'd like to thank *the writer*."

Writer: Thats very sweet.

Actor: Its a keeper, then.

Writer: No, just the one sentence.

Actor: If you dont have anything else for me to say, then I quit.

Writer
Actor

Writer: You know, some days Im alive for no reason. But Im alive that day just the same.

Actor: Can I say that? Its very good.

Writer: Yes, yes you can say it.

Actor: May I add a gesture?

Writer: Go for it.

Actor: And a little something to go in the middle.

Writer: How about a silence?

Actor: Fine. What about my costume?

Writer: Come as you are.

Actor: Thank you.

Writer: Dont mention it.

Writer goes back to writing.
Actor rehearses lines without speaking them aloud.

17 ALL THIS OPULENCE

A woman works a fan and a man eats up
a piece of paper slowly and with great care.

Fan: Do you like my eyes?

Paper: Very much.

Fan: Even when Im crying?

Paper: Even so.

Fan: Even when they go to Bermuda without you?

Paper: Bermuda?

(Rest)

Fan: Remember when we had less. That winter we had to burn the chairs to keep warm. That big bonfire in the middle of the backyard. Remember? And the gas stove's on all the time and the bill collectors calling calling calling until you ripped the phone out of the wall! Not a penny to my name. Not a penny to yrs. And now all this opulence.

> Fan rings a bell. A Servant comes in with a rope.
> Fan exits with the rope.

Paper: Wheres she gone to?
Servant: She's gone to catch herself a bigger fish.
Paper: Bigger than me? Bigger than this?
Servant: Im afraid so, sir.

> Paper continues eating paper.
> Servant awaits further instructions.

18 THE LIGHT AT THE END OF THE TUNNEL

> A Huddled Group lit by a spotlight. Theyre happy.
> They run toward the light, running in an orderly fashion,
> plenty of time to get there. Suddenly the light fades,
> their good cheer fading by degrees with the fading light.
> Then the light clicks out.

Youngest: The light at the end of the tunnel—its gone out.
Oldest: We can all see that.
Leader: Its gone out before. Not so *dramatically*, mind you, but its gone out before.
Youngest: I always remember it shining.
Oldest: Because you only remember the bright spots.
Leader: Long long ago and in another tunnel. I was with that group. Just a child, though. We were making our way through bedrock. Underneath a big city, if I remember correctly. Heading towards the light. Then darkness. Ah. It was like someone snuffed out a candle.

(Rest)

Fearful: So we'll just wait for it to come back on, then?

Leader: No—we'll keep going.

Fearful: In darkness, towards darkness?

Leader: The alternative is worse. Believe me. Hold hands. Come on, lets go.

They go.

19 STRINGS ATTACHED? NO SWEAT, CAUSE THE SOUL KNOWS NO BOUNDS

2 Men sitting on the floor. They wear blue work shirts and work pants—prison attire (at some institutions). One has the number 1 pinned to his shirt, the other, the number 2. There is a length of white string stretching from one to the other. It runs along the floor and is hardly noticeable. The Men do not look at each other. A Corrections Officer comes in. He very matter-of-factly walks by each inmate, dropping a can of tuna fish in front of them. Very quickly they pop the lids (no can opener necessary) and eat the food hungrily. They look like savages, gobbling the food. Then, both independently make sure the coast is clear, and scrabble around finding their homemade shanks. Each savagely punches a hole in the can's bottom, then threads the string through the hole, securing it with a knot. Only when theyve completed this do they relax somewhat. And then, as the lights dim, with exquisite delicacy, they pull their cans and can lines taut. And talk.

20 1 AND 2

A Man enters from stageleft walking backward 2 steps. Then he walks forward 1 step, backward 2 steps. He repeats this 1 forward–2 backward walking until he collapses from exhaustion, tearing at his hair, lying prostrate on the stage and sobbing.

21 PLENTY

A man walks onstage with a noose.
Another man comes in to watch.

Noose: Plenty of room to swing a rope.

Noose swings his rope. Perhaps playing skip the rope
with the Other. Then, when the Other gets out of breath,
Noose puts the rope around his own neck.

Other: Plenty of heart and plenty of hope, man.
Noose: You think?
Other: It worked for the folks in *Oklahoma*.
Noose: The state?
Other: The musical. And, maybe the state too.
Noose: Well, Im not in Oklahoma.
Other: Ok.

Noose hangs himself from the rafters. The Other gets up
and forms a stepstool with his back so that Noose wont die.

Noose: You wont last long down there. Yr back will tire of my feet.
Yr knees will ache from the weight. Im telling you, you wont last
long.

The Other just kneels there, exhausted already,
but not able to quit either.

22 INFLATION, OR, THE VIGOROUS STYLE OF THE MODERNS

A Man and a Woman are huddled together, bleakly watching
a Female Dancer who dances in the vigorous style
of the moderns. The Dancer's movements grow slower
and more labored. Then, finally, she stumbles, then kneels
on the ground, then, after a painful moment, she dies.

Bleak Onlookers
Modern Dancer

October

358 Suzan-Lori Parks

(Rest)

> An Army Captain in a sou'wester, all spit and polish,
> comes in. Just walking.
> He notices the body, and, after a brief inspection,
> walks off the way he came. He returns with his sou'westered
> Co-Captain. They inspect briefly, then exit the way they entered.
> They return with 2 sou'westered Troops, brief intense inspection,
> then they hold hands, forming a human chain facing offstage.
> This results in the entrance of 5 additional sou'westered Troops,
> a quick inspection of the body, and then, at last,
> the body is hoisted up by the entire Army
> and quickly taken away.

Bleak Onlookers
Bleak Onlookers

(Rest)

Man: I remember when ants were small. Tiny. You could hold a 100 of them in yr hand and some of us, the kind ones among us, although I gotta admit, there werent many, the kind ones worried, actually worried, about crushing the little hardworking creatures by accident. Say you wore a hard-soled shoe—
Woman: Shoes!
Man: You could crush one underfoot.

(Rest)

Woman: Theyre still hardworking. They havent changed. And the way they work together. You gotta admire that. Theyre separate and individual but almost part of the same organism. The queen ant and her subjects. You gotta admire that.
Man: Oh, I admire it. Im just saying, well, they used to be so *small*.
Woman: Inflation.
Man: You think?
Woman: Its hitting everything these days.
Man: Ah.
Woman: Yeah. Well.

> The Woman gets up and slowly begins to dance
> in the vigorous style of the moderns. The Man watches bleakly.

23 SALTY

Frau: You never take me no place. They all go places. Fancy vacations and whatnot. Whens the last time we ever went anyplace? Never. Our honeymoon was 3 whole years ago, Fred. Tilda and the girls, they ask me: "Where are you going this holiday?" And I change the subject. You got a wife who has to change the subject, Fred. I wanna go places, I wanna see sights, I wanna send picture postcards to all my pals, I wanna live a little, hell, I wanna live a lot, I wanna go to the seashore, Freddy! That aint too much to ask, is it? The seashore, huh?!

Freddy picks up a bucket of water and splashes her with it.

Frau
Freddy

(Rest)

Frau: Mmm. Salty. Thats saltwater?
Freddy: Yeah. Im doing my best, doll.

She licks the salt from herself. She is happy. So is he.

24 BEE

2 people talk as a Honeybee crawls across the stage.

Honeybee: Honeybee. Honeybee. Honeybee.
Man: A honeybee. Crawling. Huh.
Woman: How do you think they know where theyre headed?
Man: The sun sends them messages or—they read it or something.
Woman: Yeah.
Man: I think.

Man
Woman
Honeybee

Honeybee: Honeybee. Honeybee. Honeybee.
Woman: Honey?
Man: Mmm.
Woman: You love me?
Man: Mmm.

Man
Woman

Man: A lot. A lot. Very much. Uh—passionately. Loads. Loads and loads and loads.

The Honeybee gets overturned and writhes helplessly.
The Man and Woman watch. The Woman moves to help.
The Man stops her.

Woman: Itll die if I dont help it.
Man: Let nature take its course.

The Honeybee continues writhing, closer to death.
The Woman moves, the Man stops her, the Woman moves,
the Man stops her. The Woman struggles against the Man
and breaks free, reaching and righting the Honeybee,
who then continues on its way.
The Woman looks back at the Man. The distance between them
is an enormity. They will never be as they were.

25 PLAY HERE, PLEASE

Kids play recess games: Jump rope, jacks, hopscotch,
building blocks, tag, war.
A cannon goes off. The National Anthem plays on a scratchy
record. One Kid stops, putting her hand over her heart like her
mom and dad taught her to, but she doesnt know
what it means. The other Kids dont notice.

26 FIRST FAMILY

Kids playing. 2 Husbands and 2 Wives come in,
sitting a distance from each other. Its as if theyre having
an outdoor barbecue and theyre paired-off according
to their sexes, or however suits you.
Idle chitchat.
A cannon goes off. The National Anthem plays.
One pair of adults stands at attention. The other pair watches.
The Kid, who stood at attention last time, kicks the dog.
Other Kids keep playing.

27 THE YARD

Woman standing in the yard. Many years have passed.

Husband: What the hell are you doing?
Woman: Im looking—at the stars.
Husband: You wanna get me written up?
Woman: I just wanted to stand. In our yard. And look up. At something.
Husband: Its not our yard, hon. Not anymore. Come inside.
Woman: No.
Husband: Come inside. Come inside or I'll get me a wife who will.

She runs inside.

28 THE MONSTER OF ???

An enormous Monster follows a Little Girl wherever and however she goes. She walks through a virgin redwood forest. She hurries across the intersection of Hollywood and Vine. She swims the English Channel in winter, covered head to toe in lard to keep in her body heat. She crashes a weekend gathering of spiritualists and walks across their burning coals. She climbs every mountain. She fords every stream. And throughout, the enormous Monster follows her. When she walks, he walks. When she skips, he skips. When she twirls, he twirls. When she crawls, he crawls. Finally she turns to face him.

Girl: Who are you?
Monster: I am the Monster.
Girl: Of?
Monster: Prosperity.
Girl: The Monster of Prosperity.
Monster: Yes.
Girl: But, yr so—
Monster: Monstrous?
Girl: Bingo.
Monster: Well, what can I tell you?

She continues on. He continues after her.

29 ALMOST PERFECT

A Man holding a sign comes onstage. His sign reads:
"Almost Perfect." He looks exhausted, but, as he steps
into the light, he relaxes and, as if the light were sunshine,
he begins to feel good all over.
A 2nd Man enters. His sign reads: "Perfect."
He stands full of confidence.
At first, Almost Perfect does not notice Perfect. Then, slowly,
by degrees, Almost Perfect notices and, through the noticing,
experiences a profound erosion of the soul.

30 ALMOST EVERYTHING

A man holding a sign: "Everything" stands onstage. He is very
well-dressed but looks exhausted. Perhaps he is overdressed
for the occasion or the weather.
A 2nd man comes in with a small chair and a tin cup. He sits
down, placing his cup. He displays his sign: "Almost Everything."
Everything, with a series of little darting glances, grows anxious,
bloated, begins to sweat. He is full to bursting
and he begins to cry, but cannot cry hard enough
or fast enough and his tears arent even hot enough
to take the edge off. Such is the pressure of Everything.
Almost Everything tries to stay happy and tries not to stare.
At last, Everything either melts or explodes.

31 BOO

Producer Man: Have you written it?
Writer: Yeah.

2 actors, a Man and a Woman, come onstage.
The Writer quickly hands out scripts.

Writer: Whenever yr ready.
Man: Boo!
Woman: Ah!

The actors, finished, just stand there.

Writer: Thank you.

The actors exit.

Producer Man: Thats it?

Writer: Its a work-in-progress. Early days, still, you know. My process—

Producer Man: Thats it?!?!

Writer: Yeah.

Producer Man: Thats shit.

Writer: Writing is a process.

Producer Man: Process-schmocess.

Writer: Ever written anything?

Producer Man: No but Ive got great ideas. For example: Me-me-me-me-me-I-I-I-I-I-I-I-I-I-I-I-me-me-me-I-I-I-I-I-I-I-I-I-I-I-I . . .

Writer: This should sound as if the Producer Man is saying something. And he *is* saying something of interest, but that something is being drowned-out by his love of the sound of his own voice and the fact that, for all the good ideas he's had throughout his life, he's never managed to write anything, really.

Producer Man keeps talking.
The Writer listens for awhile then exits. She returns with a sheet
and a large butcher knife. She cuts 2 holes in the sheet,
and putting the sheet over her head, stands there.

Producer Man: Who the hell are you?

Writer-Ghost: I am the Ghost of the Writing Process.

Producer Man: Dont be silly.

Writer-Ghost: And I have come to take my revenge.

Producer Man: This scene is worse than the last one.

Writer-Ghost: Whatever.

Producer Man: Treat.

Horror music plays. The Writer-Ghost takes out her knife.

Writer-Ghost: Happy Halloween, baby. Trick or Treat?

Writer-Ghost
Producer Man

(Rest)

Writer-Ghost: Writer-Ghost stabs the Producer Man several times. It is horrible and bloody. She is thorough in her revenge. She strikes blows for writers everywhere—all their years of hard work and no respect. The Producer Man has been dead for a long long time, maybe an entire generation. Still she continues stabbing—think Medea and Clytemnestra and Lizzie Borden and the anger of the downtrodden everywhere laced with a generous dose of everyday All-American bleeding-heart liberal rage. At last she is done. She takes off her sheet and, wrapping the Producer Man up in it, drags his corpse from the stage.

Producer Man: Wow.

Writer-Ghost: Thanks.

Producer Man: Some treat. What was the trick?

Writer-Ghost: Live action.

Producer Man: Oh.

November

1 A PLAY FOR THE DAY OF THE DEAD

Downstage a Man and Woman in Halloween costumes with treat bags of candy. The rest of the stage is crammed with people: everybody with at least one large photograph of their favorite dead person. You can have more than one photo if you need to.
As the lights come up, all at once tell us who the people in the photos are and why you love them. Lights fade out before yr done.

Man: I did good. Howd you make out?
Woman: Not bad.

They open their treat bags and gobble up their spoils.

2 THE GODDESS RAINS DOWN BLESSINGS

Ted smokes. Goddess opens a liter of Diet Coke.

Ted: Im getting the 20-dollar libation, right?
Goddess: Thats what my paperwork says.
Ted: Just making sure.
Goddess: Ready?
Ted: Yeah.

Goddess: You feeling it?

Ted: Not yet.

Goddess: Now?

Ted: Kinda.

Goddess: Kinda yeah or kinda no?

Ted: Kinda sorta.

Goddess: So yr feeling lucky?

Ted: Not—completely.

Goddess: But not *unlucky*, right?

Ted: Baby, this—this tastes like Diet Coke!!

Goddess: You gotta have faith, Teddy, what can I tell you.

> She keeps pouring, perhaps opening up a new bottle
> and pouring it on. He lights another smoke.

3 SWEET (FATHER COMES HOME FROM THE WARS, Part 10)

> A Man eats slowly, but like an animal. A Woman watches.

Woman: Yr home.

Man: I know.

> His plate is empty. The Woman piles more food onto his plate.

Man: Im home but I still got the taste for killing, you know?

Woman: Lemmie put some sugar on. It tastes like shit without sugar.

> She pours a lot of sugar on his food. He continues eating.
> At last his plate is empty. He puts his knife in its sheath.

Man: Im gonna go out for awhile.

Woman: Where to?

Man: Nowhere special. I'll just, you know—

Woman: Walk around.

Man: Yeah.

(Rest)

Woman: Just smell them before you cut them, ok?

Man: Have I ever killed one of our own?

Woman: No, but—

Man: Yr talking to me like I killed one of our own.

Woman: You never done nothing like that—its just—I worry.

Man: If you kept them in the house you wouldnt have no worries.

Woman: Theyre grown. And the house is small.

Man: So I'll get us a bigger house. WHEN I GET A BIGGER JOB!
(Rest)
In the meantime, I gotta go out.

Woman
Man

(Rest)

Man: Itll wear off in awhile. The taste for it.

Woman: Lets hope.

> He goes. She frets, then cleans up the dishes.
> A Young Man enters.

Junior: Hey Mom. Wheres Pop? —

Woman: Out bowling—with his bowling buddies, Junior.

Junior: Sweet. Im history, K?

Woman: Oh no yr not.

Junior: Come on, I did my homework. And my chores.

Woman: One step out there and yr grounded, mister.

Junior: You cant ground me, Ive served my country.
(Rest)
Later. K, Mom?

> He kisses her and goes.
> As soon as he has cleared the stage, Sister comes on.

Sister: Wheres Junior and Pop?

Woman: Out and about.

Sister: Im—

Woman: Dont—

Sister: Hey—

Woman: Sure. Yr history. I know. Whatever. Sweet.

Sister
Woman

Sister goes.
The Woman very meticulously cleans up the dishes and sits.
Then she quickly gets up, puts on a coat and hat and hurries
out the door. The house is empty. No foul play will happen
to any of them, although, of course, they may cause foul play
to others, and, of course, none of them will ever ever return.

4 FATHER COMES HOME FROM THE WARS
(Part 11: His Eternal Return—A Play for My Father)

During this play we hear a war news-in-brief soundtrack,
laced with military band music thats played at
a slower than normal speed. The action is as follows:
A never-ending loop of action—5 Servicemen walk downstage
together. All wear military uniforms from the same side of
the same war, but not necessarily the same branch of Service.
They stand upstage and walk very vibrantly and heroically
downstage. Theyre returning home as heroes.
As they reach centerstage, 5 women, their Servicewives, stand
up from the audience, and run toward the men. Just as the
Servicemen reach the downstage edge, the Servicewives
meet them. The Servicemen pick up their Servicewives,
twirling them around very joyfully.
Before each Wife returns to the ground a Child comes
onstage and, racing toward its respective Mother and Father,
jumps for joy.
This action repeats. New Servicemen walk downstage,
new Wives leap up from the audience and rush into their arms,
new Children run in to cheer.
The action repeats eternally. Long after the audience has
emptied of Women; long after the Men have grown out of the
desire to be hugged and kissed and welcomed; long after
the Children have become less cheerful and more sensible and
have taken up trades, like accounting or teaching or real estate
or politics; long after the Children's Children have outgrown joy
and have all grown-up and moved away. Forever.

5 THE SIN COLLECTOR

Scene 1

The Sin Collector pins small mirrors to the inside of her coat.
Her Man reads the newspaper.

Man: You ought to do well today.

Sin Collector: You think?

Man: All those still-unsolved beachside murders. Plus, the King-President's tart made a book deal for her memoirs. Therell be a trickle-down effect.

Sin Collector: Lets hope.

Man: Youll come back home with all yr mirrors turned and yr pockets full of money.

Sin Collector: Just dont spend it before I earn it.

Man
Sin Collector

Man: Have a good day, dear.

Sin Collector: You too.

> She goes.

Scene 2

> The Sin Collector stands downstage.
> The inside of her coat is full of tiny mirrors. Someone,
> Average Joe, has just given her a coin. She unpins a mirror
> and hands it to him. Joe studies his reflection.

Sin Collector: Dont brood over it.

Joe: Right.

Sin Collector: Brooding like yr broodingll break the mirror. And thatll cost. Come on, hand it back.

Joe: Right, right.

> He hands back the mirror. The Sin Collector pins it to
> the outside of her coat, mirror-side down. We see
> she has several other mirrors pinned this way.
> It is, in fact, a good day for business.
> Average Joe goes on his way.

Sin Collector: Sin Collection! Sin Collection! Sin Collection!

> Average Jane comes up to her and gives her money.
> She glances in the mirror, returns the mirror,
> then goes on her way. The Sin Collector pins the mirror face
> down to the outside of her coat.

Sin Collector: Sin Collection! Sin Collection! Sin Collection.

The lights fade.

Scene 3

> The Sin Collector comes home.
> Her Man reads the newspaper.

Man: How was yr day?
Sin Collector: Bumper crop.
Man: Whatd I tell you.

> The Sin Collector removes her coat and hangs it on a rack.

(Rest)

Sin Collector: Did the hussy come by?
Man: What makes you ask?
Sin Collector: The smell.

Man
Sin Collector

(Rest)

> The Man tosses the Sin Collector a coin.

Sin Collector: Ive already taken off my coat.
Man: Be a sport, huh?

> The Sin Collector gives the Man a mirror from the inside
> of her coat. He looks into it. She takes the mirror
> and pins it to the outside of her coat.

Man: Thanks.
(Rest)
Ive got a roast in the oven.
Sin Collector: Thats something.

> The Sin Collector sits, takes old mirrors from a shoe box
> and starts the long and thankless task of polishing the mirrors,
> getting ready for the day ahead.

6 PUJA PLAY FOR SRI GANESHA

A Gorgeous Fat Guy with the head of an elephant,
and a Woman who speaks to him. While she speaks,
she gives him treats, which he thankfully eats. He eats a lot!
You could do a Bollywood version of this play. Have fun.

Woman:
Dear one! Dear one!
The great remover of obstacles!
Transcriber of the Vedas!
Tradition says I should of thanked you first.
My bad!
I spaced and didnt see you
even though
there you are
sitting in the middle of the room.
How could I have missed you,
shining so brightly as you do,
the son of suns?
Burn baby burn
and light up my light.
I wont mind if you send the house up in smoke
I wont mind if everything Ive purchased goes.
Its just mind
over matter.
I dont mind and it dont matter.
(Rest)
Here is a thick brick.
Ganesha: Lemmie crack it.

He does.

Woman: Here is a traffic snarl on a nearby highway.
Ganesha: Lemmie smooth it.

He does.

Woman: Here is an atom.
Ganesha: Lemmie split it.

He does.

Woman: Here are 7 conflicts in 7 war-torn countries.
Ganesha: Let me peace them back together.

He does.

Woman:
Dear one! Oh dear one!
I spent hours looking for a place called
the Center.
I was driving up and down the streets with a plastic map.
Go ahead and laugh.
Im laughing too.
Like the first time ever I saw you.
Fat boy with the elephant head resting in the arms of yr mother.
I knew you would be my pal.
And I didnt even know yr name yet.
Help me see the obstacles as opportunities.
They call artists creators, but I know Im just yr gardener.
Let me sit at yr feet
And grow yr flowers.
Ganesha: Let me help you smile.

He does.

7 7-ELEVEN

7 Actors. The Leader assigns some parts.

Leader: Ok, for the warmup today, lets do the 7 chakras:
Muladhara, the root center. Hum the sound of "lum."
1st Actor: Lum. Got it.
Leader: Svadhisthana, the personality center chakra. Hum the
sound "vum."
2nd Actor: Vum vum vum.
Leader: Perfect. Manipura, located in the solar plexus. Hum "ram."
3rd Actor: "Ram!"
Leader: Good. Anahata, means "unstuck." Its located at the heart.
Yr sound is "yam."
4th Actor: "Yam" like sweet potato?
Leader: Right. 5th chakra is Visuddha chakra, located at the
throat. Its seed sound is "hum."
5th Actor: "Hum hum hum."
Leader: 6th, be Ajna, located at the 3rd eye. Chant "om."
6th Actor: Got it.
Leader: I'll do the 7th, Sahasrara, the meeting place of Kundalini,
making all sounds through silence. Lets go.

They sit or stand or dance around, humming appropriately.
When it gets too loud or long or wild—

Leader: Now! Scene!

1st and 2nd Actors perform:

Smoker: 2 packs—Lucky Strikes and Pall Malls.
Shopkeeper: 4 packs.
Smoker: No, just 2.
Shopkeeper: Dont you try and make a fool out of me!

The Smoker and the Shopkeeper bow to the other Actors,
who flip over cards and judge them. The scores are pretty low.
The Smoker and the Shopkeeper sit down.

1st Actor: It was a dramatization of a story taken from a real life 7-Eleven.
Leader: It happened at a real 7-Eleven?
2nd Actor: Yeah.
3rd Actor: So it scores for "truth" but other than that—
4th Actor: Maybe if she had stabbed him or something.
5th Actor: Not. I mean, not, right?
6th Actor: I think it needs more love in it.

At first the Actors look at the 6th Actor like she's nuts,
but then gradually, and perhaps all in the same breath,
they get it. They do the scene again, as theyll do everything
from here on out: with more love.

8 ALL GOOD THINGS MUST COME TO AN END

A Man sits on a stool.

Woman: You done?
Man: Not yet.
Woman: Not yet? Youve been sitting there for—
Man: Almost a whole year.
Woman: That long?
Man: Yeah.
Woman: And yr not done?
Man: Not yet.
Woman: Damn.

Man
Woman

Woman: When my ship comes in, Im getting another stool, lemmie tell you.
Man: I dont mean to monopolize.
Woman: Another stool, Im getting. Mark my words.
Man: Could you get me a magazine?
Woman: I'll have to go to the store for it.

> She goes to the store. He sits there.

g **9-11**

> Upstage center, a Man in a white suit on stilts and a
> Woman in a white suit on stilts.

Stilt Man:	**Stilt Woman:**
Nein	Nein
Nein	Nein
Nein	Nein
Nein	Nein
Nein	Nein
Nein	Nein
Nein	Nein
Nein	Nein
Nein	Nein
Nein	Nein
Nein	Nein
(Rest)	*(Rest)*

> They repeat their lines softly underneath the rest of the play.
> Meanwhile downstage left, 2 boys play war games:
> toy airplane bombing and swooping. Theyre playing
> as if theyve been instructed to play quietly.
> Downstage right, 2 Mothers sip tea
> and watch their Children play.

1st Mother: I sat there watching it on the tv and, you know, when those poor people were hanging out the windows waiting for the firemen to come. And I was talking to the tv, telling the people: "Dont worry, the firemen will come for you and youll be safe."
2nd Mother: Me too.

November

1st Mother: Like they could hear me.

2nd Mother: I was doing the same thing.

1st Mother: And then they started jumping. And then, when they fell—

2nd Mother: Yeah.

Mothers
Children
Mothers

> The Stilt Man and Stilt Woman continue in the background.

1st Mother: This isnt even the anniversary. I dont know why Im thinking of it. Although I wouldnt want to just, you know, jump on some "its 9-11 so lets *think* about it" bandwagon either, you know?

2nd Mother: I think of all the people who passed before it happened. And us left behind, having to know about it.

1st Mother: "Things will never be the same." Thats what everybody's saying now, but thats always been true. Things have always never been the same.

> 2nd Mother takes out a pack of cigarettes,
> offers one to 1st Mother. They smoke.

2nd Mother: You know, this is the anniversary of the falling of the Berlin Wall. 9 November 1989.

1st Mother: Shit. Did a plane hit that too?

> 1st Child goes to stand next to 1st Mother.
> 1st Mother hugs 1st Child.

2nd Mother: Brave new world.

1st Mother: Lets hope.

2nd Mother: All I hope for is a graceful exit.

1st Mother: Go on, give it a shot.

> 2nd Mother gives 1st Mother a kiss on the forehead,
> then a reverent bow. She repeats action to 1st Child, then 2nd
> Child, then bows to Stilt Man and Stilt Woman. Then she exits.
> 1st Mother follows suit. 1st Child follows suit.
> 2nd Child follows suit and, just before exiting, blows a kiss
> and waves goodbye to the Stilt Man and Stilt Woman,
> who continue on even as the lights fade.

10 TALKBACK

The preparation for this play is as follows:
Find a large empty jar. The larger the better.
The jar should be made of some transparent material.
Ask the audience during the weeks leading up to
the performance of this play to write a question for
the playwright on a slip of paper. Ask them to write legibly.
Questions from the actors and production team
are also welcome. Put the slips of paper in the jar. At best,
the jar should be crammed with questions.
At the top of this play, the Moderator brings the jar onstage.
The Actor playing the playwright comes onstage.
The Moderator pulls a question from the jar,
asks the playwright the question,
and the playwright does her best to answer.
This should continue until the jar of questions
has been emptied.
The role of the playwright should be played by several different
Actors, all taking turns, so that everybody gets a chance to add
in their 2 cents, and so that no single person is exhausted
or overwhelmed.

11 THE BLANK BEFORE THE WORLD

A very slow light cue, as slow as possible,
from deep black to white-hot zoom.
The light reveals the stage, which is completely blank.
(Is this possible?)
The light cue is accompanied by a sound of wind—
the wind which brought most of us here to this country
or this planet. Then, the wind reveals itself to be
an enormously elongated single breath.
When the light cue has reached its maximum
and the breath has expired—the lights bump out quickly.

12 *365 DAYS/365 PLAYS*

Lights bump back up to white-hot.
Zoom.
Onstage, the manuscript of *365 Days/365 Plays*.

The Plays: A Table of Contents

The Plays: A Table of Contents

The Plays: A Table of Contents

The Plays: A Table of Contents

The Plays: A Table of Contents

The Plays: A Table of Contents

The Plays: A Table of Contents

The Plays: A Table of Contents

The Plays: A Table of Contents

The Plays: A Table of Contents

THE 365 NATIONAL FESTIVAL

The simple act of writing 365 plays in 365 days has inspired a nation-wide grassroots festival—a geographically diverse relay race which invites each theater group to produce one week's worth of plays in its own style, creating a testament not only to the daily artistic process, but also to the incredible diversity and richness of the American theatrical landscape.

As this book goes to print, we are at the starting line of this epic collaborative experiment. The 365 National Festival starts on November 13, 2006, and continues every day until November 12, 2007. With so many artists working together, it may become the largest shared world premiere in the history of the American theater. Who knows, it may also encourage us to radically change the way we produce/create/critique/enjoy/think about/talk about theater and about the world. So far, more than 600 theater companies, arts organizations and universities are involved, and the Festival is growing larger every day.

What compels these groups to join up? It starts with a shared commitment to putting art at the very center of life—not as a monument but as a commonplace necessity like fire, water, bread or shoes. Keeping the fire going requires tending, and this is a collective effort. That's why the 365 Festival relies on cooperative solutions to make it run, which means that every theater, no matter the size, has an equal role and responsibility. As one colleague in Los Angeles said recently, "365 isn't just a play, it's a movement!"

Never has a project aspired to include this many artists and audiences across the country. But the 365 Festival is not building a new community; it is revealing community where it already exists—in theaters both grand and modest, in schoolrooms, storefronts, nursing homes and alleyways. Theater touches the lives of thousands of people across the country each day. To all those who proclaim that theater is dead, this Festival shows that theater is alive and kicking up a dust storm from Hendrix College just north of Little Rock to the poetry posse of Universes in the Bronx to Steel City Theatre Company in Pueblo, Colorado. As it says in the plays, "Right on, and pass it on."

Bonnie Metzgar
Producer

Suzan-Lori Parks
Playwright/Producer

The Readings

On August 17–18 2006, the first five months of *365 Days/365 Plays* were read at The Public Theater in New York City. Bonnie Metzgar directed the reading of actors, who included: Reg E. Cathey, Gail Grate, Ty Jones, David Patrick Kelly, Joan MacIntosh, S. Epatha Merkerson, Michael Potts, Daphne Rubin-Vega and Ching Valdes-Aran. The stage manager was Stephanie Gatton.

On September 28–29 2006, a reading of the second half of *365 Days/365 Plays* took place at The Public Theater. Bonnie Metzgar directed the reading of actors, who included: Rob Campbell, Kathleen Chalfant, Jojo Gonzalez, Peter Francis James, Ty Jones, Joan MacIntosh, S. Epatha Merkerson, Adina Porter and Ching Valdes-Aran. The stage manager was Taibi Magar.

The Networks

The 365 National Festival is a big project. We are most grateful to the local hub theaters and their coordinators, who have contributed immeasurably—it could not have happened without their support. At press time, these producing organizations and angels have been helping us to coordinate the Festival on a national level: Alliance Theatre, Hilton Als, Danielle Mages Amato, Marisela Barrera, Susan V. Booth, Ben Cameron, Center Theatre Group, Emily Coates, Brenda Cook, Gordon Edelstein, Stephanie Ellis-Smith, David Esbjornson, Oskar Eustis, Carol Fineman, Vanessa Gilbert, Maria Goyanes, Sharon Graci, Mandy Hackett, Weir Harman, Carole Shorenstein Hays, Celise Kalke, Miriam R. Leal, Jason Loewith, Denee McCloud, Amy Mueller, Allison Narver, Terry Nemeth, The Public Theater, Jack Reuler, Shannon Richey, Michael Ritchie, Joseph Roach and the World Performance Project at Yale University, Diane Rodriguez, Paige Rogers, Derrick Sanders, Nick Schwartz-Hall, Susan Solt, Flora Stamatiades, Dave Steakley, Lisa Steindler, Theatre Communications Group and Chip Walton.We are thankful for the hard work of our Network Coordinators: table-work dramaturg and Coordinator for 365U, Rebecca Rugg; our National Coordinator, David Myers; and Meredith McDonagh, for her assistance. Please visit the 365 National Festival website: www.365days365plays.com

The following is a list of participating theaters and producing organizations at press time. This list will change as the year-long cycle moves forward.

ATLANTA
HUB THEATER:
Alliance Theatre
Actor's Express Theatre Company
Agnes Scott College
AIDS Quilt Project
Alliance Theatre Acting Program
Alliance Theatre Collision Project
Aurora Theatre
Big Top Theatre
Clark Atlanta University
Collection of Spelman and
  Morehouse alumni
Collective Works/PushPush Theater
Community Theater Initiative
The Company Acting Studio
Dad's Garage
Dance 101
DramaTech Theater
Emory University directing stu-
  dents
Emory University Transforming
  Communities Project
The Essential Theatre/PushPush
  Theater
Gainesville Theatre Alliance
Georgia Shakespeare
Horizon Theatre Company/
  University of West Georgia
IKAM Productions
Jack in the Black Box Theatre
  Company
Kennesaw State University
Lovin' It Live Restaurant
Multishades Atlanta and the
  Academy Theatre
NBAF (National Black Arts
  Festival)
The New Jomandi Productions
The Other Side of the Tracks
  Project
Out of Hand Theater
The Process Theatre Co.
Quality Living Services
Savage Tree Arts Project
Savannah College of Art and Design

7 Stages
7 Stages—Youth Creates
Southwest Arts Center
Southwest Arts Center featuring the
  Fresh Collective
Spelman College
Stage Door Players
Studio Zero Productions
Synchronicity Performance Group
Theater at Emory
Théâtre du Rêve
True Colors Theatre Company
Twinhead Theatre/PushPush Theater
Working Title Playwrights

AUSTIN
HUB THEATER:
Zachary Scott Theatre
Austin Script Works
Austin Shakespeare Festival
Coda Theater Project
Different Stages
Eva Street Players
Gobotrick Theatre Company
Hyde Park Theatre
ProArts Collective of Austin
Renaissance Austin Theatre
  Company
RoHo Theatre Company
Rude Mechanicals
Salvage Vanguard Theater
St. Idiot Collective (SIC)
Texas State University Department
  of Theatre and Dance
University of Texas at Austin
  Department of Theatre and Dance
UT Connections Youth Theatre
VORTEX Repertory Company
ZACH Performing Arts School
ZACH Project Interact

CHICAGO
HUB THEATERS:
Congo Square Theatre
The Goodman Theatre
The Hypocrites

Next Theatre Company
Steppenwolf Theatre Company
Uma Productions
American Theater Company
The Artistic Home
Bailiwick Repertory Theatre
Bohemian Theatre Ensemble
Chicago Dramatists
Citadel Theatre Company
Collaboraction
Court Theatre
DMG Freedom Productions
Dog & Pony Theatre Company
Eclipse Theatre Company
Estrogen Fest
500 Clown
Fleetwood-Jourdain Theatre
The Gift Theatre Company
GroundUp Theatre
HealthWorks Theatre
Illinois Caucus for Adolescent
  Health
Infamous Commonwealth Theatre
The Journeymen Theater Company
Lifeline Theatre
The Mill Theatre
The Moving Dock Theatre
  Company
MPAACT (Ma'at Production
  Association of Afrikan Centered
  Theatre)
The Neo-Futurists
New Branch Theatre Company
Northlight Theatre
Piven Theatre Workshop
Polarity Ensemble Theatre
Raven Theatre
Remy Bumppo Theatre Company
Rivendell Theatre Ensemble
Sandbox Theatre Project
Sansculottes Theater Company
Serendipity Theatre Company
Shattered Globe Theatre
the side project
Silk Road Theatre Project
Soul Theatre
Stage Left Theatre
Teatro Vista, Theatre with a View
The Theatre of Western Springs
Urban Theater Company
Victory Gardens Theater
Vitalist Theatre Company
Writers' Theatre

COLORADO
HUB THEATER:
Curious Theatre Company
The Acting Company in Loveland
Actor Group/POV
Adams State College
Aspen High School
Aurora Fox Arts Center
Bas Bleu Theatre Company
Boulder Ensemble Theatre
  Company
Buntport Theater
Center for American Theatre at
  Historic Elitch Gardens
Colorado Shakespeare Festival
Community College of Aurora, Arts
  and Humanities Department
Crossroads Theater
Denver Center Theatre Company
Denver University: Living and
  Learning Communities
Denver Victorian Playhouse
800 lb guerilla theatre
El Centro Su Teatro
Firehouse Theatre
First Strike Theatre
Freak Train at The Bug Theatre
The Grand Theatre Company
Hunger Artists Ensemble Theatre
International Theatre Collective
The LIDA Project
Madhouse Theatre
Metropolitan State College of
  Denver: Theatre Arts Program
Michael Duran
Miners Alley Playhouse
Modern Muse Theatre Company
Naropa University
New Twenty-Two Productions
Next Stage
No Credits Production, Inc.
Northglenn Youth Theatre
North High School
Notable Pirate Theatre Company
openstage etc at OpenStage Theatre
  & Company
Paragon Theatre Company
Peak Productions at Western State
  College of Colorado
PHAMALy: the Physically
  Handicapped Amateur Musical
  Actors League, Inc.
Playwright Theatre

Red Rocks Community College
Dept. of Theatre Arts
Spark Theatre Works
square productions and square
    product theatre
Stage Left Theatre Company
Steel City Theatre Company
Theatre Company of Lafayette
Theatre 13
Theatreworks
University of Colorado at Boulder
    Department of Dance
University of Colorado at Boulder:
    On Stage
Vintage Theatre Productions
Wrecking Ball Theatre Lab

GREATER TEXAS
HUB THEATER:
La Colectiva Performance Group
Alamo City Rollergirls
Amphibian Productions
Borderplex Electronica
CAM San Antonio
The Chinati Foundation
Circle Theatre
Comedia A Go-Go
Cuento Theatre
Echo Theatre
Jump-Start Performance Co.
Los Maestros Teatros
Mildred's Umbrella Theater Company
M3 Productions
Palo Alto . . . On Stage
Rose Theatre
San Pedro Playhouse
The Strand Theatre
Trinity University
University of Texas at San Antonio
    architecture students

LOS ANGELES
HUB THEATER:
Center Theatre Group
About Productions
Adam, Eve, & Steve Productions
Alliance Theatre Company
Angry Bubble Productions
Ark Theatre Company
The Black Dahlia Theatre
Blank-the-Dog
Bootleg Theater
Buffalo Nights Theatre Company

Center for New Performance at
    Cal Arts
The Chance Theater
Circle X Theatre Co.
Circus Theatricals
City Garage
Company of Angels
Cornerstone Theater Company
Critical Mass Performance Group
Deaf West Theatre
East LA Repertory
East West Players
The Eclectic Company Theatre
Elephant Theatre Company
Empire of Teeth
Ensemble Studio Theatre—LA
Filament Theatre Company
Geffen Playhouse
The Ghost Road Company
Greenway Arts Alliance
Highways Performance Space
Mr. and Mrs. Kickass
LA Stage Alliance
Latino Theater Company
The Mad Scene Theatre Company
Terence McFarland
The MET Theatre Company
Nest Arts
Odyssey Theatre Ensemble
Open Fist Theatre Company
Pacific Resident Theatre
Playwrights' Arena
REDCAT
Repertory East Playhouse
Sacred Fools Theater Company
Smart Gals Productions
Son of Semele Ensemble
Alexander Yannis Stephano
The Syzygy Theatre Group
The Theatre @ Boston Court
Theatre of NOTE
Towne Street Theatre
24th Street Theatre
Unknown Theater
Watts Village Theater Company
Zoo District

MINNEAPOLIS
HUB THEATER:
Mixed Blood Theatre Company
The Children's Theatre Company
Commonweal Theatre Company
Emigrant Theater

Frank Theatre
The Guthrie Theater/University of
   Minnesota Partnership
Illusion Theater
Kulture Klub Collaborative
Macalester College
Mu Performing Arts
Nautilus Music-Theater
Park Square Theatre
Pillsbury House Theatre
Red Eye Collaboration
Stages Theatre Company
Theatre Pro Rata
Thirst Theater
Youth Performing Company

NEW YORK CITY
HUB THEATER:
The Public Theater
Ars Nova
Atlantic Theater Company
Banana Bag & Bodice
Barrow Street Theatre
blessed unrest
Blue Box Productions
Boomerang Theatre Company
The Brick Theater, Inc.
The Civilians
Classical Theatre of Harlem
Clubbed Thumb
CollaborationTown
Desipina & Company
Dixon Place
The Drama League: The Directors
   Project
duende arts
Alec Duffy
Engine37 (Neal Freeman)
Epic Theatre Center
The Faux-Real Theatre Company
The 52nd Street Project
The Foundry Theatre
Galapagos Art Space
Gansfeld
Genesius Theatre Group
Guerrilla Girls On Tour
The H.A.D.L.E.Y. Players
HERE Arts Center
Hip-Hop Theater Festival
Hourglass Group
INTAR Theatre
LAByrinth Theater Company
LightBox

Lucid Theatre
Ma-Yi Theater Company
MUD/BONE
Naked Angels Theater Company
New Dance Group Arts Center
New Georges
The New Group
The New York Neo-Futurists
New York Theatre Workshop
Partial Comfort Productions
Pig Iron Theatre Company
Polybe + Seats
Pregones Theater
The Public Theater Shakespeare Lab
Queens Theatre in the Park
RACCA's Seaport Salon
Rebel Theater Company Inc.
Rising Phoenix Repertory
Robot Vs. Dinosaur
Salt Theater
Scenedowntown
SITI Company
SLANT Theatre Project
TADA! Youth Theater
The Tank
The TEAM
Temporary Theatre Company
3-d
Universes
Untitled Theater Company #61
viBe Theater Experience
Vortex Theater Company

NORTHEAST NETWORK
HUB THEATERS:
Perishable Theatre
Long Wharf Theatre
World Performance Project at
   Yale University
Brown University
Hartford Stage
Mount Holyoke College
Trinity Repertory Company
Yale Repertory Theatre

SAN FRANCISCO BAY AREA
HUB THEATERS:
The Cutting Ball Theater
Playwrights Foundation
The Z Space Studio
American Conservatory Theater
   MFA Program
Crowded Fire Theater Company

Elastic Future
foolsFURY Theater Company
Golden Thread Productions
Just Theatre
Katy Hilton & Co.
Magic Theatre
Marin Theatre Company
mugwumpin
The New Conservatory Theatre Center
Opera Piccola "Small Works"
Phoenix Arts Association
Rough and Tumble
Shotgun Players
6th Street Playhouse
Ten Red Hen Productions
TheatreFIRST
Thick Description
Women's Will

SEATTLE
HUB THEATERS:
Central District Forum for Arts and Ideas
The Empty Space Theatre
Seattle Repertory Theatre
Town Hall
Braden Abraham
Absurd Reality Theatre
ACT Theatre—The Hansberry
  Project
Akropolis Performance Lab
Annex Theatre
Baba Yaga Productions
Josh Beerman
Timeca Briggs
Brownbox Theatre
Capitol Hill Arts Center
Crispin Spaeth Dance Group
Eclectic Theater Company
EXITheatre
Festival Sundiata
4Culture
Intiman Theatre
KUOW-FM
Langston Hughes Performing Arts
  Center
Live Girls! Theater
Leticia Lopez
Wade Madsen
The Mahogany Project
Mirror Stage Company
Megan Murphy
North Seattle Community College
Northwest Film Forum

Nu Black Arts West Theatre
On the Boards
Our American Theater Company
Outsider's Inn Collective
Pat Graney Company
Susie Polnaszek
Rainier Valley Youth Theatre/
  Rainier Valley Cultural Center
ReAct Theatre
Daveda Russell
Samba Del Sol
Allegra Searle-Lebel
Tikka Sears
Seattle Arts & Lectures
Seattle Children's Theatre
Seattle International Children's
  Festival
Seattle Public Theater at the
  Bathhouse
SIS Productions
Smack Productions
Spectrum Dance Theater
Strike Anywhere Productions
theatre simple
University of Washington School of
  Drama
Washington Ensemble Theatre

SOUTHEAST NETWORK
HUB THEATER:
PURE Theatre
Art Forms and Theatre Concepts,
  Inc.
Balagula Theatre
Barter Theatre
Burning Coal Theatre Company
College of Charleston
Common Ground Theatre
Firehouse Theatre Project
Footlight Players
The Little Green Pig Theatrical
  Concern
Manbites Dog Theater
New Theatre of Coral Gables
NiA Company
Amanda Reyelt
The Roxy Regional Theatre
Theatre Alliance of Louisville
Theatre 99
Theatre/verv/
University of Kentucky
University of North Carolina at
  Chapel Hill

The 365 National Festival

University of South Carolina
The Village Playhouse
Virginia Commonwealth University
   Guild of Graduate Students
Walden Theatre
The Warehouse Theatre
Wofford College

**UNIVERSITY NETWORK
HUB THEATER:
World Performance Project at Yale
University; New Haven, Connecticut**
Allegheny College; Meadville,
   Pennsylvania
Association for Theatre in Higher
   Education
Barnard College; New York, New
   York
Berea College; Berea, Kentucky
Borough of Manhattan Community
   College; New York, New York
Bowdoin College; Brunswick, Maine
Bowling Green State University;
   Bowling Green, Ohio
Brandeis University; Waltham,
   Massachusetts
Brown University; Providence,
   Rhode Island
California State University,
   Bakersfield; Bakersfield,
   California
California State University,
   Fullerton; Fullerton, California
California State University,
   Sacramento; Sacramento,
   California
Chester College of New England;
   Chester, New Hampshire
Clemson University; Clemson,
   South Carolina
Colby College; Waterville, Maine
College of Staten Island, City
   University of New York; Staten
   Island, New York
Columbia University; New York,
   New York
Columbus State University;
   Columbus, Georgia
Dalhousie University; Halifax,
   Nova Scotia, Canada
Hendrix College; Conway, Arkansas
Hunter College, City University of
   New York; New York, New York

Immigrants Theater Project at
   LaGuardia Community College,
   City University of New York;
   Long Island City, New York
Kennedy Center American College
   Theater Festival; Washington,
   D.C.
Lafayette College; Easton,
   Pennsylvania
Lock Haven University; Lock
   Haven, Pennsylvania
Louisiana State University; Baton
   Rouge, Louisiana
Missouri State University;
   Springfield, Missouri
Mount Holyoke College; South
   Hadley, Massachusetts
New WORLD Theater at University
   of Massachusetts Amherst;
   Amherst, Massachusetts
New York University, Tisch School
   of the Arts; New York, New York
Northwestern University; Evanston,
   Illinois
Penn State Berks; Reading,
   Pennsylvania
Purchase College; Purchase, New
   York
Rutgers University; New
   Brunswick, New Jersey
Saint Joseph College; West
   Hartford, Connecticut
Spelman College; Atlanta, Georgia
Texas Christian University; Fort
   Worth, Texas
Texas Women's University; Denton,
   Texas
University at Buffalo, State
   University of New York; Buffalo,
   New York
University of Alabama at
   Birmingham; Birmingham,
   Alabama
University of California, Davis;
   Davis, California
University of California, San Diego;
   San Diego, California
University of Dayton; Dayton, Ohio
University of East Anglia; Norwich,
   UK
University of Iowa; Iowa City, Iowa
University of Massachusetts Lowell;
   Lowell, Massachusetts

The 365 National Festival

University of Montevallo;
Montevallo, Alabama
University of Notre Dame; Notre
Dame, Indiana
University of Rochester; Rochester,
New York
University of Windsor; Windsor,
Ontario, Canada
University of Wisconsin—Fond du
Lac; Fond du Lac, Wisconsin
Vanderbilt University; Nashville,
Tennessee
Virginia Tech; Blacksburg, Virginia
Wake Forest University; Winston-
Salem, North Carolina
Washington University in St. Louis;
St. Louis, Missouri
Wesleyan College; Middletown,
Connecticut
William Paterson University;
Wayne, New Jersey
Women and Theatre Program of the
Association for Theatre in
Higher Education; Boulder,
Colorado

WASHINGTON, D.C. AREA
HUB THEATERS:
**The African Continuum Theatre
Company**
Round House Theatre
Signature Theatre
The Studio Theatre
Woolly Mammoth Theatre Company

Actors' Theatre of
Washington/Warner Theatre
Bowie State University
Catalyst Theater
Chevy Chase Players
Corcoran College of Art and Design
The DC Cabaret Network
Dominion Stage
Folger Shakespeare Theatre
Georgetown Black Theatre Ensemble
Horizons Theatre
Howard University Players
The Keegan Theatre
Longacre Lea
MetroStage
Northern Virginia Community
College
OutOftheBlackBox Theatre
Company
Rep Stage
Rockville Little Theatre
Run of the Mill Playhouse
Shakespeare Theatre Company
Silver Spring Stage
Sol & Sol
Synetic Theater
University of Maryland—
"Kreativity"
University of Mary Washington
Venus Theatre
Washington Shakespeare Company
Washington Women in Theatre
Young Playwrights' Theater

Suzan-Lori Parks is a playwright, screenwriter, songwriter and novelist. In 2002 she became the first African American woman to win the Pulitzer Prize in Drama for her play *Topdog/Underdog*. Her other plays include: *Fucking A*, *Imperceptible Mutabilities in the Third Kingdom* (1990 Obie Award for Best New American Play), *The American Play*, *Venus* (1996 Obie Award), *The Death of the Last Black Man in the Whole Entire World* and *In the Blood* (Pulitzer Prize finalist), among others. The majority of her plays are published by Theatre Communications Group. She is the subject of the PBS Film *The Topdog/Underdog Diaries*. A graduate of Mount Holyoke College, where she studied creative writing with James Baldwin, Parks has been awarded grants by the National Endowment for the Arts, the Rockefeller Foundation, the Ford Foundation, the New York State Council on the Arts and the New York Foundation for the Arts. She is a recipient of the MacArthur Foundation's "Genius" Award, the Lila-Wallace Reader's Digest Award, the CalArts/Herb Alpert Award, the PEN/Laura Pels Writing Award and a Guggenheim Foundation grant. She is an alumnus of New Dramatists. Her work for film and television includes *Girl 6* (directed by Spike Lee) and the adaptation of Zora Neale Hurston's *Their Eyes Were Watching God*, for Oprah Winfrey Presents. She has also written scripts for Jodie Foster, Denzel Washington and Brad Pitt. Her first novel, *Getting Mother's Body*, is published by Random House. She has taught writing in colleges and universities, including the Yale School of Drama. Currently she is writing *Ray Charles Live!*, the book for the Ray Charles musical (for the film producers of *Ray*); she is also working on a new play and another novel. She lectures worldwide via www.barclayagency.com. Parks lives in Venice Beach with her husband, blues musician Paul Oscher; their pitbulls, Lambchop and Boogie-Woogie; and their black cat Houndog.